The Writing Workshop

THE WRITING WORKSHOP

Working through the Hard Parts (And They're All Hard Parts)

Katie Wood Ray
Western Carolina University

with

Lester L. Laminack
Western Carolina University

National Council of Teachers of English
1111 W. Kenyon Road, Urbana, Illinois 61801-1096

Prepress Services: Precision Graphics
Staff Editior: Tom Tiller
Interior Design: Precision Graphics and Mary C. Cronin
Cover Design: Jenny Jensen Greenleaf

NCTE Stock Number: 13176-3050

Library of Congress Cataloging-in-Publication Data

Ray, Katie Wood, 1964–
The writing workshop : working through the hard parts (and they're all hard parts) / Katie Wood Ray with Lester L. Laminack.
p. cm.
Includes bibliographical references.
ISBN 0-8141-1317-6 (pbk.)
1. Creative writing (Elementary education) 2. English language--Composition and exercises--Study and teaching (Elementary)
I. Laminack, Lester L., 1956– II. Title.

LB1576.R383 2001
372.62'3044--dc21

2001018710

For Beverly Busching

KWR

For those writers who allow us to look over their shoulders and learn from their experience

LLL

Contents

Acknowledgments

I would like to thank Beverly Busching for all the kind ways she supports teachers to be the best that they can be. This book is dedicated to her as a small token of appreciation for her years of dedication to others. My teaching is what it is today because of all the ways she supported me as a graduate student at the University of South Carolina.

For all the hundreds of teachers who have allowed me to spend time alongside them in their teaching of writing, thank you. If I started to name you all, I would surely get into trouble. But if it weren't for all of you whom I've met in your actual classrooms, in professional development settings, graduate classes, and by wonderful happenstance, this book would not have been possible. Thank you for doing such smart things, for asking such smart questions, and for making such smart connections for me. But most of all, thanks for being willing to do what it takes to work through all those hard parts in the best interest of the children you teach.

To Kathleen Burda, Margaret Johnson, and Kirsten Morgan, whose classroom stories very specifically inform this book, a special thank you for letting me write about you and for the ways your teaching informs mine, again and again.

To the students in my EDEL 606 Advanced Language Arts class in the fall of 1999, thank you for reading and responding to early drafts of this manuscript. And my apologies for not knowing which ones of you to thank personally. I have so many wonderful different handwritten comments for those early drafts (that really helped in later revisions), but I don't know who the different ones belong to. Thank you so much, anyway, all of you who responded.

Thank you, yet again, to my friends and colleagues through the years at The Teachers College Reading and Writing Project at Columbia University. You continue to push me, and thousands of other teachers, to the very edges of what we know and can do, helping us find our own miracles in the teaching of reading and writing.

A special thanks to Pete Feely at the National Council of Teachers of English, who asked that this book be written and who supported it all along the way. And to the editorial board members who gave me such thoughtful feedback on the manuscript, an anonymous thank you (since I don't know who you are but appreciate you nonetheless).

Lester Laminack, friend, colleague, and co-conspirator on this project, I couldn't have done it without you. Your boundless energy, your wonderful sense of humor, and your endless belief in me as a person have helped me be the best that I can be. I can never thank you enough.

My family, the Woods and the Rays, always stand behind me through the thick and thin of projects like this. Many people don't realize how much being able to write a book like this is a family affair. They have to understand when you can't come out to play. They have to listen when you suffer from writer's block or a serious case of self-doubt. They have to push you to get back to work when you really want to do anything but that. And they have to believe that all of this matters enough—in the whole scheme of the world—to put up with you for the many months it takes to get it done.

And finally, thanks to my husband and B.F.L., Jim Ray, who lets me be whatever I need to be and just keeps right on standing there by my side. Thank you for making my dreams your dreams, for believing in my work as a writer, and for helping me co-author this wonderful life we are living.

Introduction

If it were easy, everybody would be doing it.”

This is one of my husband’s favorite sayings. He thinks it’s motivational. He likes to say it right when I’m in the middle of doing something hard and I want to give up: trying to walk up our mountain, helping him lift his camper top off his truck, focusing on writing all day long. My typical comeback is to roll my eyes at his overly predictable line and say, “Well, I want to do what everybody else is doing. I’m *lonely.*”

Imagine my surprise not long ago when I heard his familiar line coming out of my mouth. I was talking to teachers. I was talking about teaching writing. I guess I thought it would be motivational. And it seemed to be, but that may have been because it was a Saturday. If I had caught them on a Wednesday, right in the middle of a day of such challenging teaching, they might have responded more like I usually do to my husband. Doing the really challenging work of teaching writing can be so lonely when, day in and day out, you seem to be making things more complicated for yourself while everyone around you is doing stuff that just seems, well, so much *easier.*

If you have a writing workshop in your classroom now, or if you are thinking of starting one, it’s because you have developed a particular knowledge base about writing, about learning theory, and about teaching practice to believe this is the best way to go about the teaching of writing. There is no other reason for you to be working so hard except that you are following your teaching convictions.

It's funny, but as they are learning about writing workshops, my teacher education students almost always say at some point in every semester, "But it's so much more fun for the students to teach writing this way." They are indignant and unable to understand how a teacher could possibly choose not to have a writing workshop when it's so much more fun for students than doing language arts exercises from a textbook. And then I have to do my big blowup: "You think teachers have writing workshops because they're *fun* for students? Is *that* what you think this is about? If that were true we might as well have them all line dancing! Line dancing is *fun!*"

I have to help my students understand that teaching writing in a workshop setting is highly theoretical teaching. That's why we do it—because it's theoretical. Every aspect of the workshop is set up to support children learning to do what writers really do. The teaching is challenging because what writers really do is engage in a complex, multilayered, slippery process to produce texts. The writing itself is very satisfying, even fun at times, but that's the *truth* of writing. It's not some motivational game we set up to keep children's interest. If that were all we wanted, we would do things that were far less challenging for us as teachers.

The Writing Workshop: Working through the Hard Parts (And They're All Hard Parts) was written to support both new and experienced teachers facing the challenges of the writing workshop. It is not meant to be a book that changes essential beliefs about teaching writing. I'll leave that to the brilliant teachers and writers who have offered us the most essential understandings in the teaching of writing in the past two decades: Lucy Calkins, Nancie Atwell, Donald Graves, Jane Hansen, Donald Murray, Janet Emig, and on and on. It is not meant to be a book that *introduces* readers to the essential methodologies of workshop teaching: mini- or focus lessons, conferring, inquiry, writing for publication, peer response, group shares, and so on. This book assumes that readers have a belief system about teaching writing and that there is a set of methods already in place, or at least that one has been introduced through professional reading and through experiences in writing workshops.

The Writing Workshop: Working through the Hard Parts (And They're All Hard Parts) is a book about being articulate, about being able to think through what we are doing as we are doing it so that we can improve our practice. It's a book to go back to when things are getting hard, a book that will help us think through, "Now *why* was I doing this?" In the highly politicized world that we live in, it is more important than ever that we be articulate about our practice, and being articulate is what helps us keep our faith when things do get hard or when we feel threatened from the outside about our beliefs. We need to be able to explain to ourselves and to others very clearly both how and why we are doing what we are doing. It steadies us to be articulate.

In writing this book, I draw from my experiences first as a classroom teacher, then as a staff developer with The Teachers College Reading and Writing Project, in which I demonstrated teaching and explained every move I made to others, and then as a teacher educator trying to explain the entire writing workshop process to students very new to the idea. Through this various work, I've been privileged to stand alongside many brilliant teachers who meet the challenges of workshop teaching day after day, and I have learned so much from each of them. In this book, I've tried to gather some of what I have learned from working alongside these teachers and from my own experiences as a teacher of writing, and lay it all out in a format that walks the reader through the day-to-day teaching in a writing workshop. I make no claims of knowing "the way" to have a writing workshop. As a matter of fact, I embrace the realization that there are many ways to get to the same end. I am simply offering up what I have learned about this teaching over the years, shaped and defined as it is by the particular professional communities in which I have been fortunate enough to live and learn. I don't want or need this book to be definitive. I just want it to be helpful.

My hope is that *The Writing Workshop: Working through the Hard Parts (And They're All Hard Parts)* is a book that offers teachers of writing things to think about with the work they are already trying in their classrooms or are getting ready to try. These reflections are meant to help teachers both to confirm the work they are doing and to problematize it. Some of what you read will help you to troubleshoot your work in writing workshop, as well as to think of new possibilities for that work. There are chapters on everything from how challenging teaching in the writing workshop is (and why) to how to think through what happens during writing conferences with students.

The book is made up of chapters that I hope cover the most essential ideas behind workshop teaching. The early chapters (1 through 4) explore why we have writing workshops, what workshops have in common across grade levels, and the tone of teaching that exists in a writing workshop setting. The next several chapters (5 though 8) help readers think through the workshop as a predictable event in the life of a classroom where students work independently on projects that matter to them. Developing the curriculum knowledge necessary to do writing workshop teaching is the subject of Chapters 9 through 12, and Chapters 13 through 16 examine the parts of the workshop where students and teachers talk about writing: focus lessons, conferences and share times, and lesson planning to support each of these. The ending chapters (17 through 19) are meant to help readers work through issues related to the ongoing work that students are engaged in during writing workshop, particularly assessment and evaluation.

A Writer's Voice

My colleague Lester Laminack is one of the most passionate readers I have ever met. He is a passionate reader in part because he is a passionate writer. Author of numerous professional books and articles and, most recently, of children's picture books, Lester supports his writing life by filling his heart and mind with the voices and insights of other writers. He loves southern writers most, and anyone who's ever met him knows why, of course. Their voices match his own.

When the idea for doing a book about writing workshops began, Lester and I knew we wanted to collaborate. The whole idea behind writing workshops in classrooms grew out of the understandings that *people who teach* developed when they looked at what *people who write* do. And the best writing workshops I know never stray far from that mission: to match the work in the classroom to the work of writers in the outside (of school) world. My book *Wondrous Words: Writers and Writing in the Elementary Classroom* (1999, NCTE) has as its central theme learning to write from writers. In this book, I knew I wanted the voices of people who write to surround all of these reflections for people who teach, and Lester is a perfect spokesman for writers' voices. Not only can he speak from his own experience as a writer, but also he has spent countless hours talking with other writers and reading books that writers have written about their processes.

As each of the chapters on teaching was evolving, I handed it to Lester and said, "Find out what writers have to say about this." And he did; and what he found is very interesting. The writers' voices you will find woven throughout the chapters in this book will illuminate, extend, and sometimes even contradict what is offered in the essays about teaching. Their strong voices will leave you with your own reflections and will, I think, open up professional conversations about writing workshops that have the potential to extend what we know in significant ways. Here we have tried to create almost a "talking back" between writers and teachers—a book for many voices, if you will. I have written the essays on teaching in the writing workshop, and into these pieces, Lester has woven many writers' voices for your reflection.

My deepest hope is that this book be *helpful.* If it helps even one teacher get through some of the challenging parts of teaching writing more easily, it will have been worth the effort it was to write it. I also hope this book keeps you company. I know how lonely workshop teaching can be. I know that teachers like you and me buy books like this, in part so we don't feel so lonely in this kind of teaching. But I also know how rewarding such challenging teaching can be. So before you even start to read through, pat yourself on the back and remember: If it were easy, everybody would be doing it. . . .

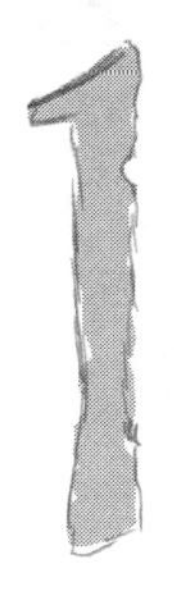

Understanding the Essential Characteristics of the Writing Workshop

Imagine this . . .

You're in a fourth-grade classroom. It's a little noisy in the room, but it doesn't seem like a misdirected, off-task kind of noise. Just the hum of noise you get when people are working alongside one another. The students are in different places around the room, and they seem to be involved in some different kinds of things. You can pick the teacher out because she's, well, a lot older than all the rest of them, but you have to look to find her. She's over behind the bookshelf at a table with Mary Ann.

Over in the far corner, two girls are flipping through sports magazines looking for pictures that show women or girls involved in some sports action. When they find a picture like this, they discuss its merits and its possibilities, and from time to time they cut a picture out and put it aside. Over the next few days these pictures will be used to illustrate an anthology of sports poems that they have co-authored (co-poeted) during the last few weeks.

At a nearby table, two children sit and listen as Dylan gets ready to read to them from a draft of a story about his grandfather's experiences in World War II. "Stop me and tell me whenever anything doesn't make sense," he tells them before he begins to read. They listen intently (well, mostly intently, except for when the guy mowing the lawn passes by the window).

A little further over, Brianna sits reading from a book about hot air balloons, taking notes from time to time in a tiny blue notebook. Next to her, two classmates write in similar notebooks, making lists of strong, descriptive verbs and trying them out in sentences as their teacher demonstrated in the focus lesson that day. They takes turns reading them to each other, and this is usually accompanied by some laughter.

Jimmy and Kelvin sit side by side, close but not really interacting, each drafting on long, yellow draft paper. Kelvin is working on a story for a fiction series he's writing about a group of boys who get in many misadventures together. He writes slowly, stopping often to stare off and think. Jimmy writes much faster, working back and forth between his notes on Florida theme parks and the draft of the travel essay he's working on.

Keisha, Donna, and Tremaine huddle close together around a copy of another Gary Paulsen book. They have been reading first chapters of Paulsen's books all week, discussing them, and trying to learn something about leads, about how to start a good story. They all love Paulsen and want to learn to write like he writes.

Mary Ann is having a conference with the teacher, and they are looking through the draft of the picture book she is writing (in both English and Spanish) for her young brother. Together they search for places where she might use today's focus lesson on strong verbs in her revisions.

Out of earshot, Todd and Karen speak in low voices as they discuss whether Todd still likes Anna (Karen's best friend) or not, since he didn't sit with her at lunch yesterday. They'll get back to their writing soon. . . .

Imagine all this.

How much you have to stretch your imagination to imagine this might depend on your experiences with *writing workshop*. This is a snapshot of a writing workshop, and it may look like nothing you've ever seen, or it may look like what you remember from yesterday in your classroom. The students in this classroom are doing what they do every morning at this time. They are working on various writing projects of interest to them. At times during the year they have studied different genres together and written pieces in these genres, but regardless of the focus of study in the room, the students have maintained their ongoing project-like work. Each student is able to bring his or her particular interests to the workshop and explore those interests through writing.

If you were to look at the products of this student writing, you would see both a real range of developmental writing skills (as you would in any classroom) and the tracks of all the teaching of writing that's been going on in the room. But the products themselves are not nearly as significant as the child standing behind each one of them. While Brianna's piece about hot air balloons might look a lot like a piece stuck in a whole class's set of papers where everyone had to "describe a hot air balloon as it looks in the sky," the fact is, hers is not one in a stack of papers. Her piece is her piece, chosen as a writing project for a number of significant reasons important only to her. And that's what is important to her teacher.

Brianna's teacher has a writing workshop not because she believes it's some "magic potion" that will guarantee her students overnight success as writers, though she believes the workshop will raise the levels of their writing in significant ways through her teaching during the year. No, she doesn't see the workshop as magic, and she understands that her students are fourth graders after all, so she makes a place for them to be just that while they gain the experience they need to become good writers *over time* with her teaching. Her most important goal is that her students write with purpose and intention first—to enrich their lives in significant ways—and that out of this they learn to write well.

Writing Process or Writing Workshop?

In my experiences working with many different teachers and students in many different classrooms, I have found all kinds of writing instruction that goes on under the name "writing workshop" or "writing process." More than once I have been told, "We do the writing process in my classroom." What does that mean exactly, and is there a difference between "doing the writing process" and having a writing workshop?

I have seen many classrooms where students "do the writing process," and the focus is on *pieces of writing* and how to take those pieces of writing through each of the steps of the writing process—prewriting, drafting, revision, editing, and publication. Sometimes there is some fabulous teaching that supports students' growth in different parts of this process, and sometimes there is very little teaching around it at all, but either way the focus is very much on the steps of the process and its products. Students move from one piece of writing to the next, faithfully taking each one down the line. Students leave these classrooms with the central impression that writing is a process of getting an idea and then "moving that idea down the line"; learning how to do this is the focus of the instruction.

This down-the-line kind of emphasis can be contrasted to a writing workshop where the focus is very much on *writers* rather than on the process that leads to finished pieces. Now, without a doubt, students in writing workshops utilize all the steps of the writing process—their teachers give them lots of instruction around the process so they can get pieces ready for publication—but it's not as though they really *do* the writing process. It's more like they *use* the writing process to get other things *done*. Now, I know that may sound like a subtle difference, but I really believe that the difference in those words—*do* and *use*—represents a huge shift in how we go about teaching writing.

In a writing workshop, one of the main goals teachers have is to help students find good reasons to write. These teachers feel that nothing else matters if students aren't finding writing projects in which they can become deeply involved. Many of these teachers have worked on personally meaningful writing projects in their own lives and have seen firsthand how the writing process can be used to say big, important things in their lives and to make important things happen. They see the writing process as a tool they can give their students to use when rocking the world, not just as something to learn to do. That knowledge at the forefront of teaching, that knowledge that writing is this amazing, powerful tool you can use to rock the world, *changes everything*.

Students in writing workshops are nurtured in so many important ways that go beyond their just moving through the steps of the writing process.

They are encouraged to reflect often on where they have been as writers and on where they are going. They learn about all kinds of things outside the down-the-line process, things that support them when they do begin to ready a piece for publication: writer's notebooks, genre studies, and craft studies, to name just a few. They are asked to begin working on pieces of writing with some real-world outcome in mind, some purpose for the writing beyond just "getting it finished."

Because the focus is on writers in a writing workshop, the environment of the workshop is often filled with so many more possibilities than is a room where students do the writing process. In writing workshops, teachers invite children to do all the things a writer really does: research, explore, collect, interview, talk, read, stare off into space, co-author, and yes, prewrite, draft, revise, edit, and publish. These teachers have studied writers' lives and habits and know that living a writing life includes a lot more than just always being in one of the stages of the writing process. Writing process classrooms sometimes present children with a very limited view of a what a writer really does when they send the message that writers simply move through these steps, over and over.

Now, my whole argument here has been based on very particular terminology that you may not even use in the same ways I have. It may very well be that when you think about your own teaching and the beliefs behind it, you feel that you have a "writing workshop" philosophy (as I've described it) but that you've been calling it "writing process" or something else. And of course, the labels don't matter as much as what's behind them that drives our teaching. I needed to be clear, however, about what I mean by writing workshop because that's what this book is all about—writing workshops where the focus is on *writers who use writing* to do powerful things in the world in which they live.

Essential Characteristics of the Writing Workshop

Having worked alongside so many different teachers in so many different writing workshops, I have seen a rich variety in actual teaching from one writing workshop to the next. As a set of essential methodologies, the workshop

WRITERS' VOICES ON . . .

what it means to be a writer

> What you have to do as a writer is to feel, look, and listen. Your stories then become a celebration of those observations. And, most important, a writer needs to fall in love. I'm constantly falling in love—with colors, with flowers, with wings, with bubbles, with mud, with goofy baby smiles. . . . When you're writing under the influence of love, there's a power that will weave your words into magic. . . . (*Bantam Doubleday Dell presents Elvira Woodruff*, n.p.)

Writing under the influence of love. Wow, what a notion for the classroom. When in your lifetime did you write in school because you had fallen in love with something and needed to examine it more closely, to know it more intimately, to become part of it and to make it a part of you? Mem Fox speaks to this same notion in *Radical Reflections* when she says that a writer must "ache with caring" (3). Have you ever "ached with caring" over anything you were assigned to write? Perhaps you ached, but I'd bet it wasn't with caring. Donald Murray, in *Shoptalk: Learning to Write with Writers,* contends that

> Too often we defend writing as a skill, saying writing should be taught so that students can fill out a job application or write a letter asking someone to buy a cemetery lot. Writing is a skill on that level, but it is also a craft and an art; it satisfies an essential need of the human animal. In school and at work, writing is seen as an act of testing, the way ignorance is exposed. But writing is a way of knowing, and the knowing, the understanding, is healing. We can all learn from the needs of writers—the act of writing is constructive, helpful, and for most of us, a necessary process. (1–2)

Recall the opening vignettes Katie provides to give us a glimpse into the lives of writers in a class- ➤

serves as a model that leaves plenty of space for teachers to bring their own particular personalities, experiences, strengths, and knowledge bases to the day-to-day teaching that happens inside the workshop. But as varied as the teachers are who teach in writing workshops every day, they all share a similar focus on the students as writers, and their workshops share some essential characteristics. These things that we see again and again, across many different writing workshops, provide us with the foundation we need in order to learn from each other how to do this teaching well. They give us a place to focus our conversations. Let's look at these briefly now. What are some essential characteristics of writing workshops?

room writing workshop. I don't know if those children ached with caring, but clearly they were engaged in the work of writers. In work that mattered to them. Not work to reveal ignorance, but work to find truth and understanding. In the lives of writers there is always research to be done; exploring to do. That is the work of a writer. "One of the gifts of being a writer is that it gives you an excuse to do things, to go places and explore. Another is that writing motivates you to look closely at life, at life as it lurches by and tramps around," writes Anne Lamott (*Bird by Bird*, xii). Writers are collectors and listeners and talkers and readers. These are habits of mind that help writers to focus, to notice, and to fall in love. It is how they learn *what* to write and *how* to write. Katherine Paterson describes that exploring and collecting and noticing: "The writer of realistic fiction is not a steam-shovel operator but a treasure hunter. In finding the story, a great deal of garbage will have to be sifted through and discarded" (*A Sense of Wonder*, 88). That is the work of a writer. But it is work driven by purpose. And that purpose arises from something the writer has fallen in love with, something about which the writer aches with caring. In our classrooms, we must trust children to know their hearts and minds. We must teach them to feel and look and listen. We must teach them to explore the world, to "sift through garbage" to find treasures. We must provide them with time: time to investigate, time to read, time to think, time to talk, time to write. We must hope that one day they will "ache with caring."

Fox, Mem. 1993. *Radical Reflections: Passionate Opinions on Teaching, Learning, and Living*. San Diego: Harcourt Brace.

Lamott, Anne. 1995. *Bird by Bird: Some Instructions on Writing and Life*. New York: Anchor Books.

Murray, Donald M. 1990. *Shoptalk: Learning to Write with Writers*. Portsmouth, N.H.: Boynton/Cook.

Paterson, Katherine. 1995. *A Sense of Wonder: On Reading and Writing Books for Children*. New York: Plume.

Woodruff, Elvira. *Bantam Doubleday Dell Presents Elvira Woodruff*. Publicity brochure.

Choices about Content

In writing workshops, students decide what they will be writing about—their content—for their many writing projects across the year. By definition, writing is about having something to say, and it is the writer's right to decide what this will be, to decide what he or she wants to say. As teachers we really do not have the right to make this decision for students. We will ask students to do their best to write well in our workshops, so they need to have good reasons of their own to *need* to write well. At the very heart of needing to write well is personal topic selection.

Even when the teaching in the room is very focused on a particular kind of writing (genre) and students are required to do this kind of writing, students still can decide what they will write about in this genre. For example, if we are studying nonfiction in a fourth-grade classroom and learning to write feature articles about nonfiction topics, there is no need for me to force everyone to "choose an animal" or "choose a country" as a topic for their nonfiction pieces. Nonfiction writing isn't about animals or countries; it's about voice, structure, and the convincing balance of opinion and research in the writing, and that's what the teaching needs to be about. Any "nonfiction-y" topic in the world that children care about will do (it may be an animal or a country, but it doesn't *have* to be). And, as we said above, caring about the topic has a lot to do with how good the writing about it will be.

So while we may have curricular reasons from time to time to require our students to write in a certain genre (as in a genre study of nonfiction), we don't need to tell them *what* they have to write about. We can still teach the strategies, techniques, conventions, and understandings about writing that we need to teach, no matter what students are writing about. And the "what" of the writing really matters. The only way for students to understand writing as something they can use in their lives (the driving force behind writing workshops) is for them to have unlimited opportunities to find uses for it, to find their own "what-they'll-write-abouts."

Topic selection in writing is also rigorous curriculum; it's what writers out in the world really have to do. Most of our students don't know how writers do this, how they select topics again and again to sustain an active writing life. So right alongside our requirement that students select their own topics, we must plan for teaching that shows them how writers go about doing this. I find that this curriculum of topic selection often gets only a perfunctory "covering" in the workshop, if it is addressed as curriculum at all. We seem to want our students just to *choose something.* "You have lots of things to write about," we tell them. And they do, but there are things to know about how to choose from all they could write about. There is curriculum behind the choosing, in other words. If our students seem to struggle when it comes to selecting meaningful topics for writing, we might think about offering them more curriculum in how writers go about this.

Having said that it is critical that students choose their own topics for writing, we can get one question out of the way right away because I know someone is asking it right now: "Does this mean we should *never* give our students a writing prompt?" *Never* is a big word and one we should be wary of in any talk about schooling (or about life, for that matter). What the argument here means is that in order to teach writing, there is no need to give students topics; in order for students to learn the purposes for writing, they need to find their own material. Might we have our fourth-grade students practice writing to a prompt from time to time because they will be tested in this way come April? Of course we might. We don't want the first time they have written to a prompt to be the day they go to take the test. But this is the teaching of *testing*, not the teaching of *writing*, and we need to be very clear about that with our students and very careful to keep this teaching in perspective.

As a final note about students selecting their own topics for writing, it's important to keep in mind that this decision of what to write about is one that every writer makes as a member of the classroom community. The right to choose personally meaningful topics comes with responsibilities to this larger community, just as the right to speak as part of a literature circle, a group inquiry, or any class discussion comes with this responsibility. So in the same ways we help students negotiate their talk in respectful ways, we may sometimes have to help them negotiate their topic selections for writing. When certain topics or ways of approaching topics (e.g., violence, sexism, racism, etc.) can do damage to the community, we may feel we simply have to ask students to make another choice about what they will write about. I believe that if we must do this, we are not taking away a child's right to choose, we are taking away his or her ability to hurt another person with this choice.

Time for Writing

To gain the experience they need in writing across a school year, it's best if students can work on their writing for a sustained block of time (at least thirty-five to forty-five minutes) every day in the writing workshop. Writing is something you do, and doing it well can be fairly challenging. What all writers need is *experience*. It takes lots and lots of time over the course of years for writers to get the experience they need to become good writers. Along the way, writers need time to just write and write—a lot of it won't be

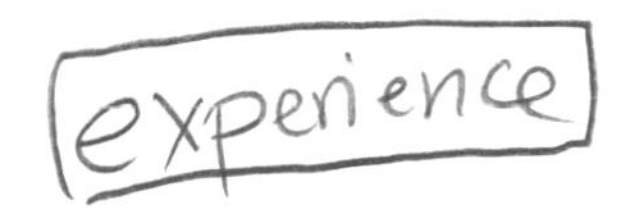

very good writing, but all of it gives writers experience. With the focus on writers in the writing workshop, teachers realize that it's okay if every piece a student writes is not a masterpiece; it's okay if students write a lot of not-so-good stuff alongside the really good stuff.

When it comes to time, writing workshop teachers go for quantity rather than quality. Let's be very clear here: When it comes to TIME, quantity is what matters. It's not that these teachers don't have high-quality expectations for the work that students do. They do. They would just rather have students spend lots and lots of time writing, knowing that not all of it will be so great, than spending just a little time writing and getting everything perfect. They also know that professional writers say they spend lots of time just "fooling around" with writing before they get to the really good stuff. So they do what it takes to open up spaces of time for their students to get the writing experience they need.

WRITERS' VOICES ON . . .

writing through the bad stuff

I feel a need to try to describe a process I don't understand. It's something like a seed that grows in the dark, and one day you look and there is a full-grown plant with a flower on it—or a grain of sand that keeps rubbing at your vitals until you find you are building a coating around it. I think that's why it takes me a long time to write a book. The physical act of getting it down on a page doesn't take so long, but the growth of a book takes time, and most of it happens out of sight like a kind of dream work. I read, I think; I look, I listen, I hate, I fear, I love, I weep, and somehow all of my life gets wrapped around the grain. I don't get a perfect pearl every time, but then, neither does the oyster. The trick is to know which ones to string and which ones to cast away. (Katherine Paterson, *A Sense of Wonder*, 36–37)

Wow, isn't it a comfort to know that Katherine Paterson doesn't get it perfect every time. Doesn't that just lift a burden right off your shoulders knowing that you don't have to have that expectation of your students? I know that as a student, I would certainly appreciate being relieved of that pressure. In fact, I would probably write more, take more risks, try things out a bit more if I were assured that every piece didn't have to end up perfect.

Katie reminds us that lots of the writing our students do will not be very good writing. She assures us that this will be OK. She's right of course, and I'm not just saying that because we are writing this together. Listen to Christopher Paul Curtis:

> I'd tried to write fiction before but it never worked. Writers know when what they've written is bad. In my twenties, I wrote stories and

Teaching

There is a lot to learn about writing, and students need teaching that supports their writing every single day. Writing workshops have lots of rigorous teaching going on. This teaching happens in several forms. There is whole-class teaching in the form of focus lessons, small-group teaching, and individual teaching in the form of one-on-one conferring, as well as the teaching that results when students share from the strategies and techniques they are using to get their writing done. There is hardly a moment during writing workshop when the teacher or a student isn't teaching others in any one of these forms.

Teachers find curriculum to teach in the writing workshop by reading books about writing, by drawing from their own experiences as writers, or by drawing from the experiences of current or former students. They teach about everything that has to do with writing—from how to get ideas for

> they were terrible. In my thirties I wrote stories and they were terrible. It wasn't until I was about 40 that I felt like what I was writing was good. (in Diana Winarski, *Teaching K–8,* 44–46)

Anne Lamott adds,

> Almost all good writing begins with terrible first efforts. . . . A friend of mine says that the first draft is the down draft—you just get it down. The second draft is the up draft—you fix it up. You try to say what you have to say more accurately. And the third draft is the dental draft, where you check every tooth to see if it's loose or cramped or decayed, or even, God help us, healthy. . . . What I've learned to do when I sit down to work on a shitty first draft is to quiet the voices in my head. (*Bird by Bird,* 25–26)

Kaye Gibbons says,

> I have a file in my computer called "Decent Outtakes" and I throw everything in that. And so far with this novel I've had 175 pages, and I have 65 pages of "Decent Outtakes." . . . Dr. Rubin at Algonquin taught me never to throw anything away. It can be plowed under. When I can't create, I open my "Decent Outtake" section, and I grab a page and figure out how to work it into what I've already done. (in Dannye Romine Powell, *Parting the Curtains,* 180)

So, every writer writes a lot of stuff that is not so good. We have to; that's how we get to the good stuff.

Lamott, Anne. 1995. *Bird by Bird: Some Instructions on Writing and Life.* New York: Anchor Books.

Paterson, Katherine. 1995. *A Sense of Wonder: On Reading and Writing Books for Children.* New York: Plume.

Powell, Dannye Romine. 1995. *Parting the Curtains: Voices of the Great Southern Writers.* New York: Anchor Books.

Winarski, Diana. 1999. "Author Interview with Christopher Paul Curtis." *Teaching K–8* 30, no. 2 (October): 44–46.

writing out in the world, to how to craft leads or use telling details, to how to punctuate dialogue. In the best writing workshops I have seen, the teachers have spent a lot of time developing their curriculum knowledge—many of them because they realize how limited their knowledge base was from their own experiences with writing instruction as students in schools. Most of these teachers have completely reeducated themselves about writing (or really, educated themselves for the first time about it) by reading widely from books about writing and by writing themselves. This is one of the most challenging aspects of this teaching: continued development of a knowledge base about writers and writing that helps us meet the teaching demands of writers at so many different places.

Talking

Writers need to talk about their writing, and the thing that seems to make or break many writing workshops is the presence (or absence) of productive talk. Writers just need to be heard; they need listeners who will nod or laugh or cry or wince at what they have written. They need listeners who will say, "This sounds great" or "The other way sounded better." They need people who will listen and understand when they need to complain about how they're not getting anywhere. Even though the specific act of writing might be a mostly silent activity, the life of a writer around that activity is often filled with talk, and because writing workshops nurture writing lives, they need to have lots of talk.

Different writers need different kinds and amounts of talk to support their writing lives. Some writers want someone to read most every sentence before they go on to the next one, and some don't want anyone to see anything they've written until it's almost finished. Some writers will want to talk out an idea before they begin writing about it, and others will need to get it down first and then talk it through. In writing workshops teachers make room for students to get the different kinds and amounts of talk that they need as writers, rather than forcing everyone into a single format for writing talk.

Periods of Focused Study

A year in a writing workshop is made up of periods of focused study around topics of interest and necessity to writers. Much like "units" in social studies or science, the writing workshop needs ongoing units of study at all times.

The teachers in these workshops plan with some kind of whole-class instructional focus in mind. These focused studies can cover a wide range of topics such as: the writer's notebook; various text structures in writing; some aspect of the language system such as punctuation; point of view in writing; the process of publication; the craft of writing; or a particular genre study of writing such as poetry, memoir, or fiction. Some of these studies (such as genre studies) require students to do a certain kind of writing as part of the study, but many of them do not dictate this; they simply support the ongoing work that students have as writers.

During a focused study, the teacher will do lots of very direct teaching, offering content to support the study in a series of focus lessons over several days or weeks. Many focused studies, however, will evolve from inquiry that students are asked to do as part of the writing workshop: looking at texts during a craft study, for example, or immersion in reading examples of a genre during a genre study.

Publication Rituals

Writing workshops operate with the expectation that students will be working toward publication on various writing projects throughout the year. It is only through taking a piece all the way through to publication that students learn both the process of writing and the rewards of seeing that process through to its completion. Most workshops have some publication deadlines that students must work toward—often these are tied to the periods of focused studies—and many also have minimum production requirements that students must meet, not only for finished pieces but also for things like volume in writer's notebooks. These publication rituals and expectations help students maintain the independent part of the writing workshop by helping them understand the outcomes that are expected. In some ways, there is a "publish or perish" mentality that exists in the workshop, and most writing workshop teachers tie at least some grading and evaluation criteria to publication expectations.

High Expectations and Safety

While students have many choices in the writing workshop, choosing not to write is not one of their options. Everyone writes in the writing workshop. We believe that by writing, students will get better at writing, so we require them to do it. Now, having said this, writing workshop teachers have to make a place in their classrooms where it is okay for everyone to write, where it is safe for everyone to write, no matter what that looks like when a student does it. It needs to be okay for even the most struggling student to do what he or she is capable of doing with writing. It needs to be okay for a student who is not yet proficient in English as a second language to write in his or her first language or to mix the two. We can expect everyone to do his or her best work, and we should have high expectations for that. But evaluation should match, at least in some ways, the students' efforts to do their best work. We must also realize that "best work" may look different for different students.

If struggling students realize that their very best work will never bring them rewards because it just doesn't come close to the writing of the other students, then they will quickly learn that their best work is not valued, that it is not safe for them to try in this place, and they will likely stop even trying to grow as writers. Similarly, if very gifted writers realize they can get by without doing their best work, then they will not grow as much as they could in the writing workshop either. If what we really value is writers' best work, and if we show we value this in every interaction with the children in our writing workshops, then we make the writing workshop both a safe place and a challenging place for *every writer there.*

Structured Management

It may be that this should have gone first because so many teachers say, "I would love to have a writing workshop, but I just need more structure than that." Ralph Peterson (2000) has pointed out that what these teachers need is not more structure; they need more control. A teacher telling everyone what to do every moment of the day is actually a very low-structured classroom—the only structure in place is the teacher giving directions!

The writing workshop is a highly structured place. There have to be all kinds of management structures in place for students to know how it works and how the workshop will be maintained. Students in writing workshops learn how to use the room during the workshop, how to manage the supplies needed for their writing, how time is managed in the workshop between teaching, writing, and sharing, what the publication expectations and structures are, how to figure out what to do next in their writing. For the writing workshop to be successful, it must be highly structured and must work the same way basically every day so that it could almost run itself independent of directed activity.

And that's it. Across many writing workshops with teachers who have very different styles of teaching, I have found these essential characteristics in place and manifesting themselves in various ways as children write daily. Let's list them for one more look:

Choices about content
Time for writing
Teaching
Talking
Periods of focused study
Publication rituals
High expectations and safety
Structured management

This list helps me think through my teaching of writing in significant ways. I often ask myself, "Am I honoring all these essentials in my day-to-day work with writers?" The answer to that question helps me refocus and redirect my teaching when I need to, and to celebrate the rewards of honoring these essentials when I see what they mean in the writing lives of my students.

Reference

Peterson, Ralph. 2000. Smoky Mountain Language and Learning Institute, Western Carolina University, Cullowhee, N.C., June 29.

2

The Necessity of a Writing Workshop in a Day Already Full of Writing

"My students write all day long in all content areas. I'm not sure why I would need a writing workshop."

This question has been raised countless times and is a very significant one to consider. If students are writing all day long in all content areas, do they really need a separate time for writing workshop? Obviously, as the writer of this book, I believe the answer to this question is "yes." There does need to be a time devoted only to writing and the teaching of writing. But because I also have lots of respect for this question and for so many of the people who raise it in important ways, and because I have seen students use writing in such powerful ways in all content areas, I have had to really think about why I believe writing workshops are necessary. And while I know that most people who have chosen to read this book also believe writing workshops are necessary, I have chosen to include this chapter because I have so much respect for this question. My hope is that this very personal articulation will help others think through their own important reasons for believing in the necessity of the writing workshop. We need to know why we are engaging in this challenging teaching.

TWO KINDS OF WRITING

First, I believe it is important to think about the kinds of writing that exist in the world and the kinds of writing students are doing across the curriculum. When I look at lives outside classrooms, I see that there are two main kinds of writing that people do:

- They write to support their lives (writing to live).
- They write to communicate ideas to others (composition).

Let me define the difference I see. Writing that supports our lives is usually some form of simply writing things down or filling things out. We use this kind of writing to hold some meaning in place and bring order to our lives. We may write things down to help us (or someone else) *remember* something (grocery lists, telephone numbers, people's names, reminder notes), or to help us *figure things out* (planning lists, household budgets). Writing done in journals, notebooks, and diaries is writing that helps us remember and figure things out. It's writing done just for the one writing it, with no worries about following the chaotic pattern of thoughts because it is just for the writer. Even when the ideas from this kind of writing are shared with others, there hasn't been an effort to organize those ideas to stand alone with an audience.

We *give information* too as we write to support our lives, usually by filling things out: checks, official forms, labels, and addresses. Some of this writing may have an audience in the sense that someone else will read it, but when there is an audience, the purpose of the writing is not to make another person understand or feel something (composition); it's just to give the reader the information requested.

In classrooms there is a lot of writing to live that happens throughout the day, to support both a learning life and a community life. Students write reflections or explanations (to figure things out); make notes from readings, lectures, and observations (to remember); fill out logs or surveys; sign up for lunch, library, or center time (to give information). There's hardly a time in the day when some kind of writing to live is not required to support either the learning or the community.

But what about that other kind of writing—writing to communicate ideas, writing designed to make others feel or understand something. What about writing as *composition?* Writing as composition is writing that begins with an idea a writer wants to communicate. The idea is developed in the writer's thinking, and then, at some point, the move toward composition is made. This move is the beginning move toward an audience, toward readers. This move means that the writer will now have to take this idea he or she has developed and begin to shape it with genre, form, sound, and the conventions of the language system all working together to produce a piece that has the desired impact on readers. This move begins the very complex act of writing as composition, and it is very different from the writing done to support our living. For one thing, it's a whole lot *harder.*

In classrooms, students may do some composition to support other areas of the curriculum, such as writing up the results of a science inquiry, writing position papers in social studies, or writing answers to essay questions on tests. With these kinds of writing across the curriculum, students are certainly taking ideas and expressing them in ways that make readers understand or feel something. But if this kind of writing isn't given its own space in the day, I believe it has many drawbacks for students if we hope for them to grow as writers. Let me explain what I believe these drawbacks to be.

Focus on Writing as Composition

First, I think we have to look at sheer proportions. How much of the writing students do "all day long" is actually the real, hard work of composition? My experience has shown me that not much of it is. Most of the writing students

WRITERS' VOICES ON . . .

the importance of rituals and routines

> Early each morning, Patricia [Polacco], dressed in a comfortable sweatsuit, will sit in a rocking chair and rock rhythmically, back and forth. This is her time—a time for gathering energy, thoughts, and dreams. . . . "When I am composing a story, I sit in one of my rocking chairs and dream it up. For me, rocking is important to the process. I have twelve rocking chairs in the house, and I keep small pads and pens next to them, in case a real good idea springs into my head." (Patricia Polacco, in Deborah Kovacs and James Preller, *Meet the Authors and Illustrators,* 49)

Routines seem to be like shoes—they have to fit the individual to be useful. One thing is clear from reviewing what writers have to say about their work habits—there is no such thing as one size fits all. What strikes me most about this quote from Patricia Polacco is the fact that she makes time for thinking, reflecting, and gathering energy a part of her writing ritual. That commitment to time is essential. She isn't doing the dishes or some other chore. She is writing. She has set aside this time—every morning. This ritual of rocking and thinking is part of her writing routine. As writers, how we use our time might differ from one individual to the next. However, the fact that we set aside time for the work of writing is noteworthy.

Mem Fox, we are told, needs solitude, silence, and a clean workspace:

> I always write in pencil first so that I can rub out as I go. My early drafts are incredibly messy. . . . I'm not one of those disciplined writers who sits down at a blank piece of paper or a blank computer screen and says, I'm not moving until I've written 500 words. I could sit there for a *month* without writing a word. (in Deborah Kovacs and James Preller, *Meet the Authors and Illustrators,* 25).

By contrast, Reynolds Price says,

> My daily routine remains what it's been almost all my writing life, except more so. . . . I'm at work, at the desk, by nine in the morning . . . and I just word process the rest of the morning. And then around twelve-thirty, I have a mineral vitamin drink and fruit juice. . . . That's my lunch. . . . Then I lie down for about an hour and a half, and I read, and I watch *The Young and the Restless.* And then I get up and I work the rest of the afternoon, and then we eat supper around six-thirty or seven. And then, after supper, I like to see friends, watch a movie, work a little bit more if I'm particularly into it that day. (in Dannye Romine Powell, *Parting the Curtains,* 368).

➤

are doing is done in support of something else. They write reading responses to bring to literature study groups or explanations for math solutions to help them think through their process. When writing is seen as something that is simply attached to everything else during the day, it usually only gets little slices of time and you can't do composition work in slices. It's writing to sup-

Both Mem Fox and Reynolds Price are accomplished writers and each has a particular way of working, a way that works for them. Yet it is clear that each of them sets aside time devoted to the work of writing. Anne Lamott describes her routine this way:

> I sit down in the morning and reread the work I did the day before. And then I wool-gather, staring at the blank page or off into space. I imagine my characters, and I let myself daydream about them. A movie begins to play in my head, with emotion pulsing underneath it, and I stare at it in a trancelike state, until words bounce around together and form a sentence. Then I do the menial work of getting it down on paper, because I'm the designated typist. (*Bird by Bird*, 56)

Christopher Paul Curtis explains that his writing actually began during breaks when he worked in an automobile factory warehouse outside Detroit, hanging doors:

> I'd do every other car for ten hours a day. My friend and I decided it would be much easier if each of us did thirty in a row instead of every other one. That way we'd get half of each hour off. To pass the time I began keeping a journal. I found that this made the time fly. . . . In essence, I was practicing, serving an apprenticeship. (in Martha Davis Beck, *Riverbank Review*, 12–15)

Later he took a year off from the factory to write *The Watsons Go to Birmingham*. During that year he "woke every day at 5 A.M., edited and rewrote his previous day's efforts and then at eight, headed to the children's room at the public library . . ." (in Diana Winarski, *Teaching K–8*, 44–46). Both Anne Lamott and Christopher Paul Curtis begin each day by rereading the work from the previous day during the time they set aside for writing.

Time, it's all about time. This work is important. If we fail to set aside time for getting the work of writing done, we send the message that we don't value the work. We see from the writers above, and those mentioned throughout this book, that dedicating time to the work of writing is essential.

Beck, Martha Davis. 1999/2000. "Interview with Christopher Paul Curtis." *Riverbank Review of Books for Young Readers* 2, no. 4 (Winter): 12–15.

Kovacs, Deborah, and James Preller. 1993. *Meet the Authors and Illustrators: 60 Creators of Favorite Children's Books Talk about Their Work*. Vol. 2. New York: Scholastic Professional.

Lamott, Anne. 1995. *Bird by Bird: Some Instructions on Writing and Life*. New York: Anchor Books.

Powell, Dannye Romine. 1995. *Parting the Curtains: Voices of the Great Southern Writers*. New York: Anchor Books.

Winarski, Diana. 1999. "Author Interview with Christopher Paul Curtis." *Teaching K–8* 30, no. 2 (October): 44–46.

port a learning life, not writing to really compose ideas. And we have to remember that while writing to support a learning life is important writing, it's also *easy* writing compared to writing to communicate ideas effectively. Writing observations and reflections is a piece of cake compared to developing an argument convincingly for an audience. Composition is very hard and takes years of experience to learn to do well. From what I have seen, without writing workshops students just don't get enough experience with this kind of writing.

Another problem is that when writing is done only across the curriculum, then the curriculum of writing itself gets lost. There isn't time to focus on the things one can learn in order to write well (the curriculum of writing) because writing is seen only as a means to other curricular ends. All of the things students could be learning about voice, style, genre, structure, craft, and so on—all the things that could be helping them learn to write well—typically get pushed out of the way when writing is not seen as a content area by itself, even when students are composing in other content areas. Without daily time for writing and the focus lessons, conferences, and share times that accompany it, there may be some rushed attempts to teach writing curriculum as students are preparing their history papers, but they often fall flat. Writing is seen as this thing you do after the real thing is over—not as the real thing itself. Rather than writing *across* the curriculum, I believe we need writing *as* curriculum if we hope for our students to learn to write well.

"But what about integration?" you may ask. "Isn't the best classroom one that is fully integrated and one where the lines between all content areas are blurred?"

"Not when that integration spills over into reading and writing," I would say. Let me explain. I believe reading and writing, as content areas, are different from others because they are things you do, not things you know. There are things to know about how to do them and these make up the "content" of this content area, but it's the doing that matters. That's what a *workshop* is all about—it's where you do the work of writing. And from experience I know that when I'm writing to communicate ideas to others (composition), I'm *writing*. I'm not doing anything else but that. I may be thinking about all kinds of things as I'm doing it, across many different disciplines in my life, but I'm doing that thinking to serve my writing. I may be reading books to see how other writers write well or to research certain ideas, but I'm doing that to serve my writing, too. To get composition done, I have to make space in my day for *just writing*.

Let me explain it this way. Writing is kind of like going fishing. "Going fishing," where I come from, represents a very conscious decision to take yourself somewhere and do something. You step away from everything else and you say, "I'm going fishing," and when you do it you're *just fishing* and it's very much a state of *being* and *doing* that separates you from any other activity (well, maybe except being with your daddy, which is why I go fishing).

And writing is a lot like that. When my husband asks me what I'm going to be doing on a given day and I say, "I'm writing," he knows just what that means. He knows I'll be starting about 8:30 (if I don't get an early start, I can't get going). He knows it means I will dress in sweatpants and a tee shirt, if I dress at all—pajamas are good writing attire, too (I have to be comfortable when I write). He knows I'll unplug the phone and plug in the little space heater by my desk (I write better when my feet are really warm). He knows all kinds of tiny little house chores will be taken care of during the day (I have to stop and think a lot while I'm writing, and I like to do mindless things while I'm thinking). He knows I'll be finished sometime around 4:00 and I'll be very hungry when I'm finished (and I'll probably want to go out for dinner because I'm too tired to cook when I've been writing all day). When I say, "I'm writing," my husband knows what that means. Writing for me involves all my little rituals and routines, and it's unlike anything else that I do in my life. I'm *writing*.

I just don't think you can integrate that with anything else. Not the doing of it anyway.

"Integration" in classrooms across content areas makes sense because that's how we think and learn. We connect ideas across all the disciplines of our lives. The connections are natural, effortless, instinctive, and are waiting there for teachers who are watching for them in students' thinking. But I believe the recognition that we think and learn in integrated ways shouldn't stop us from spending focused time *doing* some very specific things—like writing. I think we need to let ourselves know that it is OK for our students to be doing writing and *nothing else*, because it is only with the experience of doing it that we can really hope for our students to grow as writers.

Another drawback of integrating writing with everything else is that when students don't spend large blocks of class time writing, we lose most of the opportunities to teach them individually while they're in the act of writing, and teaching them individually is a very wise way of teaching when anyone is learning how to do something. The teaching we do around writing in other content areas almost invariably focuses on the content rather than the writing itself, so even though these chunks of time may be large, if the focus isn't on writing we are steered away from the teaching of writing. We need students to be writing regularly both so they can get the experience they need and so we can get the teaching time we need to help them learn to write well.

Finally, when we attach writing only to other content areas, we almost always lose what I think is one of the most important aspects of the writing curriculum, the one that will make it likely that students will pursue writing for important purposes throughout their lives. In writing across the curriculum, students are almost always writing to fill some curricular goal that exists outside their own purposes and intentions. They may have all kinds of choices about the writing within that curricular goal, but they are still making those choices for someone else's purpose.

When all students do is write across the curriculum, they never learn the important lesson that writing is also a way to get things done in your life, a way to follow your own dreams or passions, a way to be heard when you want someone to hear you. Most writing across the curriculum classrooms (and I'm sure that notable exceptions exist) don't have room for students' sometimes wonderfully reckless, wild, on-the-edge, and, I would suggest, *very important* reasons to write. And if we don't make room for these in our classrooms, then students likely won't make room for them in their lives.

Which leads us to another question. Is it important that students grow up to be the kinds of people who make room for purposeful writing that *enriches* their lives? Or should our teaching be more pragmatically focused on writing that simply *maintains* their lives? This is a question of value. There is not a single right answer to it. I can tell you that those who believe writing should be taught as something that enriches a life (as well as maintains it) are usually those who have done writing that has enriched their lives in some way. They're the people who know the satisfaction of writing about the things they are most passionate about just because they're passionate. They're the people who write letters to the editor because they're incensed, who always buy blank greeting cards, who write the stories of their childhoods because they just don't want to forget. They are also the people, of course, who write personnel memos and letters of application and legal documents.

I guess what it comes down to is a belief that writing can do more than support a professional life where you write because you have to *get your work done*. It's a belief in writing that also supports a personal life, the kind of life you want to live. It's writing to *get your life done*. I believe the writing workshop makes room for that in a way that writing across the curriculum cannot.

So, let me step back now and pull out the important threads of my argument. Why are writing workshops necessary when students are writing in other content areas all day long? (And by the way, I think students *should* be writing to support their learning lives in content areas, all day long. The workshop doesn't replace that.)

I believe writing workshops are necessary because . . .

- Writing to communicate ideas to others (composition) is different than writing to support a learning life.
- Writing to communicate ideas to others takes more time than is generally given when it is spread across the curriculum.
- When writing is done only across the curriculum, then the curriculum of writing itself is overshadowed or lost completely.
- Writing is something you do, not something you know. Students need time to *just write* so they can gain experience as writers.
- We can do our best teaching when we catch students in the act of writing (as we can in the workshop).
- We value that students learn to use writing to enrich their lives and not just to maintain their lives.

Sometimes all these reasons make sense to us as teachers and it's still hard to decide to have a daily workshop. I think it's hard sometimes, not because we believe that writing across the curriculum is really sufficient for our students to learn to write well, but because we are uncomfortable with writing ourselves and so we're uncomfortable giving over our teaching time to it. We may feel like we just don't know enough about writing and can't imagine what our teaching part in an *every-day* workshop would be. Many of us who have writing workshops now started with just those feelings. We just had to trust that students would benefit from *time spent writing* while we gave ourselves the time to grow into good teaching around that. We've spent years growing our own knowledge bases so we were comfortable with writing and our teaching of writing in a workshop.

WRITERS' VOICES ON . . .

writing routinely

Anybody can write a book. . . . I mean, look at me. Over 60 books and not one bit of talent. . . . I know it sounds funny; but I really do believe it. Writing is something you have to learn. It is a craft. It takes practice. If you set your mind to something, no matter how hard it is, you can do it. That's my message to kids: *Go for it.* If you want something in life, work at it and you can get it. . . . I don't think writing is a gift. We learn to speak, we learn to read, we learn to write. Writing is a natural thing, not a special talent. . . . Writing is something you learn to do because you do it all the time. (Patricia Reilly Giff, in Deborah Kovacs and James Preller, *Meet the Authors and Illustrators,* 28)

Writers are people who write, right? Well, yes, and in our classrooms we can have a community of writers. A key point from the quote above is the notion that writing is "something you learn to do because you do it all the time." Developing an identity as a writer (in life or in the classroom) assumes that you participate in the act of writing regularly. We are not likely to see ourselves as writers if we simply write the morning message from the board each day and copy questions from our textbooks to answer for homework. To develop a sense of self as a writer, to have that identity, we must live in a place where we have demonstrations of what writing well looks and sounds like. In our zest to help students develop that sense of self, that identity as writers, we would be wise to listen to Flannery O'Connor, who ➤

Time is another issue. I know a lot of us feel like we just don't have time to squeeze a writing workshop into our already crowded days. And we're probably right—we can't squeeze one in and keep everything we've got too. We'll have to do as Lucy Calkins says and "take carloads of curriculum to the dump" if we're going to make time for a writing workshop. But what's interesting to me is—and I don't want to step on toes here, though I fear I might—what's interesting is that I've never met a teacher who really wanted to teach writing who didn't find time to do that. While the demands placed on our time in schools can be extraordinary, too often we use this as a convenient excuse not to do things we don't want to do or feel uncomfortable doing. As my friend Randy Bomer is fond of reminding us as teachers, we can never have more time. There's no such thing as "more time." There's only time (no more or less) and we have to decide how we'll use what time there is.

once wrote that "[f]ew people are interested in writing well. . . . They are interested in BEING a writer" (in Rosemary M. Magee, *Conversations with Flannery O'Connor,* 13). Clearly, we want our students to be interested in being writers. But we must also understand that is not enough. We have to lead them beyond the romance of the identity and move them toward the action of the lifestyle. That is, living like a writer in a classroom and the world beyond:

> Being a writer means paying attention to what strikes you. What you notice comes from your core. It's not going to be what other people notice. People are different from each other. In order to embrace that fact, it's important for an artist to be very sensitive to what is striking him or her. (Clyde Edgerton, in Dannye Romine Powell, *Parting the Curtains,* 119)

As teachers, we must be sensitive to what might strike our students. We must recognize that in a community of writers there will be a range of passions and interests and pursuits and we must find ways to support those so that our students will have purposeful reasons to write regularly.

The writers I know, and many others whose work and interviews I've read, indicate that they write routinely—some every day, some on a schedule. Some indicate various patterns and routines. However, one thing is clear: Writers have a sense of themselves, an identity in the world as ones who write.

Kovacs, Deborah, and James Preller. 1993. *Meet the Authors and Illustrators: 60 Creators of Favorite Children's Books Talk about Their Work.* Vol. 2. New York: Scholastic Professional.

Magee, Rosemary M., ed. 1987. *Conversations with Flannery O'Connor.* Jackson: University Press of Mississippi.

Powell, Dannye Romine. 1995. *Parting the Curtains: Voices of the Great Southern Writers.* New York: Anchor Books.

I guess what it comes down to is that teachers who have found significant reasons to have writing workshops make time during their days to have them. Sometimes they give up some of their writing in content areas to make time. Sometimes they require students to write (as part of the writing workshop) a few pieces during the year that represent their learning in various content areas, careful to leave wide-open spaces for their own purposes and intentions. But whatever they have to negotiate to get their time, they get it so that students can spend time *just* writing and they can spend time *just* teaching writing.

3

Teaching and the Development of Writing Identities

"And the plain truth is, not everyone can be a writer."

I didn't say that. Cynthia Rylant said that in an article she wrote for teachers of writing ("The Room in Which Van Gogh Lived," 1990), and I remember being just distraught the first time I read it. I was reading the article with a group of teachers, and when we got to that part, it was sort of like the waters parted between us. Half of us were distraught, the wind knocked out of our sails, and the other half (who had always had their doubts about this whole writing business) were joyous. "*See,*" their faces seemed to say, "this is what we've been telling you all along." As if that settled it. It didn't help matters any that I was known in the group as a devoted Rylant groupie. But that didn't settle it for me. I knew I had to figure out what she was saying, and either I had to understand her or I had to just flat out disagree with her. Her comment had shaken me, but it didn't break me.

For months after encountering Cynthia Rylant's article, I thought and wrote and talked about this question, "What does it mean to be a writer?" Part of the accepted "talk" of writing workshops has been to refer to all of our students as writers, but what do we really mean when we say that? And why have some of us never accepted that talk very willingly—because we don't think of ourselves as writers? After muddling my way through this question for a long time, I believe I have come to a place of understanding that has made a significant difference in my teaching. Before I can explain that difference, I'll have to share with you the understanding I have found.

What does it mean to be a writer? I think it comes down to the essential nature of writing. Writing is something that you *do,* not something that you *know,* and when you think about it, that is an incredibly important understanding for us to have as teachers of writing. You see, as we move through our lives, we *define* both ourselves and others by the kinds of things we do in life. Take our friend Frank, for example. If you asked me to describe Frank for you, one of the main ways I would describe him would be to tell you about the things he does. Frank is a lawyer, a motorcycle rider, a golfer, an avid reader, a history buff, a kayaker. . . . I can tell you a lot about him by simply telling you what kinds of things he does.

So we create these spaces in our rooms known as writing workshops where we say to children, "Be a writer here." We ask each of our students to *be* a certain kind of person, a person defined by an activity we require them to do. Presumptuous of us, huh? But we are called on to teach writing, and writing is something you do. So how can we ask students to do it very often without also asking them to build an identity around their work? A person can't do something *a lot* without that happening. And so in the simplest sense, we can begin by saying that, in our classrooms, our students are people who write every single day.

But when you think about the subtle difference between doing something a lot and having it as an identity for yourself, you begin to complicate the issue. For example, I cook almost every day. But if you asked me, "Are you *a cook?*" I might really have to think about that. I might think about how you would define that, or I might think only about how I would define "a cook," but either way, the fact that I do it every day doesn't necessarily mean I will give myself that identity, that label. We can split hairs over that label.

I believe Cynthia Rylant is using the label "writer" differently from the way we have been using it to talk about teaching. I think she is using a much more narrow definition for what a "writer" is than "someone who writes often" (as we've been defining it). Does she mean a professional writer like her? Does she mean a great writer who will write pieces that will be published by the millions and win awards? Does she simply mean "Be a writer who writes well"—a gifted writer? I think she may mean some combination of all these. And that's not the working definition I need to help me understand what's happening in a writing workshop where everyone is asked to write. Maybe we need different language to talk and think about the ways that writing is connected to identity.

It's interesting to me that many, many adults will define themselves as "readers" but not as "writers." Why is this? It may be that they read a lot more than they write and that they feel much more comfortable with this activity. But I think it's also because the label "writer" is actually a profession you can pursue in a way that "reader" is not. (I wish there were a job you could get as a professional reader—I'd apply.) They may write a great deal both to maintain and to enrich their lives and still not be willing to say, "I'm a writer" because they don't write professionally or for publication. Also, they most likely think of writing as something you can clearly do well or poorly, and this is not a feeling most readers have about reading. The status label "reader" is connected more to quantity of reading than to quality of reading in most people's minds, and this is not as true of writing. So I believe that the "public at large" mostly uses the definition that Rylant was apparently using for a writer: someone who writes really well for audiences made up of lots and lots of people.

The label "writer," used in just this narrow way, can really limit our understandings as teachers of writing. I believe that if we engage in any activity over time, we develop an identity related to that, whether we label ourselves "a cook" or "a writer" or not. I have some very clear understandings about who I am and what I can do when I cook. Because I'm in the kitchen so often and have so much experience there, I know myself *in that way,* whether I call myself "a cook" or not. I make good biscuits, but not as good as my mother's. I never get gravy right. I cook vegetables to a slow delicious death, and I can do a chicken like nobody's business. . . . I am a person who cooks, and I know about myself in that way. Likewise, in our classrooms, our students are going to be *people who write;* and, over time, they are going to develop identities related to writing and come to know themselves in that way. There's no way around that. If you do something enough, it happens.

WHAT DIFFERENCE DOES IDENTITY MAKE?

What does all this mean to our teaching? Well, we need to find our focus, our goals for teaching writing, in thinking about our students as people who write. Our writing workshops are going to be "doing" places where identities will develop from that "doing" over time, so we need to think about the *kinds of writers* we want our students to become over time. We need to fill in this very big blank for ourselves: "Over time in my writing workshop, I hope to see students developing. . . ." What? What do we hope to see them developing? Where do we hope all the curriculum we offer them will lead them as writers? What kind of people do we hope they will become as they are becoming people who write? We have to remember that all the day-to-day curriculum we offer in the writing workshop is helping to sketch out a bigger picture of development in our students' writing lives. We have a responsibility to know where we want that teaching to lead our students. This is why the answer to that question is so important. Whatever you fill in that blank with *leads all your teaching.*

In the early years of my teaching of writing, I had a lot of trouble knowing exactly what I hoped to see students developing. But because I have developed more and more focus through the years, I have found I am able to help students grow so much more. I have a reason I can articulate for whatever I am doing with students in a writing workshop, and it always comes back to this vision I have for the kinds of writers I want to see them becoming. Let me describe that vision for you now. First we'll just look at all of it at once, and then we'll open each part up a little.

Over time in a writing workshop I hope to see students developing . . .

- a sense of self as writers, as well as personal writing processes that work for them;
- ways of reading the world like writers, collecting ideas with variety, volume, and thoughtfulness;
- a sense of thoughtful, deliberate purpose about their work as writers, and a willingness to linger with those purposes;
- as members of a responsive, literate community;
- ways of reading texts like writers, developing a sense of craft, genre, and form in writing;
- a sense of audience, and an understanding of how to prepare writing to go into the world.

These are the aspects of identity that I want students to develop in the writing workshop over time. Over a long, long time. Notice that there is no grade level or ability level tied to this vision. Writers grow in these aspects throughout their whole lives, with every writing experience they have. As a teacher, I know I need to foster students' development in these areas, whether they are seven years old or seventy years old. How I go about that will be developmentally appropriate, but the kinds of development I want to see don't change based on age, experience, or ability. This is my vision for all writers, and every bit of teaching I do in the writing workshop—every experience I set up for students to have as writers—should encourage development in one or more of these areas.

A sense of self as writers, as well as personal writing processes that work for them

Because there are so many different ways of working as writers, I want my students to develop habits of work and habits of mind that are personally effective for them in lots of different situations. Knowing the ways they work best as writers will help students manage their writing lives throughout their lives. For example, as a writer I know that I work best when I have big chunks of time to work on big pieces of writing. I don't do well in short spurts. So to write these kinds of pieces, I have to schedule whole days, and several in a row (sometimes a whole summer!), just to write. My colleague Lester, on the other hand, is more of a "spurt" writer. If he has only an hour, he can use that hour effectively to work on a piece of something. We have developed very different ways of working as writers, and we each have to manage those ways to get our writing done. With experience, I want my students to know what ways work best for them.

I also want students to have a good sense of their strengths and weaknesses as writers so they can capitalize on the strengths and manage the weaknesses. For example, one of my strengths as a writer is organization; I'm good at making lots of different chunks of a text work together. I know this about myself, and I have a lot of faith in this when I write. I use this faith to help guide my writing. On the other hand, I have a weakness in spelling that I have to be very careful to manage with technology and the support of my friends—especially when the audience stakes are high and warrant caution. Another weakness is that I can be hopelessly redundant, so I have to really watch where I'm saying things more than once. The point is, I know these things about myself as a writer. This is what I want for my students. I want the writing workshop to be a place where they come to know things about themselves as writers so that they can manage their writing lives more efficiently.

I also want my students to have a sense of themselves as writers over time, to see themselves from a historical perspective. I'd like them to have a sense of what is new and what is familiar territory. For example, the kind of writing I am doing here is very familiar territory. I fall into it easily with lots of faith gained from experience. If I suddenly decided I wanted to be a writer of fiction, however, I would be making a decision to get into something very new. I have written very little fiction in my life, so I would have to go about it quite differently, spending lots of time finding support in the work of other fiction writers before I even started. I know I would also need to give myself lots of room to write bad fiction before I wrote any good fiction. Knowing where you are on the timeline of your writing life can be a big help in managing your future writing, and so I work to develop this same sense of history in my students as writers.

Ways of reading the world like writers, collecting ideas with variety, volume, and thoughtfulness

This goal has to do with habits of mind. I want my students to learn the habits of mind that writers use to fill their lives with important writing. I want students to know that so much important writing work happens away from writers' desks as these writers move through the world, watching and noticing and thinking deeply about what they see. Donald Graves says this of writers reading the world: "Writing comes from the events of our daily lives, from what appears at first to be trivial. . . . [T]he writer's first act is to listen and observe the details of living" (*A Fresh Look at Writing,* 1994, 36).

This is one of those aspects of our work with children as writers that extends across all other areas of their learning lives. Watching, noticing, and thinking deeply will help them be better writers, but it will also help them be better scientists, sociologists, historians, mathematicians, and on and on. Watching, noticing, and listening—reading the world—is what smart people do. All of the work teachers have been doing with writer's notebooks and lifebooks and journals is in support of this goal. Over time, we want students to develop more and more ways of finding important ideas to bring to their writing desks. This will give them power throughout their writing lives, as it will help them find purposes, ideas, and intentions as writers.

A sense of thoughtful, deliberate purpose about their work as writers, and a willingness to linger with those purposes

My friend Isoke Nia, writing teacher extraordinaire, calls this sense "developing rigor and stamina" as writers. She wants the students she teaches to learn, over time, to write a lot, to write for a long time, and to carry ideas out through long pieces of writing. She wants her students developing and following through with bigger and bigger plans and projects as writers. To put it simply, she wants to see her students pushing themselves to do harder and harder work as writers.

Many of our students come to us in the middle- and upper-elementary grades never having been in writing workshops, and they have very little rigor or stamina as writers. Watching them write is like watching someone try to hike up a steep trail when that person is very out of shape. They keep stopping to ask, "Are we there yet?" And we have to do all kinds of prodding and nudging and outright pushing sometimes to help students grow in this area. We help them develop a sense of purpose by constantly pounding away at this notion of "Why are you writing this? What's your purpose? What plans do you have for how you're going to work on this?" We need to ask them these kinds of questions about every piece they decide to work on for publication.

Developmentally, "lingering with a purpose" might range from a first grader working on a piece for more than one day to a sixth grader writing and anthologizing a whole series of short fiction stories. But wherever we have to start our nudging, we must start, because without the challenges that come from doing harder and harder work as writers, our students won't grow very much, and they'll never know the rewards that can come from doing that hard, intensive, purposeful work.

As members of a responsive, literate community

Over time, I believe it is important that my students learn ways of living and being in a community of people who write, because for as long as they are writing as a part of their schooling, they will be part of a writing community. They can't choose to "go solo"—they must necessarily live in a space with twenty to thirty other people who are writing. How will they live productively in that space?

Students need to learn how to share their own ideas and listen to the ideas of others, ask important questions, support those who are struggling, give many kinds of feedback during all stages of the writing process, learn from other writers, and teach other writers what they know. Students need to learn some sense of responsibility for the community's well-being, doing their parts to make the community a safe, happy, and productive place. They need to learn to do things like clip out newspaper articles they think another writer would be interested in, or suggest a crafting book to a student who needs one. They need to learn to respect the space and materials in the workshop and to use them both in ways that are considerate of other writers.

Basically, over time, I hope that my students learn better and better ways of working alongside one another—another writing workshop goal that spills over into so many other areas of our learning and working lives. Many writers do join writing communities at various times in their lives for several weeks or even months, communities where they can get the kind of support from other writers that we hope our students get every single day in our writing workshops. But members of responsive, literate communities aren't born overnight. We have to nurture students' development as members of the community through teaching that grows from this focus.

Ways of reading texts like writers, developing a sense of craft, genre, and form in writing

Here's where we look at the products of student writing. We do hope that, over time, students will be able to develop better and better pieces of writing. We want them learning to write *well,* and so we teach them how to study the texts of other writers to see how they have written well. We encourage them to try out the crafting techniques they see other writers using to make their writing lively, interesting, compelling. We study various genres throughout the year so that students can grow in their understanding of the potentials of different genres and can learn which genres they feel most comfortable using. We spend lots of time looking at form and structure in writing so that students will learn to shape and organize the pieces they are writing.

The focus here is always on students' developing sense of what it takes to write well, rather than on single pieces of writing. Although many of the markers of what a student knows about writing well will be found in actual pieces of writing, the pieces of writing themselves are not the focus of our teaching. It's not our goal to see to it that every single published piece a student writes is absolutely the best piece of writing it can be. Our goal is to see evidence that, in writing any single piece, a student is pushing forward in his or her understanding of what it means to write well. If we can see evidence that this is the case, we let other things go and celebrate the new development we do see. Understanding this goal takes so much of the burden off of us. It's not the same as when we were in school and only wrote a very few pieces, feeling that they all had to be as perfect as possible. Remember that we are helping students learn to write well *over time,* not all today, tomorrow, next week, or even all year. Our writing workshops are just one step on a long journey of learning to write well. We have to do as much as we can to help students learn all they can, but we don't have to do it all for a single piece of writing.

A sense of audience, and an understanding of how to prepare writing to go into the world

Well now, isn't it also important that students know how to make their subjects and verbs agree? And we all want to say, "Well of course it is," because we just need to say that. But what if someone said, "Why?" Can we be articulate about "why?" We need to be in order to be purposeful in our teaching. One of the things I hate to hear most is someone telling older elementary kids that the reason they need to spell correctly is so that people will be able to read their writing. That's nonsense. Most of the misspellings that more experienced writers make are quite readable. That's not why writers need to mind their spelling. Writers need to mind their spelling, and their subject-verb agreement, and all those other conventions because certain audiences in the world expect them to, and for their writing to have power with those audiences, it should be conventional.

Now this means several things. For one, it means that we need to teach students to "read" an audience and find out how high the stakes are for the writing to be "right." Too often in schools, we go from one extreme to another. Either we act as if everything children write is for this really high-stakes audience where everything matters, or we throw up our hands and act as if nothing conventional matters at all. And that just doesn't match what people have to do to manage writing out in the real world. Writers have to have a very clear sense of the stakes for the writing audience, and then act accordingly. I write for many low-stakes audiences where editing for convention just isn't that important—in my notebook (that's writing for me), as well as in notes or letters or e-mails to friends or family members. I also do some high-stakes writing, like committee member memos to my colleagues, articles and books I submit for publication, and flyers that go out to several hundred people advertising a summer writing workshop. My process of editing for convention is different based on the stakes of my audiences—lots of exhaustive attention if the stakes are high; hardly any if they're not. Over time, I want to see students developing a sense of audience, and I want to see them manage their writing to fit the stakes associated with that writing.

A big part of learning to write for different audiences is developing a sense of when to get help with writing. We want to see our students developing, over time, a sense of what kinds of proofreading they are likely to need help with, and of the stakes for writing that warrant their seeking this help. We need them to understand when it makes sense to have an outside reader go through a whole piece just to see if they missed anything—not doing the proofreading work for them, but simply checking behind them because the audience for the writing warrants this kind of attention. And we need to teach them as much about convention in writing as we can along the way, in the context of their writing, so that they can feel confident in their knowledge of how the language works and how audiences expect it to be used.

We need to be very careful not to lose sight of why understandings about language conventions are important. They serve a specific purpose—they aren't ends in themselves. If our students aren't finding audiences who are important to write for, then we've got no business teaching them the "skills" writers use to prepare writing to go into the world. And if our students aren't learning to write with style and voice and focus and a strong sense of craft, what difference does it make if their subjects and verbs agree and everything is spelled correctly? Who would want to read it?

BACK TO THE "PLAIN TRUTH"

"The plain truth is, every one of my students writes."

I did say that. And I have to keep on saying it and thinking about it so that it reminds me of the huge implications our teaching of writing will have in students' lives. Under our care, they will come to know themselves as people who write, and so we have a responsibility to help them care for themselves as writers.

Sometimes my teacher education students ask me if it should worry them that they are the only teachers their students ever have who teach writing this way (in a writing workshop). "What if they get to the next grade level and the teacher doesn't do this at all?" they ask. "Well, thank goodness they had *you* then," I say. It seems to me that if I were my students' one shot at this kind of teaching in their whole school lives, teaching that would nurture their ways of being in so many important ways, that would be even more reason for me to stick with it. That sense of self, that sense of being "one who writes" that is nurtured in a writing workshop, is a hard thing to lose. Our students will take that sense of self with them once they leave us, no matter what happens in the next year and the next. So even if that one year they spend with us is the only year in school they ever feel like writers, that year *matters*. Maybe more than any of us will ever know. . . .

References

Graves, Donald. 1994. *A Fresh Look at Writing*. Portsmouth, N.H.: Heinemann.

Rylant, Cynthia. 1990. "The Room in Which Van Gogh Lived." In *Workshop Two: By and for Teachers, Beyond the Basal*, edited by Nancie Atwell, 18–21. Portsmouth, N.H.: Heinemann.

4

The Tone of Workshop Teaching

Most anyone who's ever spent time in a writing workshop comes away from it knowing that it just *feels* different from a more traditional classroom. A friend of mine recently showed me a written evaluation from an administrator who had observed her writing workshop and written that very thing, "Your classroom has a different feel to it." We think it was a compliment.

That a classroom has a certain feeling to it is a hard-to-pin-down idea, but one that's worth thinking a lot about if we hope to have successful writing workshops. The feeling in any classroom comes mostly from the tone of the teaching that takes place there. What do we mean when we say "the tone of the teaching"? I use this expression to mean the sum total of the presentation of teaching—and this doesn't mean teaching *as* presentation, like with an overhead and lecture notes. This means how the teaching presents itself: the sound of the voice, the body language, the position of the teacher in relation to the students, the eye contact, the content of the message, the absence or presence of humor, tension, compassion, and so on. All of these are things that come together to give the teaching—or any interaction with others, for that matter—a certain attitude, a certain feeling.

The tone of any interaction begins with how those involved feel about each other, how they identify with each other. Teachers who genuinely like their students will have a different tone to their teaching than teachers who think their students are "little troublemakers." Teachers who think their students are very smart will have a very different tone to their teaching than teachers who think their students "just don't have any skills." And what's interesting is, the tone of teaching can change dramatically in a single day, for example, when a class of students changes to a teacher who views them differently. I've seen this happen many times.

The tone of writing workshop teaching, then, begins with teachers seeing their students as writers, an identity we explored in detail in the last chapter. Because we view our students as writers, we ask them different kinds of questions from the ones other teachers ask—questions such as, "In what genre do you feel most comfortable writing?" We ask our students, our writers, to spend their time differently from the ways they spend time with other teachers: "Every day you will have forty minutes to spend working on your writing." We give our students different kinds of homework: "Take your notebook somewhere interesting at home, and see what kinds of entries you can gather there." We talk to them differently from other teachers: "I know just what you're feeling. I find fiction so challenging too. . . ." And on and on. The tone for every single interaction in the writing workshop is set by the fact that we view our students as writers.

But what about how they view *us*? We have said that the tone of interactions is set by how those involved feel about each other. We have thought a lot already about the need to think of our students as writers, but to establish the tone that we want in our workshops, we will really have to think about what our students see when they see us teaching them. This idea is very significant; let's really slow it down and think it through. We'll start with a teaching story that, I think, will bring up some significant issues related to this matter of tone.

A Teaching Story about Tone

In her fourth year of teaching, Margaret Johnson was determined to get a writing workshop up and running in her third-grade classroom. In her first three years, she had had her students "doing the writing process," but she wanted to shift that focus and make her classroom a place where students lived with writers' purposes and intentions. She wanted a place where she could teach them daily about what it means to really *use* writing in powerful ways to do important work in their learning and in their lives. Margaret had discovered this power of writing for herself, and she wanted to turn her personal understandings about writing into teaching.

Early in the year, in a genre study of poetry, Margaret noticed her students doing what most young students new to poetry will do: They were writing poems that rhymed but made very little sense. As a writer herself, Margaret could remember feeling "at the mercy of rhyme" in the past, and so she smartly decided to do a focus lesson on this very issue. In her notebook, she played around at writing some poems where she totally let the rhyming scheme drive the word choices. She wanted to experience this feeling again as a writer, just as her students were—this feeling of rhyming at all costs. She came up with several very bad poems.

Margaret chose what she thought was the worst of her poems—one that not only sounded silly, but also that didn't say *anything*. Her plan was to read the awful poem to her students, and after they had surely seen how bad it was, she was going to talk with them about how, as poets, they needed to be so careful with words. They needed to pay attention to both sound *and* meaning. They needed to choose words so carefully in order to help them say what they wanted to say in a poem—word choice she thought was so obviously missing from her poem. It was going to be a great lesson.

Margaret gathered the children around, and when everything was quiet, she read to them—from start to finish—her horrible, terrible, no-good, very-bad poem. Collecting her thoughts in the moment of silence that followed the last line of the poem, Margaret looked around at her students. Her students looked back at her, and then, as one, they burst into applause.

Why the Applause?

The group of teachers who were gathered laughed with Margaret as she told us this story from her teaching life. "You just can't believe how awful this poem was," she said. "And they clapped for me! My whole lesson was ruined!" We laughed with Margaret because, well, sometimes that's all there is to do when something like this happens in our teaching. We laugh. And then we get on to the business of trying to figure things out. Why did Margaret's students applaud her awful poem?

An easy explanation would be that Margaret's students didn't know a good poem from a bad poem. But I don't like that explanation. I'm sure Margaret's students were still growing in their sense of knowing what good poetry was supposed to sound like, but I think children are smarter than that. I'm always reluctant to go for the "They just don't get it" explanation. I've learned from experience that most things go so much deeper than that.

Perhaps, still attached to a childhood where word play and sound play are games they love to play, they really *liked* the poem. Children have this remarkable ability to find the good in things, and maybe they simply focused on the playfulness of the poem and didn't feel a need to search for deeper meaning. Or maybe Margaret's students hated the poem but recognized what a risk it had been for a writer to read something aloud that she had written. Maybe they were applauding their teacher's effort—her risk—because they were trying to support her, despite her obvious poetic deficiency. Maybe most of them were just clapping because someone else, possibly motivated by one of the reasons above, had started it. Perhaps most of them had just been joining in.

Maybe there were as many different reasons for the applause that morning as there were pairs of hands creating the thunder of it. Most of the dozens of little stories that make up our teaching days have layers and layers of plot explanations running underneath them. And so, at the risk of oversimplifying what happened that morning in Margaret's classroom, I'd like to suggest another possibility for why the students responded with applause, a possibility that will help us think about the tone of writing workshop teaching.

In the background of this story, it is important to know that not only was Margaret new to workshop teaching, but that workshop teaching was new to her students as well. This group of children had three years of school under their belts, and they had come to understand the most basic things about school in some fairly traditional ways. One of these basic things was, of course, the definition of *teacher:* someone who knows most everything and will tell you if you listen. This was the working definition that they had when they entered Margaret's classroom, and as it was early in the year when they listened to her read them a poem from her notebook, it was the definition that most likely guided their response. They were still thinking of their teacher as "the one who always gets everything right," and they were responding to that—to her *right-ness* as the teacher—as much as they were to her poem.

Margaret was at the beginning of a long journey to help her students redefine the teaching-learning relationship. She wanted her students to come to see her not as someone who had all the answers, but as someone who had had a lot of experience struggling with the same things they were struggling with as writers. She wanted them to see her as being *like them* in that way. She wanted her students to see her as *a writer*—not necessarily as a great writer or as a published writer, but simply as someone who wrote because writing meant something to her. She wanted them to see that she was teaching out of her own writing experiences, rather than out of some magical book of right-ness that belonged to teachers.

Helping her students see her in this way would take time, but Margaret knew that the time was worth it. "Ruined" lessons like the one that morning were worth it. Until her students came to see her differently, came to see her as being like them—someone who did this thing called writing—Margaret could not change the essential tone of her teaching. And the tone of the teaching matters enormously; Margaret and other good writing workshop teachers know this.

The best way I know to explain this situation is to think about a teaching setting outside of school. My friend's nine-year-old daughter Sara takes dance lessons twice a week. When this beautiful, graceful little girl tells me about her dance teacher, she tells me all about him as a *dancer*. She knows about what roles he has danced in different ballets. She knows about how he fell in love with ballet as a young boy when other young boys were falling in love with different things. She knows about a recurring injury that sometimes makes certain moves difficult for him. She knows about how he traveled a lot as a professional dancer, and how he saw interesting places and people in between long practices and grueling schedules. She knows he gets a certain look in his eyes—"a twinkle," she says—when the music is just right, and everyone is moving to it, and the world feels "full of gracefulness." She sees her teacher as a *dancer,* and that is the point of departure for her whole learning relationship with him. He is someone who does what she is learning how to do.

And oh, the feeling of that dance studio when "class" is underway. You watch, and what you see is a *dancer* teaching *dancing.* He moves in and out and around his students, showing them how to hold an arm and bend a knee and make a sweeping gesture with their whole bodies without moving their feet. The students are watching him and listening to him, and you can just feel it in the room—*the energy of all of them dancing together.*

You have this feeling that it would never occur to these dance students to applaud for their teacher in the midst of his teaching. They are much too focused on trying to understand what he is showing them and telling him. They want to be able to do what he does, to know what he knows and feel what he feels about dancing. Their response to his teaching is to turn it upon themselves immediately, to start trying it themselves. They don't have time for applause. Your heart kind of flutters at the sight of it, the remarkable beauty of this teaching.

Think about how *basic,* how *essential,* it is to Sara's learning to dance that she sees her teacher as a dancer.

I feel this way, this heart-fluttering way, whenever I watch really good writing teachers. Though very different from a dance studio, their workshops have this same feeling—this same tone about them as Sara's dance classes. When you watch them, what you feel is *the energy of all of them writing together.* You can watch students leaning into what their teacher is saying because they see her as someone who represents what they are trying to become. If you ask them about their teacher, they can tell you about why she chose the purple notebook and how she takes it along to the laundromat every Saturday morning, because the most interesting characters are there. They can tell you about the article she had rejected from a teaching magazine and about the historical novel she wants to write someday. They can tell you that she always has to recite "*i* before *e* except after *c*" for every single word with those vowels in it, and they can tell you that she's not too good at writing funny stuff (but she tries really hard). They can tell you about the memoir she wrote about her mother that was so good it made them all cry.

In the best writing workshops I have ever seen, the students can tell you all about their teacher as a writer, and that teacher can tell you all about his or her students as writers too. *They know each other in that way,* and this changes everything; this changes the whole tone of the classroom. Students can see the real work of a real person in what their teacher says and does, and teaching is not seen as the performance of right answers that deserves applause. Students take to the teaching so differently when they see their teacher as being like them and like the writers they are trying to become.

I guess, with all of this talk about tone, it sounds as if I am making rather short order of the much-debated question, "Do teachers of writing need to be writers themselves?" However, I don't think there is really a single dichotomous answer to that question—a single yes or no. What I do think is that the tone of the teaching in a room where the students know their teachers as writers will always be different than the tone in rooms where the students know their teachers as people who ask them to do something that they don't actually do themselves. Can you imagine Sara's dance teacher standing at the front of that studio, never moving, never even dressed in proper dance attire, and lecturing to his students on how to dance? Of course we can't imagine this. I don't think my friend would even have signed her daughter up to take dance classes from someone who doesn't dance.

I believe that to set the best tone in our writing workshops, then, our students need to see us as people who write, just as we see them in that same way. Now take heart. It is not at all necessary that they see us as great writers. It is *fine* for them to see us struggle as writers, to see us write things that make us (and them) say, "Oh my, that's awful!" What is so much more important than that we be great writers is that our students see us as people who think writing is a worthwhile thing to do, as people who believe in the effort it takes to write things that really matter.

If our confidence is low and we feel as though we have a long way to go as writers ourselves, then we can be the Pied Pipers in the room who lead that journey. Many of our students will feel the same way. Over time, as we teach writing more and more, and as we learn alongside our students, we come to feel that we have more "expertise" to offer them. Our identities and our confidence as writers will change and grow with time, just as our students' will, and our teaching will change because of this. But that bottom line—that we are people who believe writing is a worthwhile thing to do—will stay in place. And that is what we need in order to set the right tone for our teaching.

What Tone Looks Like and Sounds Like

Thus far, we have established the idea that in order to think about the tone of our teaching, we must start by thinking about how we view our students and how they view us. But what lies beyond this starting place? What are some things we can think about when we think about setting the right tone for our teaching? Whenever I am in someone else's writing workshop, or whenever I am reflecting on my own, here are some things I watch for and listen for that help me put my finger on the tone of the classroom, the feeling of it. I try to imagine the classroom as students would see it, thinking of all those unspoken messages behind what they see in this classroom.

- I look to see what's on the walls and hanging around the room. Does this look like a place where, even if I struggle as a writer, my work to become a better writer will be valued? Or are only the best writers valued here? Are first languages other than English valued here?
- I look at the geography of the room. Does this look like a place where I am supposed to work with other students or where I should stick to myself? Is there a place for all the students to meet together? Are there tables where I can sit with another student if I want to work with someone? Is there anywhere in the room that looks *comfortable?*
- I look to see where the teacher is in the room. Is she out where the students are, teaching alongside them while they work? When she talks to the whole group, does she sit or stand? Where is she in relation to the students at different times?
- I look around to see what materials are in the room. Are there books, magazines, newspapers, and other kinds of things with writing in them? Do these look as though they are used, or are they hidden away? Do I see dictionaries and thesauruses and sticky notes and correction fluid and

other things that writers need? Do I see resources written in languages other than English?

• I look to see how neat or how cluttered the room is. If twenty or more people are really up to something in this room, then there is bound to be some clutter associated with all that busy-ness. Overly neat rooms are sometimes a good sign that nothing very interesting is happening anywhere in the room.

• I listen. What kind of talk is going on in the room? Is *any* talk going on? Who is talking? What are they talking about?

• I listen. When the teacher talks, is it loud and direct like she thinks no one really wants to listen anyway? Does the teacher look at her students as she talks to them? Does it sound like she likes them? Does it sound like she is interested in what she is saying to them?

• I listen. Does anyone ever laugh in this room?

• I listen. What kinds of questions does the teacher ask his students? Are they questions he already knows the answer to? Or are they genuine questions, questions that show he is interested in what they are thinking?

• I listen. Does the teacher's response to his students show that he was *really* listening to them? Or does he seem more interested in what he is saying than in what they are saying?

• I watch to see how students carry on in this classroom. Does it look like they know what to do if they run into a problem? Or do they seek out the teacher to solve every little difficulty?

• I keep an eye on the clock. How is time used in this classroom? Does the use of time show me that the teacher believes the students are capable of deep, sustained engagement in writing? Or does the teacher seem to believe that they are only engaged when he or she is talking to them or having them do something they were specifically asked to do?

• I look at what students are working on in their writing. Does it appear from their work that they see writing as something worthwhile to do?

• I ask a student to tell me about writing workshop in this class and I listen. Does the student understand what this time is for, what it's all about? Does he or she have a sense of where all this is leading?

WRITERS' VOICES ON . . .

the importance of teachers as writers

> I told them I intended to begin, and work beside them, on a new novel. . . .
>
> Yesterday my writing class discussed their reactions to the first part of the novel. . . . Their finds were almost entirely helpful—the usual crop of typos and minor inconsistencies but, most encouragingly, the fairly palpable sense that they weren't just complimenting the teacher blindly but had really been led on through the scenes by an already strong narrative compulsion.
>
> Their approval has strengthened my sense of the rightness now of a leap some thirteen months later to the wedding of Roxanna and Palmer. (Reynolds Price, *Learning a Trade,* 585, 587)

Reynolds Price understands the importance of tone in a writing classroom. Through their work and work habits, he comes to know each of his students as writers. Perhaps more important, he makes himself a living demonstration of what he expects from his students. Their honest reaction, their willingness to question and critique, speaks to the tone of the classroom as a safe place to share their words and their work. Through living alongside him as he writes a novel, reading his drafts and reacting to them, his students come to know him as a writer as well. Mem Fox speaks very directly to the importance of the teacher as a living demonstration in the writing classroom:

> Teachers of writing who have been soldiers themselves, engaged in a writing battle, must be able to empathize more closely with the comrades in their classroom than teachers who are merely war correspondents at the hotel bar, as it were, watching the battle from a safe distance, declining to get in there themselves and write. (*Radical Reflections,* 11)

Fox, Mem. 1993. *Radical Reflections: Passionate Opinions on Teaching, Learning, and Living.* San Diego: Harcourt Brace.

Price, Reynolds. 1998. *Learning a Trade: A Craftsman's Notebooks, 1955–1997.* Durham, N.C.: Duke University Press.

There's so much to listen for and watch for and wonder about. We need to put our fingers on the pulse of our classrooms. What is the beat we can feel running underneath the things we can see? What do our classrooms *feel* like? What is the tone of our teaching? No lesson we teach, no structures and routines we put in place, no materials we gather, nothing we do matters more than the physical and emotional space we create to carry out our teaching days in our classrooms.

5

Time in the Workshop as a Predictable Event

"The writing workshop is a lot like lunchtime."

The first time I tell this to my preservice teacher education students, they look at me kind of funny. It's obvious they are thinking, "What on earth is she talking about?" Of course, I have to explain. For someone who knows schools but doesn't have any experience with writing workshops, I think lunchtime may be the time of day that most closely resembles a humming, productive writing workshop. Anyone who has ever spent time in schools has a working knowledge of how lunchtime goes, and we can use this knowledge to help us imagine how a writing workshop works.

Class schedules can vary widely from day to day in many schools. Special programs keep students coming and going at different times on different days: Monday there's Art at 10:30; Tuesday there's D.A.R.E. at 9:00 and PE at 1:45; Wednesday has Shakespeare in the Schools from 2:00 until 3:00; Thursday has Music at 8:30 and Spanish at 10:15; and Friday has club meetings first thing in the morning and reading-buddy exchanges at 12:30. Teachers juggle curriculum time like skilled acrobats from day to day, squeezing in as many quality minutes as they can in between the comings and goings of life in school. Some days, there are only fifteen minutes for students to work on inquiry projects. Some days, there's no time at all for math centers. Some days, it's hard to remember what day it is. The only thing it seems you can count on is lunch. Lunch happens always, every day, at 11:45.

The ideal writing workshop would be as dependable as lunchtime is in schools. It would begin at the same time each day and would become, in students' minds, simply "What we do every day at 10:00." We want it to have that accepted, routine, sunrise-sunset kind of dependability in students' understanding of how the day goes. Writing workshops break down when they lose this quality, when they become questionable, when there's a chance the teacher may decide "We're not having it today." Just as we wouldn't make that decision about lunchtime, we don't make that decision about writing workshop time, because if we do, we break students' trust in the fact that we expect them to know what to do and how to be during this time every day.

Now, the reality of schools is that having writing workshop at exactly the same time every day is more unlikely than it is probable, but that doesn't mean the workshop won't be successful. Ideally, we would like it to be governed by the clock so that students can know what to expect and be more planful about their work during the day. But if that's just not possible, then what's important is that students know exactly what it means when someone says, "It's writing workshop *time*." Let's think about lunchtime again. Sometimes, on an early dismissal day, everyone has to go to lunch an hour early, but only the time of day for lunch changes. The way everyone spends that time stays the same. You do lunch just like you did yesterday, only an hour earlier. Similarly, though the time of day for writing workshop may have to be changeable, the way you spend that time doesn't. You see, the most important thing is that students understand the writing workshop as a block of time governed by *rituals and routines*.

One of the first things a new student at a school has to learn is how to "do lunch." Every school has its own lunchtime rituals, and as varied as these may be from school to school, one thing is constant across all schools: lunchtime is *ritualistic*. There's a method to it, and the same method is followed each and every single day. Students often begin the day by systematically choosing from menu options; then head counts are forwarded to the lunchroom staff. At a certain time in late morning, classes begin to go to lunch, always in a set order. Students know what to do when they get there: which lines to get into, who to pay if they want extra cookies, where to sit, what to do when they're finished, where to put paper products and empty trays. Students know that lunchtime is just that—a *time*. You don't hear students saying to teachers, "I'm finished. Now what do I do?" They know the range of options for how they might fill up the thirty minutes of lunch time. They know what to do with themselves, and they see what they are doing as being bounded by *time,* not by a set of directed activities.

Have you ever thought about why lunchtime is so ritualistic in all schools? We have lunchtime in schools for several good reasons: Students need nourishment; they need to interact; they need a break from the rigors of classroom work; we need a break from them. We believe that engaging in the life of lunch is an important thing that happens each day, and the "each-dayness" of it is why we develop the rituals behind it. We see that if we are going to be doing it every day, we might as well do it the same way every day so that students can do it fairly independently of our direction. We bring a shared, accepted order to this time of day so that we can repeat the desired outcome over and over, every day. People eat; they are nourished. The menu may change, but the method of pursuit for the desired outcome stays the same.

In much the same way, teachers who have ongoing writing workshops have them for several good reasons: they know that students need lots of (daily) experience actually working on writing; they know that students need someone to teach them about writing; they know that students need to talk to others frequently about their writing; they know that students need reading and inquiry that supports their writing. These teachers believe that engaging in the life of a writer is an important thing that happens each day, and the "each-dayness" of it causes them to develop rituals behind it—just like lunch—so that students can handle writing workshop time without new directions for it each day. They bring a shared, accepted order to this time of day so that they can repeat the desired outcome over and over, every day. Students write; they grow as writers. The focus for the workshop may change, but the method of pursuit for the desired outcome stays the same.

For the workshop to be successful, teachers must help students understand that writing workshop is a *time* set aside in the day, not a new set of directed activities to be completed each day. Students who come into our workshops from classrooms where they have spent their days completing work (the questions at the end of Chapter 6, problem numbers 13 to 27 in math, the assigned chapter for reading homework, the worksheet on pronouns, the spelling words written five times each, etc.) often have problems at first adjusting to the workshop routine where they must find work to do on a continuous, daily basis. There is no completion of their work during the workshop; there's only a completion of the *time* spent on doing writing work. It is a time each day when every student must find some work to do as a writer, and, just like lunchtime is not over when you finish your sandwich, writing workshop is not over when you finish editing your draft, come to the end of a peer response group meeting, or get a bad case of writer's block. And just as students know a range of options for how to spend their time at lunch—they may go outside, talk quietly to friends at their table, return to their classrooms, go to the library, and so on—the key to a successful writing workshop is for students to know a range of ways they can spend their time productively so that they know how to use the block of time given to them each day.

In the earliest days of the workshop, then, we must establish the understanding that there is no such thing as "I'm finished" during the time set aside for writing. Everyone is "finished" for the day when the clock says it is time for the workshop to come to an end.

ESSENTIAL COMPONENTS OF THE WRITING WORKSHOP

We all know what kinds of activities make up lunchtime in schools. Basically, if you think of lunchtime as being made up of segments of time, each with its own rituals, you've got these segments: getting there, getting the food, eating, disposing of trash, socializing after eating, getting back to the classroom. Similarly, a writing workshop is a block of time that is made up of smaller segments of time, each with its own rituals. Unlike lunchtime segments, the writing workshop segments may be arranged in different ways on different days, but their presence is nevertheless consistent and constant. The day-to-day block of writing workshop time is made up of these segments, and they often happen in this order:

Focus lesson

The whole group of students is engaged in a directed lesson, usually by the teacher, but a lesson may also be taught by a student or a guest. It includes rituals for gathering in one place in the room, and perhaps also rituals for recording the lesson. The focus lessons are part of a larger unit of study in writing that is going on in the room.

Independent writing time

Students work as writers (which may include both time to write and writing inquiry) while the teacher confers with individuals or small groups. It includes rituals for using space and materials in the room, expectations about the range of work that students may engage in, and expectations about publishing finished pieces.

Sharing

Students share strategies, problems, and insights from their day's work as writers. Sharing may be done as a whole group, in smaller groups, or in pairs. It includes rituals for gathering in share groups and turn taking for sharing.

Basically, in the time set aside for writing workshop, these three things happen every day. It is the routine, everyday feel of these workshop components that help it to run smoothly. There are also times spaced throughout the year when the block of writing workshop time will be used for publication celebrations. Publication will happen in many ways, most of it without an official classwide celebration. But there are likely to be a few times during the year when all the students gather—often with invited guests from outside the classroom—to read selections from finished pieces of writing, much as an author would do at a bookstore or a poetry reading.

Balance of Time

Because all of us have to work with different schedules and other time constraints, it is important to think of the balance of time for these segments rather than specific amounts of time. I think a good rule of thumb to follow is to have at least as much time spent on independent writing as is spent on the focus lesson and sharing *combined*. Regardless of the block you can find to work with each day, following that rule will help ensure that you don't take over the most essential parts of the workshop—the time that students need to spend getting experience as writers, and the time when you do your individual and small-group teaching. This means that in an hour-long workshop, you might have a ten-minute focus lesson, forty minutes for independent work on writing, and ten minutes to share and bring closure to the day's work. If you need to spend a longer time in a focus lesson one day, then you might buy time from the share segment, or vice versa.

When I have taught writing on a junior-high-type, fifty-minute-a-day schedule, I have sometimes segmented the *week*, rather than a single day, with this balance in mind by doing a full day of combined focused teaching and inquiry, three solid days of independent work on writing, and then a long end-of-the-week sharing time from our work as writers. I certainly don't like this time option as much as having each component each day, but it is a compromise I have found I could live with in a pinch. With whatever time we have available, the most important thing to keep in mind is the balance of how we use that time.

Although big chunks of time are better than small chunks, there are some commonsense bottom lines to think about. For example, would three hour-and-a-half workshops a week be better than thirty minutes a day? Perhaps they would. Perhaps what we would gain from the luxury of deep, sustained engagement on those three days would be worth it. Well, then, what if we could devote all of Friday morning to writing workshop—four hours. Would it be all right to have only that time during the week? I think the answer is "no." We would be giving up way too much of the "day-to-dayness" we need to develop the habits of writing if it only happened once a week, even if it were for four hours. We need lots of time and we need regular time for students to grow as writers. We have to make the best commonsense decisions we can in order to get both of these for our students.

The thing is that none of us teaches with a perfect schedule for all we'd like to do. This is why we have to make decisions about how we will use time, getting rid of much of the fluff and frill that we can do without in order to buy time for more important things. We also have to make noise and speak up when none of our needs for big blocks of time with our students is being met. We shouldn't just passively accept a horrible, constantly-moving-from-place-to-place schedule; we need at least to try to talk through other possibilities. Most administrators have great respect for teachers who want big, uninterrupted blocks of instructional time for big, important work with their students. Once we have negotiated all we can, gotten rid of all we can, and are left with whatever time is in front of us for the year, then we have to do the best we can in order to give over as much time as we can afford to the writing workshop. We also need to remember that all subject matters beg for as much time as we can give them.

We need to keep the time that we give to writing workshop predictable and routine. If someone from outside were to walk into our classrooms, any one of our students should be able to explain exactly how writing workshop works. Like the promise of sunrise each morning, writing workshop teachers and their students have learned to see the beauty in repetition, have learned to feel the peace of knowing what to expect.

6

Getting Started with Independent Writing Time

Of the three basic components of writing workshops—the focus lesson, independent writing time, and sharing—the part that seems scariest when you first start is the time when you will send students off to work independently on their writing. Teachers who have writing workshops share a fundamental belief in the need for writers to *spend time writing* in order to grow, and so independent writing time is where this happens. It's the time when writers write. It is also the least directed component of the workshop because, unlike all other components, it's the time when students are on their own and not doing anything *with* anyone else. They lose the group or "herd" mentality of so much classroom activity and cannot simply gather around whatever activity everyone else is engaged in; we lose the comfortable feeling of directing everything. So the challenge is there: We must teach students how to direct their own work for a large chunk of the time we will devote to writing workshop. And it can be a challenge. But it in order to teach well in January and March and May, we must meet this challenge head-on in September and October and November—however long it takes to teach children to engage independently as writers.

Our goal for the independent writing part of the workshop is for students to know what to do when we say to them, "Here. Take the next forty minutes to work on your writing." Imagine that. That is all we would say: "Work on your writing." And students would go to it. Now, to those accustomed to thinking of school as a day filled with following step-by-step instructions, it may be hard to imagine how this goal might be achieved. And I'm not just talking about teachers here. Many students come to us in the middle and upper-elementary grades having already learned that school is a place where they will be told what to do each step of the way. These students are several years removed from the primary grades when they had no trouble at all imagining what to do with forty minutes of time in blocks, or housekeeping, or the art center. It may take time to help these students understand how to use a block of time like that, but, as we said above, if we want our writing workshops to be successful throughout the year, we must first establish the independent writing time in the workshop.

I have found that there are two main understandings about the independent part of the workshop that I have to get in place right from the start: what the "work" of the workshop is, and what the range of activities for getting this work accomplished is. Now, each of these understandings will need to be developed in significant ways throughout the year—both informally and formally with units of study. But at the beginning, we want to give students just enough explanation to get them started. Our goal is to get them doing what we want them doing: filling up independent writing time with purposeful writing work. At this point, we don't need to worry about whether they are doing it *well* or not. That's what our later teaching is for: to help them develop the understandings that will help them do things well. At first we just need to get them started.

The Work of the Writing Workshop

So our first challenge is to help students understand what the "work" of the workshop is for writers. The best way I know to explain it to children is to say that it is a place and time for *projects,* a place and time when they can make "writing kinds of things" and spend time being what a writer is and doing what a writer does. We may explain to students that writing workshop is a place where we want them to have *plans* as writers. Plans may range from writing the short story or play or poetry anthology they have always dreamed of, to writing a piece about a great-grandfather who was a soldier in World War II, to writing a manual on mountain biking (a passion), to writing children's books for three-year-old twin sisters, to writing and illustrating a series of comic books, to researching and then writing in many genres about rain forests or oceans or Australia or whatever interests them, to writing essays and editorials aimed at convincing the town to build a park where children can play together safely. . . . We need to tell them, "If you can do it with writing, then the writing workshop is the place to try your hand at it."

We want this conversation about what they'll be doing in writing workshop to help children focus on very purposeful *reasons* for them to write: audiences, occasions, forums, passions, a desire to try a certain genre. This is the project like mentality that makes a workshop hum with purpose. We don't really need brainstormed lists of "topics I could write about" because we don't want them just to write "stuff." That's not the point. We want them to *work as writers,* and this is quite different. It's purposeful, and it involves them having agendas to fulfill as writers. So instead of thinking of topics, we can ask them to think about questions like these as they imagine what they might do each day in writing workshop:

Who are the audiences I might write for?

What passions are in my life that I might pursue with writing?

What genres would I like to try?

What stories do I need to tell?

What causes could I address with writing?

What have I never done as a writer that I'd like to try?

Where would I like to try to get my writing published?

What occasions are in my life this year that I might serve with writing?

We need to present the writing workshop time to our students as a place where the proverbial sky is the limit. Then let them know they can try *anything*. Now, you may be thinking, can nine-year-olds really do all these kinds of things with writing, even if I give them time each day to try them? To write plays and editorials and poetry anthologies? And the answer to that is, "They can if WE can accept that they will do them like nine-year-olds."

Think of it this way. What if, instead of writing workshop, we had a building workshop every day in our classes. We had all sorts of donated and scrapped materials and tools available for them to work with, and we said to them, "Here. Build things. Every day from 2:00 to 3:00, you can build things." How long do you think it would be before some of them announced, "We're building a house." We wouldn't even think of saying, "Why, you can't possibly build a house! You don't know how!" No, we would say, "Great. Have at it!" And they would proceed to build a house like nine-year-olds. And with some teaching alongside their house building, they would probably build a pretty good nine-year-old house and learn a lot about building in the process. This is exactly the same vision we want for our writing workshops.

If we trust that students will learn from trying to build a house or write a short story collection, then we embrace their developmentally appropriate efforts to do these things and teach, teach, teach alongside them. How would students know what to build in our building workshops? They would pull from the range of "building possibilities" they have known in their lives, of course: houses, churches, skyscrapers, boats. . . . The same will be true in the writing workshop. Early on, students will choose writing projects based on the kinds of writing they know best from their reading and writing experiences: stories, poems, picture books. . . .

As we said above, once we're up and going, we will need some very specific teaching and inquiry that will broaden their understandings of what projects they might pursue and why. But just to get the workshop going and to get students working on something, we'll give examples of possibilities like those above and show our students examples of things either that we've written ourselves or that our former students have written in the past. One teacher might show students the family story she wrote down as literature for her mother for Mother's Day. We might show them the poetry anthology several children wrote on soccer, the play one child wrote and had others act out, the letter to the editor a group of teachers wrote for the local paper. We might show them books by professional authors who have stories we know about why they wrote these pieces. Or we might choose any piece of writing that we know the story behind—that's the critical part. We'll explain *why* the writers chose to work on these projects. We'll push for purposeful work right from the start, showing them writers' purposes and reasons for pursuing various projects.

The Range of Workshop Activities

Once we have established this understanding in a very beginning way—that the writing workshop is a place for students to pursue writing projects—our next goal is to help them understand the *range of activities* that they can choose from during this time to help them with these projects. In other words, we need to help them envision what kinds of things they can do to fill up their writing time each day. Now, our goal is certainly not to have students just filling up writing time, but until they find some work that really catches them and gets them going on a specific writing project, they need to know just that: how to do purposeful things as writers that fill up the independent block of writing time.

During the early days of the workshop, we want to focus on helping students learn what this range of acceptable writing activities is—just enough to get them started—and on helping them know that we expect them to find productive work for themselves within that range. Again, once we are up and going, we will need units of study on most all of the activities within this range. For example, later in the year we will probably need to look very closely at how writers use tools like notebooks to collect ideas, freewrite, and try things out. We'll need to study how writers use reading to support their writing and what the best ways are for one writer to help another. We'll need to study how a writer actually takes a piece through drafting stages, and how different genres have different forms and components. Our students will need to learn lots about all these things and more, but they don't need to learn all those things *before* they can get started. We'll let them just start with whatever they know, and then we can *teach into* that as the year progresses. At the beginning, we just name the range, give a little explanation of what's possible, and get students going on trying to do what we want them doing.

So what might a range of writerly activities be? From studying what writers say they do when they work on their writing, and from my experiences working in classrooms, I can offer the following list of things students might be doing during independent writing time that would support their plans, their productivity, and their growth as writers.

What writers might be doing during independent writing time

• **Freewriting in a notebook or journal to develop, play around with, or extend ideas.** Many of these ideas will be ones that have come to the writer *away* from the desk, while living out in the world as a

WRITERS' VOICES ON . . .

reading as a writer's work

> Still, I began to do what I always do when I start a book. If I start a book about a fox, I read fox stories, fox articles, fox books. I want to know everything there is to know about a fox. . . . Even if the setting of the novel is familiar—like the beach—I start reading books about beaches. I read about them until I can actually feel the sand between my toes, though I'm sitting at home in the middle of January. . . . For me, reading books and writing them are tied together. The words of other writers teach me and refresh me and inspire me. (Betsy Byars, *The Moon and I,* 27)

Katie mentions reading as one of the ways students might use time wisely during independent *writing.* This might have surprised you, but it shouldn't have. Writers are lovers of words. Words standing alone. Words carefully placed together in a marriage of rhythm and image. Writers notice, collect, savor, share, and work with words in the ways artists work with color, musicians with sound, and dancers with movement. Clearly, Betsy Byars demonstrates the influence of reading on her work as a writer. She is reading to gain greater knowledge of her subject. She is reading to transport herself to the world of that subject. Writers like Betsy Byars read deliberately.

Reading influences writers in other ways as well. Note, for example, how through reading, Jacqueline Woodson discovered she could be a writer:

> Eventually, three books helped convince her to make writing her career: *The Bluest Eye* by Toni Morrison, *Daddy Was a Numbers-Runner* by Louise Merriweather, and *Ruby* by Rosa Guy. Before reading these books, Woodson thought that only books featuring mainstream, white characters, or works by William Shakespeare constituted valid literature. But in these three books, Woodson saw parts of herself and her life, and realized that books could be about people like her—and she knew she wanted to write them. (*Bantam Doubleday Dell Presents Jacqueline Woodson*, n. p.)

➤

writer. Good writers need to bring lots of ideas to their desks, not sit there and try to think things up. The desk time is used to explore the ideas and see what potentials may be there. This kind of writing is usually collected in a notebook or journal because writers freewrite with intention. They know they may someday use some of the collected ideas that have been written freely in notebooks in actual drafts.

• **Writing exercises.** Many writers "work out" by giving themselves exercises to do. For example, Natalie Goldberg's book *Wild Mind: Living the Writer's Life* (1990) is filled with "Try this" exercises that she does for writing workouts: writing for ten minutes without stopping and

Andrea Davis Pinkney says that her writing has been influenced by the writings of Virginia Hamilton, Patricia McKissack, Avi, and Maya Angelou. She says that Avi

> never does the same thing over and over. It's always fresh, new, different. . . . even though I'm doing a little bit of a track record—doing nonfiction, doing biography—I'm always looking for ways to break out and do it differently. Maya Angelou has taken her roots and made . . . literature. And she's a great storyteller. (in Betty Roe and Mike Roe, *Tennessee Reading Teacher,* 22–24)

Andrea says she reads Cynthia Rylant's work because Rylant has excellent voice in her writing. Kaye Gibbons was influenced in a similar way:

> What literature did for me was to say, "There is a way out, and it's in this book." It wasn't that I dreamed of living with Louisa May Alcott. I didn't dream about living in the Puss'n'Boots palace. I just dreamed about using language the way they did. To write myself out of it. (in Dannye Romine Powell, *Parting the Curtains,* 160–161)

In the writing workshop, we must make room for reading. Reading like writers. That means that we must make books available to our students and that we must select those books wisely, as they may well become the most influential teachers in the room. "I read a lot, which helps me to know how to write as well as what to write about," says Mem Fox. "My best advice for anyone who would like to be a writer is: Read!!!" (in Deborah Kovacs and James Preller, *Meet the Authors and Illustrators,* 25).

Byars, Betsy. 1991. *The Moon and I.* New York: Beech Tree.

Kovacs, Deborah, and James Preller. 1993. *Meet the Authors and Illustrators: 60 Creators of Favorite Children's Books Talk about Their Work.* Vol. 2. New York: Scholastic Professional.

Powell, Dannye Romine. 1995. *Parting the Curtains: Voices of the Great Southern Writers.* New York: Anchor Books.

Roe, Betty, and Mike Roe. 1997. "Meet the Author/Illustrator . . . Brian and Andrea Davis Pinkney." *Tennessee Reading Teacher* (Fall): 20–24.

Woodson, Jacqueline. *Bantam Doubleday Dell Presents Jacqueline Woodson.* Publicity brochure.

filling in the line, "I remember . . ."; or having "waking daydreams" where she writes in first person, present tense "I am . . ." about something she dreams of being. In any writing workshop, I always keep a good supply of books like this by writers who describe their writing workouts and other processes. Students are invited to use these books if they want to learn from these writers and try the things the writers suggest on their own. When the books are too adult in content for young writers, I will copy out various "Try it" exercises and other writing suggestions that make sense for my students, laminate them, and keep them in baskets for students to use as resources during the workshop.

• **Reading to support writing.** There are a number of different reasons writers might be reading when they are working on their writing. They might be doing research and collecting information for a piece they plan to write. They might be reading to see how another author has crafted a piece of writing or handled a similar topic. They might be reading to immerse themselves in a genre they want to write in. They might be rereading their own writing to find direction for their next writing move. The point is, the reading that happens during a writing workshop needs to be purposeful and intentional in direct support of some *writing* goal.

• **Staring off into space.** Sometimes writers just need to think. I know this because I write, and I value the time just to sit and stare . . . thinking. Sometimes I have to take a quick "thinking walk" around the house when I'm heavy into drafting. I get up and think something out, and then come back and get it down in the draft. I always like to make "thinking spaces" an explicit choice students can make in the writing workshop. Of course, like all choices, this one comes with responsibilities. I tell students they must be *thinking* and not thumping someone on the head or doing their math homework. Also, students are expected to be productive during workshop time—evaluation is tied to that—so if they choose some thinking time for themselves, they will need to balance it with some highly productive writing.

• **Drafting a writing project.** During independent workshop time, a student might be working on a draft of a project she wants (needs) to take through to publication. She might actually be generating the draft, or she might be going back through it to make revisions and edits.

- **Having a conference with a peer(s).** Writers need to get feedback—they need to be heard. And using some workshop time to get or give feedback on an idea or a draft is certainly an option for how time might be filled. Many workshops have structures in place to organize and support the peer-to-peer work in the room. Some require students to sign up for response meetings. Others have certain corners or tables of the room designated as conference places, and students must go to empty conference areas to talk through a draft. Others have a certain block of time set aside during the workshop for students to meet together. And many have expectations that students will simply find a quiet place and a partner for a conference when one is needed.
- **Publishing a writing project.** Students may be using their writing workshop time to finish a piece for publication. This could include everything from word processing a final draft, to drawing pictures for a picture book, to making a book binder for a collection of poetry.

Basically, that's it. If I look around the room, I want to see children engaged in any one of these activities. When we share a list like this with students, we have helped them know what it means (in a very beginning way) to "work on writing" so that when we say, "Here is some time to work on your writing," they can envision what they will do.

In a poetry-writing workshop I did for third and fourth graders this past summer, I went over this range of activities on our first day together, explained each one, and then gave the children the small reminder shown in Figure 6.1 to paste in their notebooks.

On the first day of this workshop, I knew there were things on this list that some children knew very little about, depending on their experiences as writers. Most of the children, for example, really didn't have much of an idea about what they might write in a notebook. But I still didn't go through a whole big "curriculum dump" about what goes in a notebook at the beginning. I went ahead and started them in the workshop, acting as if they could figure this out, knowing that we would soon begin to fill the writing workshop with notebook possibilities.

We can get tons of mileage out of "acting as if" in a writing workshop. When students see, right from the start, that we *really do* expect them to take charge of this time and figure out how to use it on their own, they almost

FIGURE 6.1 Student Workshop Reminder

During independent time each day in the writing workshop, you will need to decide how you will use your time. I won't be telling you what to do with this time, but I will be expecting you to use it wisely. Remember that you want to do things that will help you grow into a very good poet. You are responsible for doing what it takes to make that happen.

Here are some of the kinds of things you might do during this time:

- Write new stuff in your writer's notebook.
- Go back through what's in your notebook already and "play with" those ideas. Write more about them or try to turn them into other kinds of writing.
- In your notebook, try some writing "exercises" recommended by professional writers. You'll find these in baskets around the room. Return these to the baskets when you're finished. You might try these with a friend.
- Work on writing drafts of poems you want to publish.
- Have a writing conference with another poet about something you are working on (either in your notebook or in a draft for a published poem).
- Read poems from the books we have in the room. Always be sure to ask, "How did this writer write this poem? Could I try that too with my topics?"

always respond to this. We have given them the support of a clear range of choices, and we just have to stand back and let them make of that what they will at the beginning. Remember, again, that when we start, our goal is for everyone to be doing some kind of writing work that he or she has chosen. And *that's it.* That's our goal. We don't worry about whether they are doing it well or not at first; that's our later teaching job. First, we just get them doing it.

Little reminders, little things in writing like the one in Figure 6.1, can really help students manage their writing time independently in the workshop. As time goes by, the spaces in between entries and drafts in my students' notebooks and folders begin to fill up with little reference materials like this that help students manage their work. After several days in the poetry workshop, for example, I gave students the list shown in Figure 6.2 to paste in their notebooks in order to support their notebook writing.

In focus lessons and in share times, we had talked about the notebook as a gathering place for ideas, and we had looked at some of the strategies on this list for gathering notebook material, but I wanted there to be even more possibilities in the room than we had had time to talk about. So I gave them this list as a reference of other notebook strategies. This seems to be a key factor in the success of the independent writing time in the workshop—that students have access to a wide range of possibilities for their work as writers. We need to support them in any way we can in knowing what these possibilities are for their work. Chapter 18, On Loving *Worksheets* in the Writing *Workshop*, looks closely at the role of reference materials (like the ones above) in supporting students' ongoing independent work as writers.

Independence as an Act of Faith

In my summer writing workshops for children, I have no school schedules to contend with and I am blessed with the luxury of *time*. Two hours or more of it and all of it just for writing. I'm in writing heaven, and so are the students, I believe.

This past summer, as the observing teachers and I were discussing what had taken place with the children that day, one of them commented that she just couldn't believe how the children worked on their writing for so long. That particular day, we had been in independent writing for an hour and a half when I brought the children together for share time. Several of the children, wanting even more time to write, had moaned and groaned when I stopped them. "I've never seen children stay on task for so long," the teacher said.

"I guess it all depends on what the task is," I replied.

As a teacher, I have so much faith in the task of writing. I have so much faith in what I am asking students to do during writing time—explore, pursue,

FIGURE 6.2 Notebook Support

Kinds of entries you might try in your notebook . . .

- Very close observations of things, capturing sights, sounds, textures, moods, and so on.
- Snippets of interesting things people say—talk written down!
- Entries that ask lots and lots of questions about a subject, person, thing, place, and so on.
- Lists of things you want to think about later or just want to keep in lists.
- Quotations from music, movies, books, magazines, and so on that interest you.
- Writing about photographs or pictures that interest you.
- Plot ideas from things you hear on the news or hear other people talking about.
- Memories, memories, memories—ask questions such as "What does this remind me of?" Look at things from your life, and think about what they make you remember.
- Things you see that are interesting. Remember, a writer is someone who notices and is enormously taken by things other people walk right by.
- Character ideas from people you observe. Try to imagine the smallest details of their lives.
- Setting ideas from interesting places where you are writing. Try going somewhere interesting and writing about it as a setting.
- Entries about things that interest you as a person—Antarctica, inchworms, vacuum cleaners, mountain biking, soccer, snakes, WHATEVER!
- Research facts about your interests. Get them from the Internet, books, the Discovery Channel, and so on.
- Great first lines for things you'd like to write—first chapters of novels!
- Poems that just "come to you."
- Reflections (thinking) about things you see, hear, or think about.
- Play around with words you like.
- Family stories that you know orally. Write them down!
- Talk to people about a subject that interests you, then write about what they say.
- Lists of people's names and the names of places that you might like to use someday.
- Long entries about things you care about.
- Any other ways you can invent to collect material for your writing life.

WRITERS' VOICES ON . . .

thinking as a writer's work

I suppose one reason I really like writing . . . [is that] . . . what you do when you write is you let your mind play. You let yourself go to make connections. You let yourself not do the dishes or get the oil changed in your car. I think a lot of just fooling around is necessary for a writer. . . . It's play. It's creative thinking. You have to wander around the mall. You have to just let yourself go with an idea. This is the kind of time that writers have to have, and it's very hard for people who begin to write in their 40s and 50s to justify this time to themselves and their companions. Because nothing is produced. . . . I just take it. I don't do other things I ought to do. I just sit around. I watch TV. I spend a lot of time just doodling or walking around in public places looking at people. Just thinking about stuff. . . . And *play* is in a sense the wrong term, because a lot of this play is very serious. But it's very necessary. (Lee Smith, in Dannye Romine Powell, *Parting the Curtains,* 403)

Writers need time to think and reflect, time to read and connect, time to stare off into space and imagine. That *is* the task. Spending time this way helps writers come away with something to begin the process or to propel it forward. Jerry Spinelli writes,

I'll just have an idea, which may come from any source and may develop into a book. I don't try to be too calculating or measured or deliberate or organized about it at first. . . . I like to let it be chaotic so possibilities can reign and prevail. Out of that mess, gradually, hopefully, a story will begin to take shape. . . . Doing it my way, you end up with snags. I don't always know where I am going in many stories. Sometimes that can be frustrating. . . . It introduces spontaneity and fresh, unexpected elements to the story. (in Deborah Kovacs and James Preller, *Meet the Authors and Illustrators,* 128–129)

Writing is rarely orderly and neat and linear and precise. It is rarely a series of small tasks that we can direct children through. Mem Fox tells us that

After three months of thinking I sat down one afternoon to write the first draft of what I freely acknowledge to be my best book, *Wilfrid Gordon McDonald Partridge.* As I wrote I had the strangest feeling, as if the pencil on the page were being controlled by some outside force that I cannot explain. Perhaps that's the definition of inspiration. It had never happened before and it's never happened since. . . . Wilfrid is probably a once-in-a-lifetime book, but I will go on writing in case—*just in case*—there's another story like it waiting to appear in the blank pages of my future. (*BookLinks,* 31).

Think of it. Three months just thinking about the story. Not writing—just thinking! Then in an afternoon, the first draft. So ask yourself if those three months were "off-task behavior."

Fox, Mem. 1993. "On Writing *Wilfrid Gordon McDonald Partridge.*" *BookLinks* 2, no. 5(May): 31.

Kovacs, Deborah, and James Preller. 1993. *Meet the Authors and Illustrators: 60 Creators of Favorite Children's Books Talk about Their Work.* Vol. 2. New York: Scholastic Professional.

Powell, Dannye Romine. 1995. *Parting the Curtains: Voices of the Great Southern Writers.* New York: Anchor Books.

experiment, dig in to things that are meaningful to them. I also have the faith of experience. I have known what it is like to work on writing for long stretches of time myself, and I have seen so many children in so many different settings work for long periods of time on things that were interesting to them. My faith isn't shattered when I have a few students who take longer to get invested in their work or who have an off day. I just know that when they find some work that interests them, they will stick with it. They know that I know that. I wear that expectation on my sleeve.

If we have only experienced schooling in traditional ways, schooling that comes in little bites of activity off and on all day long, then it will take an act of faith to believe that our students can be engaged for long stretches of independent writing time. If we have never sat and worked at writing for hours on end ourselves, then we may have trouble understanding what that work feels like. It's hard to have faith in things we haven't experienced. But students can know the satisfaction of deeply engaging work if we exercise an act of faith and make a space in the day for them to engage in it. We need to let them know what the possibilities for that work may be, set them up to be successful in this work, and then send them out to fulfill the promise of it.

Reference

Goldberg, Natalie. 1990. *Wild Mind: Living the Writer's Life.* New York: Bantam.

7

Managing Predictable Distractions in the Writing Workshop

Once we have students up and going in independent writing time, we have to think about some management issues that will surely follow. When lots of people are working together in a relatively small space, there are bound to be some distractions: the student who is not on task and wants everyone else to join him, the student who has her work spread out and is taking up an entire six-person work table, the students who are having a great writing conference but are talking so loudly that everyone can hear them, the student who is paralyzed because he needs drafting paper and can't find it. Thinking ahead about some of these management issues can help us head off some of them and make life in the workshop a lot easier for everyone. I tell my students who will soon be teaching that there are three main things to think about when planning for good writing workshop management: presence, space, and supplies.

A Strong Teaching Presence

First, presence. Our presence in the room as the independent writing is going on helps us manage much of what is happening. We want to be very much "out among the workers" during this time. Rather than having students come to us for writing conferences, management is often easier when we move around the room a lot; as we stop to confer with individual writers, we spread our presence out across the room. And we don't ever want to think of students' independent work time as a time for us to work on other things that need doing. We need to be out there teaching, for one thing, and for another, if they sense that this is a time when we "let them loose," we will have problems. Letting them choose their work doesn't mean letting them loose.

I think we struggle with this a lot as teachers who are trying to understand teaching in different ways. We're not quite sure how to insist that students be engaged, how to be *strict* about their working, if you will, if they aren't all doing exactly the same thing. I have been asked so many times, "What do I do if a student won't write?" And I bet no one ever asks, "What do I do if a student won't do the states-and-capitals worksheet I gave out to everyone?" Why is it that we feel as though we know what to do with the worksheet slacker but not with the writing workshop slacker? Why is it that a classroom feels so much more manageable to us if everyone is doing exactly the same thing?

Perhaps we need to rethink our understanding of "on task." Writing workshop teachers have just as much responsibility to manage on-task work as other teachers. There is a very clear range of activities that are considered "on-task" work in the workshop (as outlined in the last chapter), and as the instructional leader, the teacher must insist that students are on task within that range. It's like the difference between being a supervisor on a factory assembly line, where everyone does the same thing over and over, and being an office manager in an advertising agency, where workers are engaged in lots of different kinds of work, but all in support of a common outcome. You probably remember from your courses in American educational history that schools were originally set up in factory-like models; they were thought of as learning factories. And even though we have learned so much about how teaching and learning is not a factory-like operation, we still struggle with how to be office managers rather than line supervisors.

One key (in addition to having faith that students can stay engaged in work for a long time) is a strong presence. As we work out there among the writers, we must make sure that we show, in all our actions and interactions, that we expect them to be involved in some kind of writing work. Our students should think that it is our official business, all the time, to know as much as we can about what's going on with them and their writing (even though we will feel like we can never keep up with it all, as we'll discuss in the next chapter), and they should understand that we will use any means possible to know this. When we have a situation where a student is clearly choosing not to engage in any of the sanctioned work of the workshop, we deal with this in a very serious manner. We let the student know, in no uncertain terms, that choosing no work *isn't one of the options.* Also, we must use discretion here. We have to be sure that what we are seeing is a clear case of a student not engaging. We're not talking about the normal social interactions that happen around very active work. We don't want the workshop to be an oppressive place, and we need to recognize that people working together in the same place, even if they are working on different things, need to interact in some way in order to have a healthy working environment. So we aim for a strong presence in the room that lets students know we are in there working right alongside them and that we expect them to take their work seriously. We must be *strict* about this.

Using Space in the Writing Workshop

The next issue is space. We work in all different shapes and sizes of classrooms with all different numbers, shapes, and sizes of children inside them. All we can ever do is work with whatever space we have been given. But it helps to think about our needs for space and how we can best put to use the space we have.

First, writing workshops really need some kind of place where all the students can come together. In a focus lesson or a share session, students need to come together, both literally and figuratively. It just sends students the wrong message to be spread out all over the room when we are trying to pinpoint their attention on something very important. So we need a way and a place to pull them in close. Ideally, there would be an open space in the room large enough for students to come together to sit on a carpet on the floor, or on old couches or bean bags—a meeting area. If this is not possible, then we might need a system for making an open space quickly; certain students might be assigned to push back desks and clear an area, or push several tables together that students can sit on in one part of the room. If there is any rearranging that has to be done as part of the daily routine of the workshop, we want to be sure to have a team of students who is responsible for doing that each and every day.

In this space where everyone comes together, we may find that we need some sort of system for where students sit. This is often the case when the meeting area has, for example, one couch, two bean bags, and a carpet on the floor where the rest of the students sit. "First come, first served" usually doesn't work well in this case because it can quickly become the battle of the day. We'll probably need some sort of rotating system that dictates who gets the coveted spots on the sofa and chairs, and, again, we'll want to put a student or two in charge of this system. We might even need to think about how students will be asked to sit in this space. I prefer for students to get comfortable, because I think they listen better when they are comfortable, but sometimes we don't have enough room for them to stretch their legs out, for example. As we look at the size of the space and the number of bodies we're dealing with, we'll likely need to make some decisions about this issue.

During the independent part of the writing workshop, we need as much space as possible for students to spread out and get to their writing work. We'll want to think about the fact that, at times, students may have out several pages of a draft, a draft folder, a notebook, a dictionary, and perhaps a mentor text for their writing. Sometimes, in other words, a single student may need a good bit of room. This is why many writing workshop teachers prefer to have large tables in the room where students can work, in addition to smaller, individual desks. Many teachers allow students to sit on the floor to work, if they'd like; when this is the case, it's helpful to have lapboards available for students to write on. Basically, if possible, students should be using the *whole* room as work space during the independent part of writing workshop.

Believe it or not, the space we use has a lot to do with the working *sound* of the room during independent writing time. I believe it is best if we do not aim for a "no-talking" workshop. First of all, we will spend all our time trying to enforce it, and second of all, I don't really think it makes for a healthy working environment. Instead, we can use lots of space in the room and let that space swallow up some of the natural sounds of people at work. Giving students enough room to find some space and distance for themselves will actually help them to manage their own talk in more productive ways. Sometimes they talk more because they are sitting right on top of two or three others. It's natural to talk to someone right next to you!

Now, some students will want more quiet than others during their independent writing time. Where can these students go to find some quiet space? We might want to have a few designated quiet zones, as well as some corners reserved for students who really need to have a writing conference where there will be several minutes of ongoing conversation. And, of course, there will be the students who are talking way too much and not writing nearly enough. And they will need to be asked both to correct this behavior ("Stop it") and to realize that they will be penalized in evaluation for not producing enough in writing workshop.

Just like in the meeting area, if there is some prized work space in the room—maybe a table right by the window or a fancy old writing desk rescued from a flea market—we may need some kind of system for deciding who gets to work where. Ideally, though, what we are working toward over the course of the year is students' learning to choose where they will work based on the kind of work they are doing that day. Writers in the world outside school do this—make decisions about where they need to go to get their writing done. And within the walls of the classroom, we want to give over as much of this decision-making power as we can to our student writers.

If the share portion of our writing workshop is usually done as a whole class, then we will likely just use the same meeting space that we use for focus lessons for this part of the workshop. We may want to think about whether we need a designated chair or space at the front of the meeting area where the student who is sharing sits. It may also be that the meeting area easily facilitates turning attention in different directions, in which case a centralized share place isn't necessary. If we prefer to do our share time in smaller response groups, then we will likely want to have designated areas where the groups go each day for these meetings.

Getting from Place to Place

So we've thought through the different space needs we'll have during the writing workshop, but we haven't considered yet how students will get from one space to the next. How do students know when to gather on the carpet for the focus lesson, or how do they know when to stop their independent writing, begin cleaning up, and move back to the carpet for share time? There are several ways we might go about managing these transitions. First of all, just getting the workshop started is the easiest part. Usually, it starts at a very predictable time of the day, often following the conclusion of some other segment in the day, say, right when students return from lunch or after independent reading at 9:30.

The trickier parts are having a time for writing workshop that, of necessity, varies from day to day, or, inside the workshop, getting students to finish up their independent writing and come back together near the end of it. Ideally, this transition time would be governed by the clock, but we know that many students will be involved in their work and won't pay any attention to the clock. One option is to have two or three students who are in charge of helping us manage time. These students go around to different areas of the room and quietly tell their classmates when it is time for them to begin to bring their work to a close and move back to the meeting area. Some teachers have a student put some quiet music on or dim the lights to signal the end of independent writing time. Whatever we decide, we want a way to make the transitions happen without our having to stand in the middle of the room and yell at everyone to stop everything and run. Our goal is for the workshop to be structured well enough that it could almost manage itself without our being there.

Supplies for the Writing Workshop

Finally, we come to the issue of supplies. I am amazed at how having the right supplies and having them out where students have easy access to them helps manage predictable distractions in the workshop. If we really want the writing workshop to feel like a place where students engage in thoughtful, deliberate work, then it needs to be filled with supplies and tools for them to do that work. I am always blown away by the interesting work students do in their notebooks and on their drafts when things as simple as self-stick notes, highlighters, and paper clips are made available for them to use. Supplies are very important to writers, as well as to the success of our writing workshop management. If we begin by assuming that every student will have a writer's notebook that comes and goes each day from home to the writing workshop and back again, then what kinds of supplies (in addition to writer's notebooks) will we need in our classrooms to support the independent work of our writers?

Here are a few to think about:

- **Writing tools.** Highlighters, pens, markers, pencils, paper clips, sticky notes in different sizes, staplers, correction fluid, glue, tape, scissors, index cards, and so on. The more tools, the better, because students imagine new writing work for themselves based on the kinds of tools they have available. If we show them possibilities for these different writing tools in mini lessons and conferences throughout the year, they will get more and more sophisticated in how they use them. We want even the youngest writers to use all the tools—even fat, wide markers and richly colored ink pens. (Who made that rule that little guys should only use pencils, anyway?)
- **Paper.** Students will have paper in their writer's notebooks, of course, but they will also need all kinds of paper for drafting and publishing. Many teachers buy legal pads in various colors to use as drafting paper, the colors signifying a draft in progress, and they help students see the difference between that process and notebook writing. For publishing, a wide variety of colored paper in various sizes is important, as well as

creamy white finishing paper. With our youngest writers, it's important to have many different kinds of paper around, because the paper has so much to do with what kinds of things they write. You'll want skinny paper and fat paper with drawing space at the top, round paper and paper cut out in shapes, and paper that looks like stationery. We'll want paper already folded and stapled into little books, and paper with a frame around it for a poem or an invitation. Very young writers often make important decisions about what they will write based on the kinds of paper available.

- **Work folders.** Students are going to need folders for their ongoing work: drafts of works in progress, workshop logs, assessment forms, and so on. We may want to have a central place in the room where all these folders are kept, or students may keep them in their own desks or container areas.

- **Publication folder.** Most finished pieces of writing will go out into the world or into the class or school library, but we will probably need a place in the room to keep copies of these published pieces for evaluation and assessment purposes. Expanding folders make nice containers for publications, and again, we may decide to keep these all in one place.

- **Writing support.** We will need to have dictionaries (in English *and* other languages), thesauruses, frequently used words posted where they can be easily seen, alphabet charts for our youngest writers, guides to grammatical conventions, Franklin spellers, and so on. We should have enough of this kind of support in the room so that students can help themselves and others when these writing issues arise.

Now, we have only looked at actual writing *tools* here. Later, in Chapter 9, we will consider other materials we might want to have available that provide important *curriculum* for writers in the workshop. But for now, there are several issues related to workshop supplies and tools that seem important to think about.

One of these issues is where these supplies will be "housed." Students need to have easy access to the things they need during writing workshop if they are to be independent. Because we will be busy conferring during the writing workshop, we won't be able to be the gatekeeper for supplies. If we feel we need a gatekeeper for certain supplies, then we will probably need to put students in charge of this job. Ideally, we will simply make the supplies available and let students get them as they need them, but this is sometimes a challenging area that needs a management system in place.

As we work alongside our students, we'll want to show an interest in how they are using various supplies in the workshop. This interest will send an important message about how we honor the tools and the place that these tools have in students' work. It will also help us know what kinds of suggestions we need to make about better ways to use the various supplies. In the writing workshop I did this past summer for third and fourth graders, it became the summer of the sticky notes. After I noted an interesting way one student had used the sticky notes to tab notebook pages that used language he liked and shared this with the class one day, the tool caught on like wildfire. Over the course of the next few days, students began using the notes in so many interesting ways to do so much thoughtful work at all phases of the writing process.

If we have students who are abusing the supplies we have provided, we must consider what the consequences of this should be. But we should use discretion here in how we handle things. Before we decide that a student is wasting sticky notes or highlighter ink, we should try to find out if there is some "method to the madness" we see. I have had situations where something that looked like complete wastefulness and madness was actually a very sophisticated (albeit cumbersome) way for a child to manage some aspect of writing. In this case, we want to help the child refine the use of the materials rather than just busting him for supply abuse. Related to this, as with the various space issues, if we have limited numbers of supplies, we may need to develop some kind of system for who gets to use what when.

Whenever there are supplies and tools in use, there are housecleaning issues that come with them. Folders containing works in progress will need to be cleaned out periodically; supplies will have to be returned to their containers daily; and dry pens, empty staplers, and broken pencils will have to be restored from time to time. We'll need to develop a system for managing the housekeeping issues, remembering to give as much responsibility to students as possible.

Another supplies and tools issue is the question of technology. Because we are at such different places in our technological resources in schools, I

WRITERS' VOICES ON . . .

the importance of space

> [I write] any old time. And I write longhand, so I do it everywhere. I have a desk downstairs, so I do it down there, or I do it in the kitchen. I do it in the car. I did it everywhere. I did it in a million motels. . . . That's the thing about a novel, too. You can do it anytime you want, and you can take it anywhere you are. See, that's one thing that's always attracted me about writing fiction, is just the freedom of that. Being able to do it, I always write a lot at the Chapel Hill Public Library. (Lee Smith, in Dannye Romine Powell, *Parting the Curtains,* 397)

Although it is true that in our classrooms we must work within the parameters of the physical space allotted, we must also recognize the needs of writers for finding and using personal spaces. Lee Smith leads us to believe that she is comfortable in a variety of settings and is able to work productively in any of them, though she finds the public library a special place to work. Other writers are more particular about their work spaces. Clyde Edgerton, for example, prefers a place free of distractions:

> The first thing I did was to move out of my house into an office with no windows. Flannery O'Connor wrote in front of a blank wall. She would sit down there three hours a day. I don't do exactly that when I am working hard on a novel. But I do make myself sit down and work uninterrupted. (in Dannye Romine Powell, *Parting the Curtains,* 120)

We read earlier that Patricia Polacco begins the composing process by sitting in one of the twelve rocking chairs in her home, and that Mem Fox *always* begins writing in pencil first and needs "solitude, silence, and a clean work space." Annie Dillard describes one of her favorite writing spaces as

> a pine shed on Cape Cod. . . . The study—sold as a prefabricated toolshed—is eight feet by ten feet. . . . There is a computer, a printer, and a photocopying machine. . . . The study affords ample room for one. One who is supposed to be writing books. You can read in the space of a coffin, and you can write in the space of a toolshed meant for mowers and spades. . . . Appealing workplaces are to be avoided. One wants a room with no view, so imagination can meet memory in the dark. When I furnished this study seven years ago, I pushed the long desk against a blank wall, so I could not see from either window. (*The Writing Life,* 25–26)

Wow, how can we ever accommodate the individual preferences of twenty-plus writers in our classrooms? Clearly, there is no one magic place, no single perfect spot, that all writers long for. What we must recognize is that *where* writers work matters to them. Space is important to writers. And, to the extent it is possible, we need to make space available so kids will have options to find what works best.

Dillard, Annie. 1990. *The Writing Life*. New York: HarperPerennial.

Powell, Dannye Romine. 1995. *Parting the Curtains: Voices of the Great Southern Writers.* New York: Anchor Books.

have chosen not to consider them in the list of supplies. But certainly, if we have technology readily available in our classrooms, we'll need to think of it as a tool just like the tools discussed above. If they are available, many students will be using word processors to draft, revise, edit, and publish their writing, just as many writers out in the world do. If we have in-class access to computers, we will need to consider all the space and access issues that will arise when they are available for student use.

I guess the real bottom line with supplies is this: The best way to manage "distractions" in the writing workshop is to have plenty of "attractions" for students as writers. Remember the "building workshop" we imagined in Chapter 6 as a metaphor for the writing workshop? Remember how we imagined that it would be filled with all kinds of things used in building? Well, this is the same image that we need for tools and supplies in the writing workshop. When students sit at quiet, lonely desks with only a pencil in hand and some paper, it doesn't look or feel much like a *workshop*. If our rooms are equipped like real places where writers work, then students are much more likely to think of their work there in the same way and go at it with more intention.

Helping Students Feel Responsible for the Room

Throughout this chapter we've been thinking about all these decisions that the teacher will have to make about how the room will "work" during writing workshop. And the truth is, it is our job as teachers to see that all these issues are thought through and that decisions about them are made as needed. But we don't have to make all the decisions by ourselves. We can bring students into the decision-making process, especially, as we move along during the year, when issues arise that require us to rethink some of our structural management. If there are arguments every day over who gets to use the three red markers that smell like strawberries, we can bring our students together and say, "We have this problem. What can we do to solve it?" If some students aren't doing their part to help put supplies back where they belong, or if some students are distracting others, we can bring the issues before the group and let our students help us figure out a way to deal with the problem.

Even though we need to have this strong, central presence in the room, a presence of "oppressive control" is not what we are aiming for. Instead, we want a presence that says to children, "I am right in the middle of this with you. I'll be here all the way. But I expect, I *insist,* that you help me to shape this into a happy, productive place where we can do good work together." When students see that we are adamant about this, they usually join us quite willingly in taking responsibility for the space that we occupy together for seven or eight hours a day.

8

Understanding That Slightly Out-of-Hand Feeling in the Workshop

I suppose that once enough people said that writing workshops were a good idea, someone decided to package that idea and sell it off for "easy" classroom consumption. And sure enough, you can buy a "workshop in a kit" these days. These kits usually wear writing workshop masks: children get to *choose topics* from a box of cards with topics listed on them, *talk* about their writing from a script of questions matching the stages of the writing process, and *publish* their writing on clever little blackline masters with borders. These kits have writing workshop masks for teachers too: ready-made *focus lessons* already planned out for the year and designed with John Q.

Student (fill in any name here) in mind, *rubrics* designed to match any piece of writing with *comments* on the writing already written—you just choose one!

Writing workshop kits are dangerous. Not only that, I think they are highly insulting. Like diets that promise weight loss without exercise or watching what you eat, these kits lull us into believing that we can have a "writing workshop" in our classrooms with very little of our own effort or input, and that having them will really be quite easy.

Baloney.

Planning, organizing, and teaching in a writing workshop is very challenging work. Teachers who have them (their own, not one from a kit) have spent years developing the deeply theoretical underpinnings necessary to understand the work they are trying to do with children. They spend day after day in these workshops watching and planning and redirecting and pulling back and pushing forward and just trying to keep up with all the different work children are engaged in. Every year feels almost like starting over as they feel compelled, once again, to take what they learned from last year and rethink how they will do things this year with this new group of students in mind. In fact, having a writing workshop is such complex, hard work that the best writing teachers I know sometimes spend their whole careers never feeling like they've quite got a handle on it—feeling like it's just slightly out of their control.

I think that may be how it's supposed to feel.

The workshop is highly structured and highly organized, but the work inside it—the work of twenty-five different ten-year-olds all at different places in different pieces of writing—always feels just beyond our own ability to know about it all, to control it all. And it should feel that way. I believe that is the *nature* of this thing called writing, and that, out of necessity, it's got to be the nature of the teaching of writing. Any efforts to reign it in and put it in a kit change the nature of it and cause us to teach something that looks a lot like it should be writing, but that really isn't. And until we, as teachers, make peace with this, make peace with the fact that the work that children do inside all our well-organized, well-managed structures will always feel just beyond our control and a little messy, we will never know the rewards that come from having children deeply involved in their own writing.

Writers' Voices on . . .

the chaos of writing

My most productive days are spent in chaos. Prewriting for me is a disorderly stage, first of aimless drifting, anxiously waiting, hoping to be overtaken by a tornado that will turn into a frenzy of scribbled notes on scraps of paper. It's feverish work when anything that comes my way, when everything I see or hear or taste or smell or touch or think or dream, seems intimately connected with my story. Only when the storm's blown over—however long it takes, the fever cooled, does a new stage begin in which I pick my way carefully among the pieces, torn scraps, stacks of paper, trying to see what's left that may be worth saving, hoping it will be sufficient; hoping, too, that as I sit or stand or lie or walk or sleep or eat or read, it will be revealed to me what I must do with it. (Barbara Ann Porte, *BookLinks*, 21)

Did you hear that? Her most *productive* days are spent in *chaos!* Do you think she means the frenetic scurrying with absolutely no plan of action? I don't. I think she means exactly what Katie is describing: that slightly out-of-control feeling of letting the work lead her. I think she is comfortable with the notion of making decisions on the basis of what is generated in process.

Clearly, writers must make many decisions in the process of their work. Katie reminds us that we will need to make peace with the temporary discomfort of not knowing how every decision will be made. In our classrooms, we must understand that these decisions are not ours to make. We must accept the fact that writers need to explore the options, weigh the consequences, and make decisions. Think of Barbara Ann Porte's description of her process as a tornado, a raging storm, and remember that we are asking students to jump into the middle of that, too!

Porte, Barbara Ann. 1997. "On Ideas and Webbing," *BookLinks* 7, no. 4 (March): 21.

Now, if this were a choose-your-own-adventure book, this would be a good time to offer the reader a choice. If you know you cannot ever make peace with that slightly-beyond-your-control, messy feeling, then you should choose Option A and put this book down and go out for coffee. See a movie. (If you purchased this book, I'm sorry if you feel you wasted your money.) However, if you feel like you can at least entertain the idea that you might be able to make peace with that slightly-beyond-your-control, messy feeling, then you may choose Option B and continue reading. I just want to be fair and clear with you about the fact that where we will go with this won't always be easy and will sometimes raise as many questions as it answers.

So if you're brave and willing, we'll start pushing into what's hard.

The problem is that we are dealing with a truth with two sides to it. (I hate that kind of truth, don't you?) It is true, as we said in the last chapter, that it is our job as teachers to know as much as we possibly can—using any means available, any means we can think of—to know as much as we can about the work students are doing in our writing workshops. But it is also true, at the very same time, that we can't possibly know all of that. There's no way to keep up with it all. So the writing workshop asks us to spend the rest of our careers trying to do something that we will never really be able to do, at least not all the way. We have to try to understand this intellectually, because emotionally we are feeling like, "I don't think I want to do that for the next twenty-five or thirty years."

Why is it that the work inside the writing workshop always feels slightly beyond our control? Well, because it is. We necessarily give over the work of writing to our students. They control it. It's *their* writing. The writing is controlled locally, at each desk or table with each child's agenda as a writer. They will control it like ten-year-olds. They may not control it very well, but we believe that it is only through controlling it that they will learn to control it well. You see, one of the most basic beliefs about workshop teaching is that students need lots of writing experience to grow into good writers. They need to spend years *doing what writers do* in order to become the kinds of writers who move through the world using written words to make a difference in whatever lives they will choose for themselves.

And herein lies the issue of control. When we ask our students to *do what writers do,* we open up this huge closet full of possibilities for what that could mean, possibilities that just seem to grow exponentially the more we really think about them. Although the ending place for any writer is publication, the path to get there involves a seemingly endless range of choices and ways of working. Writing kits would have you believe that the path is made up quite simply of prewriting, drafting, revising, editing, and then publishing. But if we really look at what writers do, or if we write ourselves, we know that there are so many ways a writer can go about getting from an idea to a publication. It seems like there isn't any one thing we can say for sure that all writers do when they, say, revise. We know they all do it, but there are so many ways to go about it.

Let's look at this another way. If our focus is on writers, and we decide that we will devote time daily to having children do what writers do, let's just think about the proverbial can of worms we open up in terms of all the different combinations of things that could mean.

- **Choices about daily work in the workshop.** There are all kinds of work students might be engaged in that would support them as writers, and they have to make choices (based on publication expectations) about what work they will do: write in a notebook, talk an idea through with a peer, read or research for writing, and so on. Once students are working toward publication on a piece, then we have another whole set of decisions each of them has to make.

- **Choices about content.** Students will have to choose what they will write about in their notebooks or in drafts for publication, just like writers do. They can choose from almost *any topic in the world*. That's a lot of topics.

- **Development.** As we said above, at *every step* of the way, from developing the topic or idea through prewriting, drafting, revising, and editing, there are decisions to be made, and there are so many ways students could go about each of these processes. Will the piece require research? Will the piece need feedback from a peer group? How will the student get editing assistance?

- **Genre.** Students will have to choose how they are going to write about those topics. Unless we are engaged in a genre study, they may choose any genre. There are lots of different genres they might choose from.

- **Form.** Once they've chosen a genre, they will have to decide what kind of piece to write in that genre. There are many, many ways to write a memoir, many structures a writer might choose for fiction, and so on.

- **Publication.** They will have all kinds of decisions to make about publication. Will the piece be illustrated, submitted to the school magazine, mailed to the local newspaper, placed in the class library?

If we take just these decisions (all of which are decisions writers have to make and manage) and give them over to children, then start multiplying them by the number of children we teach, that feeling in the pit of our stomachs can start fairly quickly. *How would we ever keep up with all of that*? Add to that the fact that students will be at very different places in all that decision making because development will take them varying amounts of time, and the feeling grows. Add to that the realization that this list assumes students are working on only one piece of writing at a time, when in fact they may be working on several (as many writers do), and the feeling grows. Add to that the realization that kids will be kids while they are doing all of this (we know what that can mean), and we have a full-fledged stomachache just thinking about it.

Now, I hope you don't think I'm being flippant here. I'm not trying to be. I'm simply trying to think through and understand a feeling that many of us who engage in this kind of teaching feel. If we can understand this feeling, we can make peace with it. All those students making all those different decisions can make us feel like we don't know what's going on in our classrooms, and that contradicts what we have historically believed about teaching—that we *should* know exactly what's going on.

But think about this: Maybe we do know exactly what's going on. What's going on is that our students are doing what writers do. That's exactly what's happening here. The fact that we have so many of them (students) makes it hard for one person to keep up with it all, but what they are doing is exactly what they should be doing. They are doing what writers do. That's what the workshop is all about.

Writers have to manage so, so many different decisions to get writing done. That's one of the most fundamental things about writing—making all these little decisions along the way. Anyone who doesn't understand that, that writing is a complex, recursive, ever-shifting kind of thing *you have to decide about,* hasn't written very much or hasn't listened very well when writers have explained how they do what they do. So if our students aren't making all those different decisions in the myriad ways they can make them, if they are being herded through some predetermined set of steps, then we may know what *each* of them is doing, but we cannot look at the herd of them and say, "Ahh . . . they're doing what writers do." They aren't.

You see, in a way, that feeling that things are just beyond our control is a litmus test for whether or not our writing workshop is really working. When our students don't have so many different things going on that we can't keep up with them, then something is probably awry. If we have that many people together in a room and they are all deeply involved in writing, then we're not SUPPOSED to be able to keep a handle on it all. That's its nature, and that may be exactly why we haven't had a history of more good writing instruction in schools—because they have traditionally been very controlling places.

Now, one thing to be very clear about here is this: It's all their different individual writing decisions that feel slightly beyond our control; it's not their *behavior* that feels that way. Somehow or another in our minds, we have gotten this idea from traditional schooling that the only way for students to "behave" in school is for them all to be doing exactly the same thing, quietly. We think that's what good behavior looks like, and it seems odd sometimes to imagine that an invitation to make different choices and decisions in a classroom is not also an invitation to act out. It's not. The best writing workshop teachers I know have very high expectations for student behavior in their classrooms, dealing seriously and swiftly with those who try to disrupt the work of others. So once again, it's not student behavior that feels beyond our control. It's their work as writers that always feels like we can't quite keep up with it.

Here's another thing. Because the writing act itself is not *one thing* or even one manageable set of things we can teach students, it adds to our feeling that we never quite have a handle on it all. We have traditionally liked to spend time in schools on things that make for easy curriculum: states and capitals, steps of mitosis, the order of the planets, spelling. We like teaching things that show us easily whether students have "gotten it," and writing just doesn't lend itself well to this at all. There's just so much to get and so many ways to get it, and none of those things that you get matter much by themselves because writing is something you do, not something you know. This is why the writers' voices sprinkled throughout this book are so important. We need writers to tell us how they do what they do. Their voices are in this book, not so much to support what I am saying about the teaching of writing as to problematize what I am saying—even to contradict me sometimes. I wanted those writers' voices wrapped around this book so that they could whisper, and sometimes shout, "But wait a minute. . . . That's not how I do that at all." The writers' voices are here to keep things complicated, to keep reminding us that as we think about our own writing workshops, we have to think of them as very complex places where there is always one more thing to think about, one more exception to consider.

Teaching in a writing workshop is not easy. Anyone who has chosen to have a writing workshop has had to make peace with this. I have had to make peace with this. I have pursued this kind of teaching because I believe that writing is important. I believe in deeply theoretical ways that a workshop setting is the best environment for students to learn to write in, and I believe that I have the responsibility always to act in accordance with what I believe is best for my students, even when it is very, very challenging.

But as hard as it is, I also find my teaching of writing to be one of the most rewarding things in my life. I suspect that my peers in this teaching feel the same way. When we know that a student wrote a piece that changed his life while he was in our class, we are rewarded. When we know a student wrote her first poem, all by herself, while in our class, we are rewarded. When our students care for each other because they have gotten to know each other so well through writing, we are rewarded. When a parent tells us his child is writing all the time at home now, we are rewarded. When we see students grow and grow as writers, learning over time to control more and more aspects of the whole process for themselves, we are rewarded. Teaching writing is so challenging, but so worth it. Those kinds of rewards don't come packaged in a writing workshop kit. They are priceless.

9

Getting Ready to Teach

Since so few of us had a history of good writing instruction in school, we don't have a lot to draw on when we start to think about what our teaching will look like in the writing workshop. And we know that by its very nature, the writing workshop belies a curriculum guide that will give scope and sequence to our teaching on a day-to-day basis. Curriculum guides by themselves don't know our students. That doesn't mean, however, that there are not many kinds of curriculum support for our teaching. There are. There are tons of it.

To understand what kinds of curriculum support we will need, it helps first to think through how the teaching happens in the writing workshop. We know that *learning* will be taking place all the time as students are writing and thinking and talking about writing during independent work and share times. The teaching we do surrounds that active learning and is meant to push it and support it in important ways.

A part of this teaching, the focus lesson, will look very much like the front-of-the-class, teacher-talking kind of teaching we know traditionally as *the lesson*. But this is only a small part of it, this five- to ten-minutes' worth of an hour or more of writing workshop. I worry sometimes when I have my teacher education students plan and do a focus lesson. I worry because it seems so small to them. "Is this all there is?" they seem to ask. And the answer of course is "no." There are layers and layers of "things that teach" in a writing workshop, and the teacher is responsible for thinking about and planning for them all.

When I try to help my students understand what these layers of teaching will be, I tell them that basically there are five categories, five ways of thinking about teaching and learning in the workshop: how we set up the room to teach (environment), how we live in that room (demonstration), what we teach in focus lessons and conferences (direct instruction), what investigations we plan (inquiry), and what we require as writing homework (the potential of the world). When we plan with intention for teaching to happen in each of these five ways, we create a dynamic learning space. Getting ready to teach begins, then, with thinking carefully about each of these ways of teaching.

SETTING UP THE ROOM TO TEACH (ENVIRONMENT)

Have you ever been to a hands-on science center or museum? Or maybe a place like historical Williamsburg, where you can actually live like people did in colonial times? In many ways, the kind of teaching and learning that takes place there matches what we are trying to establish in the writing workshop. These are places where you can look at things, try things out, read things, touch things. . . . You learn in these places because you are surrounded by things to learn *from*. The best writing workshops are a lot like that.

Think of it this way. Ask yourself this question: "If I locked my students in my classroom and stood outside the door, what could they learn about writing without me even being in there?" This is such a good guiding question, because it helps us think about the classroom environment that we want to set up for the writing workshop. When we think about this kind of teaching, the teaching that happens as a result of the classroom environment we create, we think not so much about "what students will *learn*" as we do about "what can I get going in the room that students can *learn from?*" Luckily, for writing workshop we don't need nearly as elaborate a setting as a re-creation of colonial Williamsburg. No, we simply need to think about what kinds of things writers could use to support their learning.

The first thing writers need in their environment is time. We know that simply by establishing the writing workshop and the expectation that students will write daily in this workshop, we are getting ready to teach. The experience students gain from writing every single day will teach them *a lot* about writing. If we did nothing else but locked them up and said, "Write," we would be teaching. So this expectation, this *requirement* that students write, is actually very important teaching work.

Beyond establishing a daily time for writing, I think about two main things that are part of the classroom environment: the instructional structures and routines I can put in place, and the material resources that students can use to teach themselves.

Structures and Routines

Good teachers of writing establish any number of structures and routines in their workshops that do important teaching work on a regular basis. The "group share" that most teachers have as some part of every writing workshop (see Chapter 15) is a great example of an established routine that teaches each day. During this predictable time, students share strategies and insights from their ongoing writing work, and, in that way, everyone has access to the learning of others. The group share is a daily routine that teaches content, but the content is not determined until the sharing takes place. Rather than "delivering" this important content, the teacher's role in this teaching is to create the daily routine and maintain a supportive classroom environment where students are willing to share. The long-range goal of the group share and other similar structures and routines is that, over time, the teacher truly could stand outside the classroom door and students could "carry on" with this teaching tool, using this routine as a vehicle for their learning quite on their own.

Here are just a few examples of other structures and routines that teachers have set up that do important teaching work as part of the classroom environment:

- visits every other Friday with students from another class where students talk about what they've been doing as writers;
- a table in the room where students may sign up to teach small groups some strategy or technique they have been using as writers;
- a basket where students may place texts with pages marked that they want copied for their own study, and an assistant who makes those copies every Tuesday and Thursday;
- a bulletin board that is changed every two weeks where various groups of students may display pieces of writing;
- "official" response groups for writing that meet once a week during independent writing time;
- a "notebook news" board where students may write new strategies they have tried for gathering notebook material; other students can use the news board to support their own notebook writing when they need new strategies;
- a student each day who is responsible for sharing with the class a quote from an author.

The best classrooms have just a few structures and routines like these in place at any given time. Whatever is put in place, we want to be very selective so as not to overwhelm the structured, routine work of independent writing. The best curriculum resources I know in order to help us imagine structures and routines that support writing are those found in professional books written by teachers about the teaching of writing. You don't have to think this through all by yourself. You can read stories of other classrooms and let them support your planning.

Material Resources

What can students get their hands on during writing workshop? One of the good things about thinking of resources that students can use is that many of these resources are the same ones we will need to use to support *our* curriculum knowledge for direct instruction. We will be learning, alongside our students, from all kinds of resources in the room, such as:

• Books, magazines, newspapers—anything with good writing in it. We need all kinds of texts around, written in many different genres. Our students can refer to these texts to learn how to write well (to study the craft of writing), and they can use them to immerse themselves in a genre. The more we have in our rooms, the better, but we can (and should) also use the school library as a resource.

• Copies of writing that students have done in the past. Students can learn a lot from looking at what writers who are a lot like them have done in previous writing workshops. We may even want to ask students to leave copies of their writing with writing advice attached to them for our future students.

• Books about writing. We won't be able to do our teaching without the help of writers like Ralph Fletcher, in *What a Writer Needs* (1993), or Robin Hemley, in *Turning Life into Fiction* (1994). We'll use books like these to support our direct instruction, but students can use them on their own too. We may just have the books out for use; we can also copy excerpts from the kinds of books that we think would be helpful for our students, laminate these excerpts, and keep them in folders or baskets in the room for students to use (as we mentioned in Chapter 6).

• Writers' *voices* in the room. We can paste quotes from writers around the room, or we can have articles with writers' interviews in them available for students to read. *Booklinks* magazine, published by the American Library Association, is one of the best resources for readable, interesting author interviews. We might also have video- or audio-taped interviews with writers that students can watch, or books full of writers' quotes about all aspects of the writing process. If there is Internet access in the room, students can get in touch with writers' Web sites.

• We can purchase copies of *Writer's Market* and other books that tell how to get published, and have these available. We might also copy various submission guidelines from different magazines, and have these in folders for students to use.

• Books or guides for grammar and convention are essential. Every writing workshop should have a copy of Strunk and White's *Elements of Style* available. It's fairly easy to read, and it covers *everything*. Dictionaries and thesauruses, of course, are important resources to have out and about as well.

- People who can talk about writing. Visitors make great resources for our students' learning. And we don't have to have access to professional writers. We might invite someone who just loves poetry, someone who writes a lot as part of his or her profession, someone who collaborates with others to help students understand these kinds of relationships—anyone who can show children what some of what they're learning looks like in the world outside the classroom.

Resources like these will set up the room as a place that "teaches" without us having to do anything. If it is a *workshop*, then all kinds of things need to be in that "shop" that students can *work* with as they go about their writing.

How We Live in Our Rooms (Demonstration)

Everything we do in our writing workshops, every move we make, teaches students. Either we can be walking, breathing, talking examples of all we advocate for our students, or we can have them sitting around wondering why we are trying to get them into something that we are obviously not into ourselves. As we discussed at length in Chapter 4, our students need to see in us what we hope for them. In that chapter, we worked through the idea that as students begin seeing us as writers, it will have a tremendous influence on the tone of our teaching. Here, however, we need to extend that idea and think about our writing lives—the fact that we have them, and how having them does important *teaching* work in the workshop.

First, anytime we work on our own writing, we are doing important curriculum work for our teaching. Teachers who have written some on their own (since they were students in school!) just know things, understand things, about writing that other teachers don't. There is just no way around that. So much of my best curriculum for writing comes from my own writing experiences. I understand and can explain so many things about writing because I've been there. Speaking from my own experiences lends an authenticity to my teaching that students get a "read" on pretty quickly and that they respect. They see me as someone who writes, which is how I'm asking them to see themselves, and this is a key ingredient in learning *anything*. They listen to me because they can see that I know what I'm talking about. You can't get that if you don't write.

Now, I don't think teachers need to be certain kinds of writers to use this as an asset in their teaching. But teachers do need to keep their own notebooks and to try, from time to time, writing out of those notebooks for audiences and for important reasons. Teachers don't even need to write all the time—they don't have time! But they can use notebooks that they have kept during the summer or poems that they wrote three years ago to do their teaching. They do need to have had some kind of a writing life that they can share with students.

I do not believe we make our writing lives a demonstration by *writing* during writing workshop time. I *teach* during writing workshop—from start to finish. After the focus lesson, I begin conferring, and I use every possible moment to get around to my students to do this one-on-one teaching. So how do my students know I write? Easy. I carry my notebook to every conference, and I refer to it often to make a point in that teaching. Many, many of my focus lessons use examples from my own writing or tell stories from my writing life to show a strategy or make a point. I share pieces I've written during writing celebrations, and I have some things I've written available for students to read on their own. I frequently share with students the ways my reading life is informing my writing life.

So, while I don't write much while my students are writing, they know all about my writing life and are able to look to me for a demonstration of how a life like that might be lived. I routinely reflect on my guiding vision for students' development as writers (Chapter 3), and I ask myself, "In my teaching, am I demonstrating to my students all these ways of being as a writer?" It is such a cliché to say that "actions speak louder than words," but you know, clichés become clichés because there is so much truth to them. Anytime we are getting ready to teach, we would be wise to remember that particular cliché and let it guide us. Our actions do a tremendous amount of teaching.

Focus Lessons and Conferences (Direct Instruction)

Whenever nothing about the writing workshop feels like traditional teaching, it may be helpful to remember that in a good hour-long workshop, the teacher will actually be engaged in direct instruction—what he or she knows best from tradition—for almost the entire hour. As we said above, five to ten minutes of that time will be direct instruction for the whole class, delivered in a focus lesson that fits with whatever unit of study is going on in the room. Once the focus lesson is completed, students move out to their independent writing work for the day, and the teacher moves out with them, continuing to offer direct instruction to individual students (conferring) and sometimes to small groups.

So while the focus lesson is planned to meet some classwide objective that the teacher has in mind, the instruction offered in a conference is given in direct response to an individual student's work at that time. The "in response to" part of direct instruction in the conference is what so often makes this feel like very foreign teaching. You can't plan for what you'll teach in conferences because you don't know what you'll have to respond to. It is important to remember, nonetheless, that the conference *is* direct instruction. Before we leave that writer, we are supposed to have taught him or her something. We will consider conferences and focus lessons separately in later chapters, since they have a whole set of considerations all their own.

Investigations We Plan (Inquiry)

In certain units of study, there will be occasions for us to get students involved in some sort of inquiry during their independent work. This too can be powerful teaching. Focus lessons are used to set up these inquiries and get students looking at something with a frame that relates to the topic under study. Here are some very common methods of inquiry: reading examples of a genre at the beginning of a genre study, asking questions such as "What makes fiction *fiction*?" or studying a single text very closely during an author study, asking, "How does this author craft his or her words?" When we plan for inquiry, we don't know specifically what content will come from the study, but we have faith that if we get materials into our students' hands and get them asking good questions, then important content will follow.

In addition to looking at texts in genre and author studies, here are some other examples of kinds of inquiries we might set up:

- In a study of their lives and histories as writers, students might look through pieces of writing they have done in the past, using self-stick notes to mark and comment on things they notice; students would then discuss what they see with a small group, asking questions such as "What have we learned along the way?" and "How are we different now as writers than we used to be?"
- In a study of what writers need to gather from the world to sustain a published writing life, they might look through stacks of texts together and imagine (make theories about) where the writers got ideas for those texts.
- In a study of writing processes, students might pore through articles by writers and dig out every mention they can find of writers describing their processes.
- In a study of how writers follow an idea through to publication, some students might look at magazines and study submission guidelines, while other students study copies of *Writer's Market* to learn about book submission guidelines.
- In a study of peer conferring, students might look at transcripts of conferences the teacher has had and study the kinds of teaching they see there; they would then make theories about what does and doesn't work in conferences, and develop some guidelines they might want to follow in their own conferring.
- In an author study, students might spend a day just looking at leads across many different texts by the author, then develop theories about how the author crafts leads.
- In a study of how writers edit their work for publication, students might look through pieces of the teacher's writing that have been edited and develop questions and insights about his process, eventually interviewing the teacher about his editing process.

Inquiries like these are very engaging for writers and are absolutely essential to some units of study (genre, author, and craft studies especially). We need to plan for some inquiry in the writing workshop during appropriate units of study, not because we need to find things for students to do, but because they can learn so much from the process of inquiry. Always, always, though, we have to keep in mind the balance of time. If students are spending so much time in writerly inquiries that they never get time to *write,* then the inquiry can't serve its purpose: to support students' work as writers.

One piece of advice that seems pertinent here is this: I wouldn't recommend setting up inquiries in the workshop that happen during independent writing time until you are pretty sure students are going to be a little miffed that you are asking them to step away from their writing for just a bit. We need to get that independent writing time firmly in place before we beg a little of it for inquiry. Remember that it is very important for students to learn, *first,* that independent writing time is a time when they will (almost always) have to decide what their work will be. So in our units of study very early in the year, we simply want to support that work with fresh new strategies, techniques, and understandings, but not with plans for inquiry that take students away from their independent work.

Requiring Writing Homework (The Potential of the World)

When most of us were in school, writing homework was usually the time when we did the actual writing. We rarely wrote in class. We would be given an assignment in class and then we would take that assignment home, do the writing (as best we could—lonely as we were there), and turn it in a few days later. Of course, this was when we were actually writing. We were also asked to do "writing" homework that came in the form of completing a set of exercises where we underlined the subject once and the predicate twice; added punctuation to someone else's paragraph; or labeled sentences as "fragments," "run-ons," or "complete."

These old models we knew for writing homework just don't make much sense for the writing workshops we teach in today. We want students doing the heavy work of writing *during* the workshop. We need to catch them in the act of this work so that we can teach directly "into" their actual processes of writing. We can't do this if they are doing their writing outside school. This is why we give them time, every single day, during the writing workshop to work on their writing. And if there are any sentences to check for completeness or paragraphs to check for punctuation, well, we want that done during the workshop too—and we'll have students do that on their *own pieces* of writing, thank you very much. That just seems to make more sense to us.

So does this mean that students in writing workshops never have any homework? No, it doesn't mean that at all. As a matter of fact, I believe that the success of the writing students do in school depends a lot on the attention they pay to writing outside school. The world outside school holds a completely different potential than the one inside school. When we recognize this and ask students to go get that world and bring it into our writing workshops, we have found the real power of homework. Let's think this through.

If you study what writers in the world outside school do, you'll find that their actual "desk work" is accompanied by lots of "world work" that happens away from the desk. Writers lead writing lives away from their desks, wide-awake lives that bring them back to those desks each day full of ideas and plans and purposes. In our writing workshops, students will be doing the "desk work" of writers, but if we want this desk work to be successful, then we have to nurture and encourage the "world work" they will do when they are away from these desks.

In writing workshops, then, the homework that is required is the actual "world work" that writers do. Writers are engaged in "prewriting" all the time. They are watching and listening and studying and gathering material and ideas wherever they go. In an interview with Beverly Cleary on *All Things Considered* (Aug. 16, 1999), the beloved author talked about how she got the idea for a chapter of her newest Ramona book from a conversation she overheard in a restaurant about a baby getting its head stuck in a cat scratching pole. Our hope for writing workshop homework is that students will be doing just what Beverly Cleary was doing in that restaurant that day—finding material out in the world that they will bring back to the desk work they do in our writing workshops.

In many writing workshops, the homework "toolbox" is the writer's notebook. Students use writer's notebooks to do all kinds of collecting out

WRITERS' VOICES ON . . .

homework

What I tell young writers is that when I see something that strikes me, I write it down. I don't ask myself, "why is that important?" I just know it's important because it's who I am that something seems important to me. It'll either be something I see or something I hear or something I feel inside. That may happen once a month. Or it may happen every day five days in a row. Whenever it happens, I make a note. Once, I overheard a woman talking about a boy getting a fishhook hung in his nose. I wrote it down. Later I was able to make a scene out of that. (Clyde Edgerton, in Dannye Romine Powell, *Parting the Curtains,* 119)

Writers are careful listeners and watchful observers of the world in which they live. They notice and note. These noticings enable writers to speak to the experiences of readers, to connect to the universal themes of life itself. It is because of this watchfulness that writers can leave a reader with the feeling of familiarity with characters, events, and place. Living a writerly life *is* the writer's "homework." Much of a writer's most important work is done away from the desk—it's homework or "world work."

Phyllis Reynolds Naylor does her homework for months, sometimes years, before she begins a book.

Whenever Phyllis Reynolds Naylor gets an idea about a particular book, she writes it down in a notebook specially set aside for that book. . . . The notebooks have pockets in them to hold relevant magazine articles, photographs that remind Phyllis of one of the book's characters, maps of the area, or pages from the area's phone book. This collecting and notetaking usually goes on for a year or two before Phyllis is ready to begin writing the book. "I know I'm ready to start writing the book when I begin waking early in the morning, thinking about it. I'm excited. I can't wait to get going." (Deborah Kovacs and James Preller, *Meet the Authors and Illustrators,* 120)

➤

in the world, which gives them the essential material they need for their desk work in the writing workshop. Teachers in these workshops expect students to collect ideas in notebooks when they are away from school and out in the world. They offer students "homework curriculum" that teaches them about the kinds of things they need to be collecting as writers when they are out in the world (see the end of Chapter 6 for a support list of the kinds of things students might gather in notebooks). These teachers make predictable times in the writing workshop when students are expected to talk about what they are collecting in their notebooks, and some part of evaluation is always tied to this homework.

Yep, you heard right, she said a year or two. Now, that's some homework.

Pat Conroy describes how he is at work even when he is away from his desk:

> Certainly, if something happens or somebody says something interesting or thought provoking, I try to write that down. . . . It can be current events, what somebody said, what somebody did. Something I want to remember I do not think I'll remember otherwise. . . . One of the notes I had in the journal was "Remember the white porpoise that used to swim between Harbor Island and St. Helena Island when you first came to Beaufort." Just that note reminded me and became the basis for the white-porpoise chapter in *The Prince of Tides.* (in Dannye Romine Powell, *Parting the Curtains,* 68)

Pat Conroy provides us with an excellent demonstration of a habit of mind, that watchful eye, that attentive ear that is so much a part of the writer's work in the world.

When we are doing our homework, what we see or overhear can spark immediate work:

> I remember at one point right in the middle of writing *Fair and Tender Ladies,* I went to the outlet mall in Burlington and nobody would wait on me in Linens-n-Things because they had this book, and they were all in there interpreting each other's dreams. It was hysterical. So I came home and wrote the story, "The Interpretation of Dreams" right then, that weekend. It was the Fourth of July weekend. . . . (Lee Smith, in Dannye Romine Powell, *Parting the Curtains,* 399)

A writer's homework is an interesting notion. As Katie reminds us, it isn't a worksheet on verbs or an exercise on describing your ideal pet. Rather, it is living in the world with a writer's eyes and ears and frame of mind. It is noticing and noting. It is trying out possibilities and exploring other options. It is listening for what rings true and what might become your next writing project.

Kovacs, Deborah, and James Preller. 1993. *Meet the Authors and Illustrators: 60 Creators of Favorite Children's Books Talk about Their Work.* Vol. 2. New York: Scholastic Professional.

Powell, Dannye Romine. 1995. *Parting the Curtains: Voices of the Great Southern Writers.* New York: Anchor Books.

Remember that with homework, the key is to get students to think of it as being work that supports the desk work they will do in your writing workshop. This is particularly true of notebook gathering. Many of my students use their notebooks just to get ideas down, and then they use their workshop time to really write and write about the ideas they've gathered that interest them.

In addition to supporting their own writing, lots of teachers also have students do homework that supports various units of study in the room. Take surveying, for example. In a genre study of poetry, students might survey as many people as they can find outside of their class, asking them how often they read poetry or what their favorite poem is. In a unit of study on writing lives, students might interview people outside class about their earliest memories of writing, or how they use writing in their professions and in their lives as adults. Students might be asked to collect and record examples of language use for a study of variations in language use. Basically, you can use any of the primary research skills—observation, interview, survey, collecting, recording—as homework assignments that can provide writing content that you just can't get if you don't go out into the world and gather it.

Teachers of writing must be aware that each day in the writing workshop is filled with layers and layers of teaching: environment, demonstration, direct instruction, inquiry, and the potential of the world. We'll want to think about and plan for each of these with intention as we start getting ready for our writing workshops.

References

Cleary, Beverly. Interview with Linda Wertheimer. *All Things Considered.* Public Broadcasting System. 16 August 1999.

Fletcher, Ralph. J. 1993. *What a Writer Needs.* Portsmouth, N.H.: Heinemann.

Hemley, Robin. 1994. *Turning Life into Fiction.* Cincinnati, Ohio: Story Press.

10

The Nature of Workshop Curriculum

In the last chapter, we looked at *how* the teaching happens in a writing workshop. Now we need to think about *what* it is we will be teaching. We have a responsibility to nurture all of our goals for students as writers with our teaching. And because of the kinds of goals we have, we necessarily will teach about lots of things that are not traditional, empirically based content. In writing workshops, we both teach how to do something and we nurture the identities that come to be because students are doing this something every day, so we need new ways to think about the content of the curriculum. What do students need to know and know how to do in order to grow into the kinds of writers we hope they will become? For me to even begin to think about this question, I have to return to that set of goals that guides all of my workshop planning and instruction. As I explained in Chapter 3, these goals are:

Over time in a writing workshop I hope to see students developing . . .

- a sense of self as writers, as well as personal writing processes that work for them;
- ways of reading the world like writers, collecting ideas with variety, volume, and thoughtfulness;
- a sense of thoughtful, deliberate purpose about their work as writers, and a willingness to linger with those purposes;
- as members of a responsive, literate community;
- ways of reading texts like writers, developing a sense of craft, genre, and form in writing;
- a sense of audience and an understanding of how to prepare writing to go into the world.

The curriculum students will need in order to grow in all these ways is varied, but I think it boils down to about five kinds of things that I teach in a writing workshop:

- strategies (ways to do things);
- techniques (ways to fashion things);
- questions (ways to think about things);
- relationships (ways to connect things);
- conventions (ways to expect things).

In all parts of their writing lives and their writing processes, students will need to build a repertoire of understandings, strategies, and techniques to support them in their work as writers. Many, many of these will come about simply because we require students to write daily. We might never do any teaching at all, and we know that students would grow as writers just from the experience of writing daily. But they can grow so much more when good teaching supports their work, so we need to think carefully about the kinds of things we will be teaching them, both in whole-class focus lessons and in individual conferences. Let's take each one of these now, think it through a little bit, and look at a few examples.

Strategies (Ways to Do Things)

We have said before that writing is something you do, not something you know, but there are all kinds of things to know about how to do it. There are strategies for writing that students can learn that will help them do many things—across all their different processes—that they might not think of trying on their own. When I think of strategy teaching, I think of lessons that show students how to do very specific things that they might try as writers. When teaching strategy lessons, I usually show students an example where either a student or I have tried a strategy. I have learned many of the writing strategies I know from books I have read by writers who describe how they go about it all. I usually read about these things and then try them myself so that, in a lesson, I can show students both the writer's suggestion and my own try at it. Some of this curriculum I have sort of invented through my own experiences with writing, and some of it I have invented based on my own teaching observations in order to help students with their struggles.

For example, to help students with their growing sense of audience and to help them prepare their writing to go out into the world, I might teach this strategy lesson (in either a focus lesson or a conference).

> Sometimes when we write, we read back over what we've written and we think to ourselves, "I'm not sure if this makes sense." We know what we're writing about so well that we know what's in between the lines that makes it make sense, but will someone else? If you are wondering this about your piece, you might try this. Have someone else read it and then ask that person to tell it back to you as they remember it. Then, you listen very carefully to hear if it made sense to this person. As she tells it, you may ask her questions about the content to see if it made sense or not, but don't ask her, "Did it make sense?" She might say, "yes it did," but you don't know if it made the sense you wanted it to make unless she tells you about it. *You* need to answer the question, "Did it make sense?" Not your reader. Just let your reader tell you about it.

I would probably follow this explanation of the strategy with a demonstration where a student reads a short piece I have written, tells it back to me, and I listen "out loud." In this way, students have access to what I'm thinking about as I figure out whether the piece made sense or not. This is a very typical whole-class focus lesson that teaches students a strategy they can use for revision.

For another example, suppose I were trying to help students learn different things they can do in their notebooks to generate material for writing. This would be content that goes with my goal of having students learn to read the world like writers. I might teach them one of my favorite collection strategies:

> Sometimes, when I'm just hanging out with my notebook, I like to do something I call "finding a story." I don't make one up out of nothing; instead, I look around me, and I try to find something that someone has obviously left behind or something that has someone's life behind it. It might be an old sweater left hanging over a chair, a picture someone has hung on the wall, an old yellow school bus with paintings all over it parked in someone's side yard. It can be *anything* I see, as long as I can imagine a person behind it. Once I've focused on something, I just start writing some person's story to go with it. For example, if I saw an old rusty bucket sitting on someone's porch, I might start like this: "Charlene had been meaning to take that bucket to the trash dump for some time. It had holes in it and was rusted all over—no good to anyone. But somehow she just couldn't throw it away. It had been her daddy's chicken feed bucket. . . ." And then I just keep writing to see where it leads me. I never know what I'll think of next for the story. Sometimes they dead-end right in my notebook, but sometimes I've gotten some great stuff too—like this one about Jack, a character I love.

And I can show them the entry from my notebook, written one day when I saw an old car with a large canoe strapped to the top of it (Figure 10.1).

This is a strategy for writing, a thing a writer can learn *to do*. We get these kinds of ideas and these how-to's into the room so that they add new possibilities for things writers might try. We look around the room to see, and we also ask our students to show us, when some of them try this strategy we have taught them (and they will—we learn to have faith in this). Those students who have a go at trying something that's been taught in a focus lesson can share the results of the strategy with others. Lots of the teaching that happens in the workshop is of this kind. We might write the explanations for strategies like these on cards, laminate them, and have them available for stu-

Everyone laughed at him for having that boat stuck on top of his car. They said, "Jack, man, it looks like you don't know how you want to travel!" But Jack didnt care. The red canoe sitting upside on his old white car made him feel safe somehow. He liked the way it split everything he saw as he drove along in two. It made him feel like there was a clear line drawn between him and the rest of the world.

So, he kept it there all the time, even if he knew it would be weeks before he'd go to the river again.

The river Ever since Stella left the river was the only place Jack could lose the memory of her— drown out the pain she'd left him with there among the rocks and rapids, drown out the sound of her "goodbye, you don't need me enough" line—the last line he would ever hear from her.

Did he need her? He didn't like

FIGURE 10.1
My Notebook Entry

dents to return to on their own during the workshop. In this way, our focus lessons on strategies can become resources that students return to independently—and this adds to the ways in which they can manage their own work in the workshop.

TECHNIQUES (WAYS TO FASHION THINGS)

Techniques are very similar to strategies in that they are also things writers can do or try, but techniques have to do with refining things, with ways writers do things *well.* If strategies are all the things they can do as writers, techniques are those approaches to writing in which they become craftspersons, usually in the service of writing for an audience. Most of these will be crafting techniques—ways to write things that are distinctive, sound good, and catch readers' attention. You needn't get hung up on the difference between strategies and techniques, however; I am sure you will quite naturally see the need for both kinds of content, even if you're not sure whether you would refer to them as one or the other. Lessons that show writing techniques are almost always tied to very specific examples from professional authors, because we learn about techniques for good writing by studying the texts of good writers.

To push students to develop a sense of craft, as part of one of my teaching goals, I might teach them this technique lesson about exploiting print and spelling to make meaning:

> Look at this sentence I ran across in Gary Paulsen's book *Canyons* (1990, 41): "It was going to be a long, loong night." Isn't that neat? The way he added that extra "o" to "loong" so it matched the meaning? Writers sometimes do this—they manipulate spellings and print to match their meanings. Remember when you were little and you saw in books that things like "hot" would be written in red letters or a word like "bumpy" would be written with the letters going up and down? It's sort of like that, except that it doesn't have to be a little kids' text. It could be one like Paulsen's novel, or one like *Sports Illustrated,* where one writer wrote "rightthisveryminute" all as one word (Gary Smith, 1998). I was looking through my notebook and found this sentence where I could try this—

"The other side of the lake looked so far away."—spacing them out like that to match the meaning. You can do anything with the print—run words together, spell them a different way, write in big or small letters—anything, as long as it captures some meaning you want to make.

So this would be the content of a lesson that teaches students a technique for writing. Technique lessons are the ones in which "Try its" often make the most sense, so we might have students see if they can think of a quick example using this technique that they write in their notebooks at the end of the lesson—but we don't have to. We can just send students back to their work with the request, "If anyone tries this, be sure to let me know." We'll want to fill the room with technique possibilities so that students know many different things they can do with writing to make it good writing.

Questions (Ways to Think about Things)

Writers—like anyone who works at something on a regular basis—ask themselves all kinds of important questions that help them manage their work. When we want students thinking in important ways about their writing, we teach them about the kinds of questions writers ask. In this teaching, the question is actually the content of the teaching (rather than the answer), because it teaches a way of thinking that writers will need to return to again and again.

Sometimes we plan focus lessons that present important questions for writers to think about. Usually, in these lessons, we demonstrate kinds of answers other writers have had, and we usually come back after some interval of time to see what kinds of answers to the question our students have found. But the focus is always on the question; we let students know we want them to continue to question themselves as a part of their personal writing process. We may ask, again, to see evidence of their questioning strategies in portfolios or other assessments.

This time, without giving the text of an actual lesson, let's look at a few different kinds of questions that might be the topic of whole-class focus

WRITERS' VOICES ON . . .

learning from other writers

I feel that the first layer of writing is art. The surge. The second layer, I come behind myself and craft what I have written. And I learn as I go from other writers. For example, right now I've kept reading Saul Bellow's *Herzog* to learn how to do density. This book that I am working on needs a weight and volume to it unlike I've had before. The weight cannot pull the story down. The anecdotes cannot be tangents that would have been better cut out and saved in the computer for another day.

It's learning how to get myself out of my chair and say, "I'm losing my way in this plot. How am I going to manage this?" And that's when I'll read an old Anne Tyler book, for example, and I'll see how she creates a plot around a simple domestic story. Or Alice Hoffman. But I wouldn't go to Alice Hoffman for a quickly drawn character. I'd go to Dunne. In the process of writing one book, I'll use ten writers, because that's about how many elements of craft there are in a novel. (Kaye Gibbons, in Dannye Romine Powell, *Parting the Curtains,* 181)

Writers are forever learners. Kaye Gibbons shows us how even an accomplished and proficient writer relies on the works of others to teach her. There are two important lessons here for our classroom writing communities. First, Gibbons knows what she needs help with and is able to recognize when that help is needed. And second, as one who reads widely and reads like a writer, she knows where to go for that help.

Eudora Welty speaks to the influence of reading on learning to write well:

> Indeed, learning to write may be a part of learning to read. For all I know, writing comes out of a superior devotion to reading. . . . The writer himself studies intensely how to do it while he is in the thick of doing it; then when the particular novel or story is done, he is likely to forget how; he does well to. Each work is new. (*The Eye of the Story,* 134–135)

Welty tells us, and Gibbons shows us, how the writer is a learner.

There seems to be one big lesson for us here. These two women, Welty and Gibbons, are accomplished and acclaimed writers, and they are still learning how to write. Now, isn't that comforting? I certainly feel better just knowing that we can't expect to teach everything our students need to know about writing in nine months. It also implies that we can't think we have taught something and just leave it. From the examples above, we can see that writers are always learning, returning to favorite writers who teach them. Perhaps the wisest teaching we do, then, happens when we show our students how to use their reading lives to support their writing work.

Powell, Dannye Romine. 1995. *Parting the Curtains: Voices of the Great Southern Writers.* New York: Anchor Books.

Welty, Eudora. 1990. *The Eye of the Story: Selected Essays and Reviews.* New York: Vintage Books.

lessons or of the content of a conference with an individual writer. These questions should give you a feel for this kind of content.

- "Am I in a rut?" is a good question that helps students as they are developing their personal writing processes. We might ask them to look at their notebooks with this question in mind, paying close attention to the kinds of entries they are making. "Do all the entries have a sameness to them that looks like someone who is just filling up pages?"
- "What words could I really do without in this piece?" is a revision question I always teach that helps students with their growing sense of craft. It is a question they should take with them to every single piece they ever write, so it's a big one. Good writing is pared down to the bare bones—only the essential words are left after all the revision.
- "What themes lie underneath and in between the entries in my notebook? What seems important here? Where are the connections?" This series of questions can help students grow in "thoughtful, deliberate purpose" as writers. These questions frame a way of looking at notebooks that helps students uncover important topics to pursue toward published writing.

Remember that the questions we teach in focus lessons are meant to develop important habits of mind. In searching out the content for these lessons, we need to ask, "Is this an important question for a writer to ask? Is this a question a writer will ask again and again?" If the answer to both those questions is "yes," then we probably want to get that question into the room as a possibility.

Relationships (Ways to Connect Things)

So much of what a writer does can be difficult to understand. Teachers in writing workshops spend a lot of time trying to help students understand this difficult work, so a lot of the content they develop is a content of relationships—helping students understand something complex by comparing it to something students know well. In a way, these lessons build important metaphors that lead to deeper understandings that students can take with them throughout their writing lives.

To give you a feel for this kind of content, we'll look at a few of my favorite relationships—ones I like to build into my teaching of writing:

- A writer's notebook is a lot like a painter's palette, or a cabinetmaker's toolbox, or a seamstress's sewing kit. The notebook is a possibility place filled with what we need in order to do our writing: words, ideas, possibilities (just like paintbrushes, hammers, and needles). This understanding helps students develop their ability to read the world and to work with thoughtful, deliberate purpose, using their notebooks as tools for that writerly work.
- Learning to read like a writer is like a seamstress visiting a dress shop. She looks very carefully at all of the different clothes, examining how each one is made so she can get ideas for her own sewing. This is how a writer goes to the library, how a writer reads—with a sense of possibility. Writers can look carefully at how other texts are written in order to get ideas for their own writing.
- Getting your writing ready to take out into the world is a lot like getting dressed in the morning. People in the world expect us to do certain things to get ourselves ready—brush our teeth, comb our hair, wear clothes, and so on—and we do these conventional things so people will respond to us positively. It's the same thing with writing. Readers expect us to have done certain things with our writing before we send it out: checked for spelling, made sure our message was right, made it easy to read, and so on. We do these conventional things so readers will respond positively to our important message.

When relationships like these are presented to the whole class in focus lessons or in individual conferences, they are meant to build important understandings that will help students grow in their sense of what they are doing as writers. There is nothing to do after these lessons at all, no "Try its"; they are just presented as something for students to think about. Often, teachers of writing return to these metaphors again and again in focus lessons, using them to deepen and refine different understandings along the way. The best writing workshop teachers I know have found the metaphors that seem to work best for them in building student understandings, and have refined their use in their teaching through the years.

Conventions (Ways to Expect Things)

The content of some lessons will be a simple explanation of how something usually works in the written language. We call these "ways that language usually works" *conventions*. If one of our goals is for students to grow in their ability to prepare writing to go out into the world, then they will need some lessons that explain the conventions that support this preparatory work. Lessons on conventions can range from an explanation of how page numbers work in kindergarten, all the way to how to make pronouns and antecedents agree, or ways to punctuate dialogue. For whole-class teaching, we want to make sure we are focusing on only those conventions that lots of students are struggling with; otherwise, these are best dealt with in small groups or individual conferences.

There are several reasons why lessons about conventions are better suited to small-group and individual teaching. One is that, unlike the other kinds of curriculum we offer in the writing workshop, there aren't a lot of ways to deepen students' understandings about conventions once they are using them just fine. There are only so many things to know about capital letters, for example, and once a student knows those, there's nowhere else of significance for the student to go in his or her understanding. Also, students come to understand conventions so much better when the explanations for them are tied directly to their pieces of writing. Teachers get a lot more mileage out of showing a single student where a subject and verb need to agree, and why they need to agree, than they do from whole-class lessons on this issue.

When deciding what lessons on conventions to do for the whole class, we need to see what kinds of conventions students need help with, being careful not to fall into the easy trap of assumptions—assuming all fourth graders must need help with subject-verb agreement, for example. Many of them may not need help with this at all. Also, in planning these lessons that explain conventions, we must be sure that the content will be something that will directly help our students as they write and prepare their writing to go out into the world. Remember, that's why we teach them about conventions. Labeling all the parts of speech in a sentence probably will not help students with their writing. We may debate whether or not this is an important thing for students to be able to do and for them to know, but labeling parts of speech is just not something that will help them write better or that will prepare their writing to go out into the world.

Here are just a few of the kinds of conventions that I have found students do need help with from time to time in their writing, all of which are presented in the service of getting their writing ready to go out into the world:

- issues of capitalization;
- issues of punctuation;
- issues of agreement (subject-verb, pronoun-antecedent);
- issues of spelling;
- issues of structure (sentences and paragraphs).

So there we have it. Basically, the content of our teaching in the writing workshop—what we teach—will present one of these five kinds of curriculum to students: strategies, techniques, questions, relationships, or conventions. Lots and lots of writing curriculum that comes in these different forms can help students grow in all the different ways we want to see them growing. Remember that the curriculum for writing is very complex—that's why we need all these kinds of content to support it. Many times, we will need to return to a specific lesson to think about it again and again with our students.

Building your Knowledge Base of Content

Having outlined all the *kinds* of teaching we'll be doing in the workshop, we are left realizing that, as nice as it may be to understand curriculum in that way, it still doesn't tell us what to teach! No, it doesn't. Writing *content* is not really the purpose of this book. The purpose of this book is to help us think about what kind of content knowledge we need and where we can go to get it. There are really only a few main resources that teachers find helpful to accumulate the content knowledge they have for teaching writing, and a lot of these resources are available for student use in the classroom as well (as we mentioned in the last chapter). Good teachers of writing continue to add to their knowledge base about writing curriculum throughout their teaching careers. We just can't know it all when we start out, and we are always finding that there is more to know as we go along.

So where does content knowledge for teaching writing come from? We've alluded to the answer to this question off and on throughout this book, but we'll spell it out very specifically here. Here's how teachers get smart about writing:

- They write themselves, and they pay attention along the way to their own writing processes. Because they are teachers as well as writers, they think of their own writing as curriculum development. They write with a sense of, "Oh, this is something I might share with my students."
- They learn from watching and listening to their students work as writers. They know that daily, in any writing workshop, there is important "curriculum development" going on all around them.
- They take courses—many of them in the summer—in writing and teaching writing.
- They take advantage of professional development opportunities in writing offered by their local schools and districts.
- They join existing study groups on the teaching of writing (or form their own).
- They talk to colleagues who are also teaching in writing workshops and learn from them.
- They join professional organizations like NCTE and IRA, go to their conferences, and read their professional materials.
- They read professional books by teachers on the teaching of writing.
- They read books, watch television programs, and visit Web sites of professional authors that address the process of writing.
- They know good literature in many different forms and genres, and they have studied this literature to develop curriculum knowledge about how to write well (craft).
- They read guides to editing and using conventions (written by real editors, not school textbook companies), and they keep these handy as reference materials.

And basically, that's it. If we do some of all of these things, we should learn, over time, all we need to know to teach writing well. Sound challenging? Don't take it all on at once. First, think about all you already know about writing. You probably know a lot more than you think. Then find one or two places to start building your knowledge base. The key is to always keep our teaching and our students at the forefront of our thinking as we use these resources to learn about writing. We always need to be thinking, "What could my students do with this as writers? How would what I'm learning help them?"

Find some way to keep up with what you're learning along the way. I know lots of good teachers who keep notebooks or folders of "stuff" they are learning about writing, usually organized in some way by where the content fits in their vision for writing development. There is no quick, easy way to get to good writing instruction, no one place we can go to find out all we need to know. That may, in fact, be one essential characteristic of being a good teacher of writing—that you have to love the learning journey.

References

Paulsen, Gary. 1990. *Canyons.* New York: Delacorte.

Smith, Gary. 1998. "Eyes of the Storm." *Sports Illustrated* 88, no. 9 (March 2): 88–93, 106.

11

Teaching a Whole Class of Very Individual Writers

"How do I teach whole-class lessons when everyone is writing about a different topic?" This is one of the biggest questions most all teachers have when they first begin to think about moving to a workshop format for the teaching of writing. When we really think about it, the question is kind of a "knee jerk" question that we just blurt out because of our experiences with writing, experiences where any writing "instruction" at all was always tied to some whole-class writing (topic) assignment. Most all of us experienced this kind of teaching as students where the topic was assigned, we wrote about it with very little (or no) teaching connected to it, and then the "teaching" was to give it back to us with all our problems noted. That was how we were supposed to learn to write, and that was what we thought the teaching was all about when we were students. And unless jolted, we carried this belief into our own teaching: I need to think of a topic to give them so I can do some teaching. Of course, the irony is that very little teaching ever happened in these situations.

In some classrooms, there was teaching going on that was connected to the writing, but still, all students were asked to write about the same topic, even though the topic wasn't really necessary to the teaching. Why was it that the lessons about things like using your five senses to write descriptively about a place were always followed by assigned topics like, "Describe your kitchen using your five senses." Was this a lesson about kitchens or about a descriptive writing technique? Of course, it should have been a lesson about the writing technique, a technique a writer could use to describe any kind of place in the world. So why were we students, all thirty of us, asked to describe a kitchen? This is a big question, and the answers are varied and complex. The answers are also important if we are to understand teaching in writing workshops, so let's think them through.

First of all, quite simply, I think we were all asked to describe our kitchens because schools were thought of as places where students should all be doing the exact same things. A classroom looked and felt "on task" if everyone was engaged in the same work. And of course, this is very questionable in itself—why should everyone be doing the same thing? But even if we let go of that radical notion, we can still have problems with the kitchen assignment. You see, what is the "work" of this lesson? Isn't it to try writing using all of your five senses to describe a place? So we could have all of our students on task and engaged in the *same work* of this lesson—the five sense description—but still not have all of them describing kitchens! They could describe parks, the insides of cars, the lunchroom at school, anyplace in the world.

Which leads us to our second notion. The kitchen assignment shows that the teacher doesn't understand that the teaching of writing is not tied to topics. The teaching of writing should revolve around strategies, techniques, and understandings that aren't connected to specific material. The teaching may be tied to a certain kind of material (genre)—such as a writing lesson on developing a character that helps you write fiction—but it still doesn't need to be tied to a topic. The focus of the lesson is on *how to* develop a character, how to do things like answer questions about what's in the character's closet, what's in her refrigerator, what station her radio is tuned to, what messages are on her answering machine, what her plans are for Friday night, what she is afraid of, what movies she is anxious to see, and on and on. The lesson shows students how to think through all the little details of the character's life so they get to know that character. But this lesson doesn't need to end with a topic that forces all the students to develop *the same* character: "Develop a character for a new person who's moving in next door." Students can find their own "topics" for characters.

Often, the teaching is tied to a very specific technique, such as learning how to show something rather than tell something (a very common writing technique), but it *still* doesn't need to be tied to a topic. Again, the teaching is focused on the how-to of this technique. We can explain clearly how to show and not tell with examples: "She was angry" (that's telling). "Her face turned a bright red, and her fists were tightly balled at her side. When she spoke to me, she hissed the words and hurled them at me" (that's showing that she's angry). But there is no reason for us to assign everyone a topic such as "Show that someone is very happy" to go with this lesson. If I want students to try this technique very specifically, they can find a place in their notebooks or their drafts where they have told something rather than shown it and try a rewrite, or they can just make up their own "showing, not telling" assignment.

Although much of our teaching will show students *how* to write things, there are hardly any good reasons for us to tell them *what* to write about. We can let go completely of assigned topics and still do very focused, whole-class teaching with all of them writing about all kinds of different things.

Perhaps the main reason the kitchen assignments came about was because they happened in classrooms where students didn't have any ongoing material of their own. The kitchen assignment doesn't even make sense in a writing workshop where students have notebooks full of writing, drafts of projects in progress, and completed pieces of writing they can return to. The *lesson* on using five senses to write a description makes perfect sense in a writing workshop, but not the *assignment* that follows it. Students in writing workshops can find their own material for using this writing strategy. When we were students in school, I don't think our well-meaning teachers just assumed we didn't have anything of our own to write about. I think that maybe they just recognized that asking each of us to find something to write about after a lesson would require an investment of time that just didn't make sense in the traditional teaching contexts they knew. The writing workshop, though, is a very different kind of place, where time has already been given over to students to find their own "somethings to write about." We don't even start our teaching of strategy and technique in the writing workshop until students have things to write about. So even though the lesson is important, the kitchen assignment that follows it is simply unnecessary in this place known as the writing workshop.

Finally, and perhaps most important, we were all asked to write about kitchens because the traditional notion of teaching held that we should all be asked to do *something* as a part of the lesson. But in a writing workshop, you see, everyone is already doing something. Remember that the writing workshop is this place, this space in the day, that we have set up for students to use for work on their writing. Like the comparisons we made earlier to lunchtime and a building center, the writing workshop occupies a space in the day where students know what to do *without our direction*. They've got things going on, and they go to work on them every day. We set that up, and we get them understanding and doing that before we do any other teaching.

Now, that should lead us to a huge insight: Whatever teaching we do in the writing workshop doesn't have to *set up the work for the day*. By the very nature of the workshop, the "work" for the day is already set up—every day. Think about that. It's huge—and it's so different from "six-point lesson plan" thinking, where guided practice and independent practice are part of our plan each day. Students are "practicing" writing (I prefer "experiencing" writing, but we'll use "practice" to make a connection to what we know about lesson planning) every day, both independently and with guidance, as a part of the natural course of the workshop.

When we plan our focus lessons for the writing workshop, we don't have to plan for students to *do anything* as a part of those lessons. We can just do our lesson and then send them back to their writing. Our aim is for students to take that teaching back to their ongoing work and "use" it when and where it makes sense for them. Not every lesson will be something to "use," and certainly not every lesson will be something that every writer *needs* to use right that minute. What if we had taught any of the lessons discussed

WRITERS' VOICES ON . . .

having a purpose for writing

> First, I wonder how often we demonstrate our crazy, private note writing to our students? It's probably not much of an option in their own lives because they don't know that it's possible, that such fun exists, and that it's rewarding for its own sake, let alone for the glorious responses it creates. I'm wrong, of course. They do know. What about all those underground notes students write to each other in class? Why can't we legitimize it? Wouldn't it make our classrooms come alive if kids giggled and shrieked in the open about writing that was written in the open instead of underground? (Mem Fox, *Radical Reflections,* 17–18).

In this chapter and in chapter 8, as well as in several other places throughout the book, Katie cautions us about falling into the seductive traps of writing kits, packaged writing workshop programs, and cute activities to build up our students' writing muscles. These activities lack an essential ingredient: purpose for the writer. Mem Fox says that real writing always hangs on an outcome—like a response to a "crazy, private note" you've written to a friend—and that a major flaw with activities and worksheets is that nothing hangs on the outcome—at least nothing with emotional weight and significance to the writer (Keynote address, Western Carolina University). Work, to be real and meaningful, must be significant to the writer:

> I am anxious about the power, or lack of it, in school writing. Power is about being able to craft a piece of writing so effectively that its purpose is achieved. *Craft* means understanding the nature and importance of leads and endings; of showing, not telling; of sharpening and tightening; of structure and focus; of purpose and audience; and of the conventions. *Craft* means being able to put those understandings into practice. *Craft* means struggling in that battlefield between the brain and the hand until the best possible draft is achieved. Children won't learn how to be powerful by writing identical letters to Mem Fox, as so often happens, alas. So depressing! (Mem Fox, *Radical Reflections,* 20)

So, do we just turn those kids loose and let them write? Do we just forget about teaching them anything? The answer to these questions is NO, of course. The big issue we can take from this example is that we need to let go of the notion that every kid needs to be writing on the same topic or doing identical letters to Mem Fox in order to learn how to write a letter. If we know *what* we are teaching, then we won't need to have everyone in the room writing about the same thing. Mem makes it clear: everything we know about writing well is taken away if the writer doesn't care deeply and find purpose in the work.

Fox, Mem. 1993. *Radical Reflections: Passionate Opinions on Teaching, Learning, and Living*. San Diego: Harcourt Brace.

———. 1999. Keynote address. Western Carolina University 14th Annual Fall Language Arts Conference, Asheville, N.C.

above—using your senses, developing a character, showing instead of telling—and at the end of the lesson just said to students, "Try this if and when it makes sense for you in your writing." In the best writing workshops I know, there is lots of teaching that does just that. It adds a technique or an idea or an understanding to the pool of possibilities in the room, and then students are sent back to work on their writing while "swimming in that pool of possibilities." Students make their own decisions about when to use the lessons we've offered them.

The important point is, because students have work going on, we don't have to ask them to do anything at the end of a lesson, and this changes how we think about our teaching in significant ways. In a writing workshop, teaching is thought of as something that supports and extends the ongoing work of student writers, not as a directed set of scoped and sequenced activities for students to do each day. Teachers look for evidence that students are making use of the teaching; they nudge them in conferences to try things and think about things that have been offered in whole-class lessons, and they often ask them to show evidence (in portfolios and other assessments) of how they are using the teaching to fulfill their own purposes.

I often recommend to teachers that they make sure to have very few (if any) lessons at the beginning of the year that ask students to do or to try specific things during independent writing time. We don't want students to think that they can count on our lessons to direct their work for the day. We want them to know that we expect them to find their own work from the range of options available to them. We use the lessons early in the year to build important understandings about that work, but not to direct it.

Once students are directing their own work each day—once they have learned to pull from the possibilities we are teaching them that support, but not direct, their work—then we can begin to incorporate some lessons that ask students to do and to try very specific things. Teachers sometimes have "Try its" right in a lesson, where students try writing something they have been shown how to do. But this is done quickly and processed quickly while students are still in the whole group so that they can move on to their independent writing. Sometimes teachers will even ask students to try a strategy or technique during their independent writing time, especially during genre study. Sometimes there is a lesson that asks students to be very specifically on the lookout for something as they work on their writing that day, such as looking for places where they have a "word struggle" to find the right word, and thinking about how they might handle that. Another lesson might set up an inquiry that will take over a good bit of students' independent time for that day, such as asking them to spend time reading and talking about examples of writing in a genre during a genre study. The key is to balance carefully the number of lessons that end with directed activity with the number that don't so that students will know, as a rule, that they are responsible for deciding how they will use their time in the workshop.

Throughout this argument, we've really been thinking about a very specific kind of teaching: that which shows students how to do something, either a strategy or a technique for writing. But as we outlined in the last chapter, there are other kinds of curriculum we offer to the whole class in the writing workshop that simply help students with different understandings. The only logical "work" that follows these kinds of lessons—lessons on relationships, good writerly questions, and, to a great extent, even conventions—is for students to simply carry on with the writing lives and projects they have going, carrying with them what they have learned in the lesson. When we think of this kind of curriculum, it is easy to see how it can be for the whole class, and how it isn't necessary for students to be writing about the same topic or even doing the same kinds of writing at all. This is curriculum that is big enough to support any writer doing any kind of writing.

In the writing workshop, we don't teach students what to write. We teach them how to write. If the content of our lessons isn't big enough to serve students across many, many different writing topics, then it's not good writing curriculum.

12

Whole-Class Units of Study in the Writing Workshop

In our conversations as a profession about the teaching of writing, perhaps the place where we are outgrowing ourselves the most is in our thinking about planning across the year for the writing workshop. More and more teachers are realizing the need to map out a year of thoughtful study in the workshop by focusing students' attention for days or weeks on issues that will really help them to grow as writers.

The time that we spend up-front, at the beginning of the year, teaching our students how the workshop "works" is an investment for our teaching during the rest of the year. Writing workshops need to be predictable places so

---

Parts of this chapter were excerpted from Chapter 11 of *Wondrous Words: Writers and Writing in the Elementary Classroom* by Katie Wood Ray (Urbana, Ill.: NCTE, 1999).

that wonderful, unpredictable things can happen in them. Setting up the management structures and routines buys us quality teaching time for later. As we have said before, we do not have to invent ways of working over and over for our students, directing every move they make during the block of time we have set aside. So in that sense, planning what and how we might study in the writing workshop looks very different than traditional planning has looked, where each segment of time, each day, is accounted for with a "plan."

But there are ways in which planning for the writing workshop should look very much like traditional planning. Namely, we need to know what it is we are "working on" with students at any given time in the workshop. While they are working on many different kinds of projects independently, we need *units of study* that surround that work where our focus lessons over a period of time work together to build big, important understandings about writing. Without units of study, our focus lessons become a hit-and-miss series of bits of teaching, isolated sound bites that don't come together into larger, more lasting understandings.

For a long time, I think we resisted thinking of writing workshops as places that needed curriculum organized into units of study. "Don't they just learn what they need to know from the experience of writing?" Well, yes. Our students learn many, many things about writing and about themselves from engaging in daily work as writers. We hold onto this time for our students as if it is sacred for just this reason. But if we accept that we need instruction around this, and if we accept that some of this will be *whole-class* instruction, then I believe we need a way of planning for that instruction that is meaningful beyond single lessons. We need big answers to the question, "Why am I going to teach this lesson?" Big answers to "What am I trying to accomplish here?"

Possibilities for Focused Units of Study

Beyond the growth that we know will happen in the natural course of the workshop, we need to use the vision we have for students' growth as writers to help us plan units of study for our whole-class instruction. A unit of study in the writing workshop is a period of time, from a few days to several weeks, when the community of writers turns its attention in a single, focused direction. All of the focus lessons, and sometimes many of the conferences and class sharing times, center around the unit of study. Sometimes the direction of the study will impact *what* students write during independent writing time, as in a genre study where they write pieces in that genre, but sometimes a unit of study in the writing workshop simply supports students' learning around all their self-selected pursuits as writers (such as a study of peer response and how to give and get help from another writer). During a study like this, students would work on totally self-selected writing projects (topic and genre) and they would use their study of peer response to support that self-selected work.

If we return to the vision we've been using throughout this book, we can think about topics for study that would support students' growth in the various areas. Here are just a few possibilities for different studies that might happen in a writing workshop:

Over time in a writing workshop, we hope to see students developing . . .

A sense of self as writers, as well as personal writing processes that work for them

- a study of writers' lives and what they say about their writing processes
- a study of writing in other professional lives (other than professional writers)
- a study of our own lives and histories as writers

Ways of reading the world like writers, collecting ideas with variety, volume, and thoughtfulness

- a study of what writers need to gather from the world to sustain a published writing life
- a study of the gathering-from-the-world habits of various kinds of writers: poets, memoirists, fiction writers, essayists, and so on
- a study of specific writers' notebooks
- a study of our own writers' notebooks

A sense of thoughtful, deliberate purpose about their work as writers, and a willingness to linger with those purposes

- a study of how writers follow an idea through to publication
- a study of how writers "live with" a topic over time
- a study of how to conduct research for writing (firsthand and second-hand research)

As members of a responsive, literate community

- a study of peer conferring and collaborative relationships
- a study of how writers work with other writers, editors, and publishers

Ways of reading texts like writers, developing a sense of craft and genre in writing

- a study of how to read texts like writers, both for structure and ways with words
- a study of a specific genre: poetry, memoir, literary nonfiction, fiction, drama, journalism, critique, editorials, picture books, description, and so on
- a study of how writers "write" without words: looking at punctuation, spacing, layout, fonts, and so on in written texts
- a study of one writer's body of work (looking at the craft of his or her writing)
- a study of text-structure possibilities
- a study of crafting techniques
- study of sentences and paragraphs and how writers build them in different ways for different effects

A sense of audience, and an understanding of how to prepare writing to go into the world

- a study of publishing opportunities for young writers
- a study of the strategies writers use to revise and edit their work for publication
- a study of what happens in the publishing process

As we look at these possibilities, we must remember that they are for units of study *over time*. During the year, there will be curriculum outside these units of study that students will need us to teach them in focus lessons or conferences to help them grow in different areas. For example, some students may need help with subject-verb agreement issues so that they can "prepare writing to go into the world," but subject-verb agreement would not be a whole unit of study because it dead-ends too quickly. It would simply be an "as-needed" focus lesson or, more likely, a conference lesson. There are only so many things to know about it because writers don't really "craft" with subject-verb agreement. We want our units of study to be "big enough" to encompass understandings of some breadth in writers' lives.

Selecting Units of Study

Even if you have not been organizing your writing workshop by units of study, you can probably imagine how we might lead our students in studies of this kind, organizing a series of focus lessons around a specific writing topic. In just the possibilities listed above, there is way more than a year's worth of curriculum. There is no "big brother" who has some magic answer to tell us what we should study with our students in our writing workshops. We will need to select units of study that make the most sense for our different teaching situations. There are several questions we can think about that will help us to select our units of study.

What are my strengths as a teacher of writing?

Whatever you absolutely love in writing, whatever you're best at, should become a unit of study in your classroom for the rest of your career. You may be the only teacher students ever have who is passionate about whatever it is—poetry, fiction, punctuation—so go for it. Your love and knowledge in this area will help you teach well year after year. Every student I have ever had has studied Cynthia Rylant's writing for just this reason—because *I love her writing*.

What have my students studied before in writing?

From first grade on, it is helpful to know as much as we can about what kind of writing instruction our students have had before they arrive in our classrooms. What we know can impact our decisions about what we will teach, and we will need to plan with our students' expertise in mind, going "deep" when we know they have a lot of experience in an area. We will want to plan for studies that both *extend* what our students have been learning and studies that *introduce* them to important new ideas. Extending means that students might engage in similar units of study year after year—this is especially true of genre study. Students could study memoir or poetry every year of their lives and continue to extend their expertise each time. So we aim for some studies that return students to familiar concepts and others that take them into new territory.

Sometimes knowing what is new territory for students can help us decide what studies we need early in the year. If, for example, we have students in our fourth-grade classrooms who have never been in a writing workshop, we will want to start with studies that build the most essential concepts necessary for their learning throughout the year: how writers gather ideas from the world, and how to read like writers. If, on the other hand, students have had several years of experience keeping notebooks and studying writing in these ways, then we might start in a very different place, perhaps with an opening study of a challenging genre.

What are my students interested in? What do they *want* to know as writers?

This is a question that we probably cannot ask before the school year begins. We will have to get to know our students for a few weeks, or even a few months, to really answer this question. For this reason, we don't want to plan out the entire year of study until after we have gotten to know our students. What we teach in April might depend on where our students' interests lie. If there is a clear area of interest among many of our students, we'll get behind the energy of this and go for it. I once had a class that got very interested in drama—they were quite the little actors and actresses. And so even though I would not have planned it on my own, a genre study of scriptwriting seemed appropriate with that group of students. The energy was there. We might have groups who are very interested in some author or genre or in getting published "in the real world"—whatever it is that catches our students' attention, we follow along behind that and focus some of the study during the year around those interests.

What are my colleagues studying in their writing workshops?

We may want to think about planning a unit of study along with other teachers in our school. If we have enough resources available, at some point during the year a "study-in-common" across several classrooms can have many benefits. It gives us and our colleagues a chance to study this teaching together and to share resources, and it gives students a chance to share their learning and ideas with students from other classrooms. These studies-in-common need not happen only at particular grade levels. Fifth graders and first graders, for example, might study literary nonfiction together in a co-genre study.

What resources do I have?

Sometimes decisions about units of study are made based on the resources we have available. I once planned a study of Patricia MacLachlan's writing because I knew she would be visiting in our area. But short of very famous author visits, there are all kinds of ways other resources might lead our planning. For example, if we have access to two writers who work together a lot, we might plan a unit of study on collaborative relationships, or if one of our friends works at the newspaper, we might plan a study around journalism. And then, of course, we will need to look at our library resources to see whether we have the texts we will need to support a particular study. This too can influence the planning decisions we make.

For what kind of writing will my students be held accountable?

If there is a particular kind of writing for which our students will be held accountable, we will want to plan a genre study of that kind of writing (narrative, persuasive, descriptive, etc.—whatever genre students will be asked to write). This is often the case in states where writing is tested at various grade levels. We slow these studies down and really immerse students in *real examples* of the genre, having them read the examples like writers (describing how they are written) and study how writers go about supporting their work in this genre. Also, if we have state or district curriculum guides that we are accountable for, we will plan units of study that get at the objectives of the guide while still turning students' attention to writers for the learning they need in a given area.

The answers we find to these questions should help us plan some units of study to get our year started in the writing workshop. Remember, there are no "right answers" to what students should study at any given time during their school years as writers. What we want is to have good reasons for why we have decided to launch a unit of study in our classrooms. Teachers can make the best informed decisions about what is right for their classrooms.

Units of Study over a School Year

To help us picture units of study over a year, let's look now at two sample year-long layouts in writing workshops (Tables 12.1 and 12.2). The first is the layout of a year in an upper elementary classroom, and the second is a year in a K–1 classroom. Notice that with each layout, we look at what kinds of writing students are doing alongside the study. We want to aim for a good mix of totally self-selected writing and required writing in specific genres under study. Topics, of course, are always self-selected, even when a genre is required. The exception to this on these layouts is a two-week genre study of testing in the upper grades, in which students learn about testing and about writing in response to prompts.

So these are examples of what a year *could* look like. The time frames in these sample layouts are based on the assumption that the writing workshop happens every day, and even then they are very approximate. Sometimes there will be real energy for a unit of study, and it will make sense to stretch it out longer than we might have planned. We should not be afraid to study one thing for a very long time if the energy is there. These are the studies students will remember for the rest of their lives.

TABLE 12.1 Sample Year-Long Plan for Upper-Grades Writing Workshop

	Unit of Study	Students' Writing
One week	Study of who we are as writers; making plans for the year	Self-selected
Three weeks	Study of what writers need to gather from the world to sustain a published writing life (notebooks)	Self-selected
Three weeks	Study of how to read texts like writers, both for structure and ways with words	Self-selected
Four weeks	Poetry genre study	Poetry
Two weeks	Study of peer conferring and collaborative relationships	Self-selected
Three weeks	Author study of one writer's body of work	Self-selected
Five weeks	Literary nonfiction genre study	Literary nonfiction
Three weeks	Study of writing in professional lives (other than professional writers)	Self-selected
Three weeks	Author study of one writer's body of work	Self-selected
Two weeks	Testing genre study	Prompt writing
Four weeks	Historical fiction genre study	Historical fiction
Three weeks	Memoir genre study	Memoir

Notice that several of the units of study are the same at both the upper grades and in the K–1 writing workshops. We plan for these in developmentally appropriate ways. For example, we want to teach both first graders and fifth graders how to read texts like writers, but we will select different texts to introduce them to this idea. For the first graders, we will need texts where a lot of the crafting is in the print and the pictures and in very obvious text structures. Similarly, the concepts of genre study and author study

TABLE 12.2 Sample Year-Long Plan for K–1 Writing Workshop

	Unit of Study	**Students' Writing**
Two weeks	Study of different kinds of writing. Imagining what's possible	Self-selected
Three weeks	Study of where writers get ideas and why writers write	Self-selected
Three weeks	Study of how to read texts like writers	Self-selected
Three weeks	Label books genre study	Label books
Three weeks	Study of collaborative relationships (helping each other)	Self-selected
Three weeks	Study of writing for audiences	Self-selected for a specific audience
Three weeks	Alphabet book genre study	Alphabet books
Three weeks	Author study of one writer's body of work	Self-selected
Three weeks	Poetry genre study	Poetry
Three weeks	Study of how writers write without words: punctuation, spacing, layouts, fonts, etc.	Self-selected
Three weeks	Author study of one writer's body of work	Self-selected
Three weeks	Study of simple text structures	Self-selected choosing structures with intention

are important across all grade levels, but we choose the genres and the authors we will study with the experience of the writers in mind.

Notice that in the upper-grade layout, there is a genre study of testing. During a study like this, we teach students about how to take a writing test. We deal with issues such as managing the time allowed for the test and writing to the prompt. In a study like this, we are very clear with students that this is *testing curriculum* and not *writing curriculum* because in some ways the two are at such odds. For example, "Don't spend more than ten minutes planning your writing" is good testing curriculum but terrible writing curriculum. But understanding the difference between testing curriculum and writing curriculum can also help us a lot as we plan our teaching. There are many, many places where the two curriculums overlap. Many of the things students need to know in order to do well on writing tests are good *writing curriculum:* writing compelling leads and endings, writing with depth and detail, writing smooth transitions, making good sentence and paragraphing decisions, and so on. If we are filling the year with rich writing curriculum in all our other units of study, we are doing very important test preparation all year long.

Rather than putting specific testing curriculum in a unit of study, some teachers are choosing to spread it out across the year, separating it from writing workshop altogether. Many of them are taking an hour slot every other week or so (in addition to writing workshop, rather than in place of it), teaching a *testing* focus lesson, and then having students practice writing to a prompt as they will on the test. These teachers carefully assess these papers to see what *writing curriculum* students need more help with, and then they plan teaching (conferences, small groups, and even units of study) in the regular writing workshop to support these areas. And if they see from this assessment that students need more help with some aspects of testing, they plan future testing focus lessons to address them.

The Frame for Genre and Author Studies

Genre studies and author studies, scattered across the year, are planned in predictable ways. These studies always begin with some time for *immersion* in the genre or the author's work. During this period of the study, the students spend a good bit of their time in the writing workshop reading and sharing around the genre or author, getting a feel for the kind of writing under study. After immersion, students begin a period of *close study* of the genre or the author. During this time, they will look closely at both the writer's processes and the craft of the texts they find in writers of this genre or of the author under study. These units of study always end with students *writing,* either in the genre or under the influence of the author they have studied.

Once this way of working through a study is established in the workshop, students come to expect and own the process, and the inquiry becomes a habit of mind for them. One of the best resources for learning about genre study is found in the August 1999 issue of *Primary Voices K–6* (available from NCTE), where Isoke T. Nia and her colleagues describe a frame for genre studies in general and for specific genre studies in nonfiction, fiction, and memoir.

Later, in Chapter 16, we will look specifically at writing actual daily lesson plans for the writing workshop. What's important at this point, before we look into the three components of the writing workshop (focus lessons, conferences, share time) in the next chapters, is to realize that what happens on a daily basis in the workshop is always part of something bigger than that one day. Any lesson that we teach, any conference that we have, has both a history and a future in the life of the workshop. Our units of study create important teaching timelines across the year.

Reference

Nia, Isoke T. 1999. "Units of Study in the Writing Workshop." *Primary Voices K–6* 8, no. 1 (August): 3–11.

13

Focus Lessons: Whole-Class Teaching in the Writing Workshop

About midway through a poetry genre study, as my third- and fourth-grade students are beginning to draft the poems they will work on for publication, I pull them together for the morning's focus lesson. I read to them an entry from my notebook about being irritated by the loud banging that the metal parts of my overalls make when I put them in the dryer (Figure 13.1).

When I'm finished reading them this entry, I begin to explain to the group of writers gathered around me:

> Sometimes we find poems in the most unlikely entries in our notebooks. Many entries that we never intended to lead us to poetry actually have poems hidden inside them, if we know how to look. When I read back through my notebook, I

FIGURE 13.1
My Notebook Entry

I hate the sound of my overalls in the dryer. All those big buckles and buttons just banging against the sides — clanging — making such a racket. I always seem to think that if I just put enough towels in there with them they will muffle the sound and not let the loud parts find the hard metal sides of the dryer. But it never works. Those overalls just seem to always work their way out to the sides, the towels go in the middle, and they clang, clang, clang. Tonight, after a long day, I decided just to air dry them — even if it takes four days for them to dry. I just can't bear to listen to them. Of course, there may be at least one thing I know of that's worse than buttony, metaly overalls — TENNIS SHOES in the dryer! Bonging from side to side like a big headache. Oh well, I guess I should just stick to sheets — sheets only in the dryer.

look for entries that have strong sound or sight or smell or touch images. I look for entries that have something like that in them—something I can really grab onto and make come to life. That's what I felt when I came across this entry about my overalls. It was just so *vivid* to me, and it had layers of meaning for me underneath—layers about how desperately I want calm and quiet in my life. So I saw this entry, and I said, "There might be a poem in there."

I took a different colored pen and began to read the "overalls in the dryer" entry aloud to myself, underlining lines and phrases that I liked. Then I went to a nearby page in my notebook and began to write some of those lines and phrases.

At this point I actually hold my notebook up so students can see where I have done this, and then I read them the collection of phrases and lines that has become the beginning draft of a poem (Figure 13.2).

I continue the focus lesson . . .

I really like what I'm getting at here. I still want to do a lot of work on this, but what's neat is that I just kind of went and found this poem waiting for me in my notebook. I'm thinking that a lot of you may have poems waiting for you in your notebooks too. They hide in the most unlikely places. Some of you might want to spend some time doing what I did—looking through your notebook for entries (maybe some of them are even ones you wrote a long time ago) to see if you can find poems inside them. Douglas, I was thinking that you might find some for sure in all those entries you wrote about Boy Scout camp! Anyway, if you find one you like, you might read it aloud like I did and listen for the lines and phrases you could pull out for a poem. Mark those somehow, and then try them out in a draft.

I know a lot of you are right in the middle of stuff you're working on, but if anyone wants or needs to try this strategy, let me know how it goes for you. I'd love to find out how you "found poems" of your own.

And with that said (in about six minutes), the students are off to work on their writing for the day, me following closely behind them to begin conferring very soon.

This is a focus lesson, a daily little "chunk" of curriculum possibility that is put into the room where students are working independently on their writing. For students' work to grow and grow and get better and better during the year, they will need daily focus lessons like this, within units of study, that

FIGURE 13.2
First Draft of My Poem

Sheets in the dryer

So soft
a muffled jumble
against the hard metal
dryer-drum.
I do not mind to dry them at all.

But overalls, with their
fat loud buttons and buckles,
Clang and bang and clang
endlessley,
metal against metal against metal.
Their noisy clatter
feels like it's inside my brain
instead of inside my dryer.
I've got
to get
them out
of there...

fill their rooms up with all kinds of writing possibilities for their ongoing work. It is difficult sometimes to understand the significance of a single focus lesson because, in good teaching, the single focus lesson is always a part of a series of lessons and conferences that the teacher is carefully weaving together to build larger, more lasting understandings. We can, however, use a single focus lesson on an ordinary day (as this one is) as a "text" to help us think about focus lessons more generally. So let's do that now. What are the important issues related to the planning and delivery of focus lessons?

Pulling Students Together

Because students get so spread out into their different work once the workshop begins, many teachers feel it is important to bring students together (physically) in one place in the room for the focus lesson. The physical coming together serves as an important metaphor for the more important *intellectual gathering* of a community of people. We should be careful not to underestimate the value of pulling students together in one place where they are all very *focused* for just a few minutes on a single thing—the lesson. Most teachers have some kind of gathering place in the room, often carpeted so students can sit together on the floor. Often, there is an overhead projector in this gathering place, since lots of lessons use that medium to show a piece of writing to everyone at once, and there is almost always some chart paper nearby in case some public writing needs to be done as part of the focus lesson. The best writing workshops have structures and routines for gathering students for the focus lesson, so we shouldn't be afraid to spend a lot of time at the beginning of the year getting the management for this gathering running efficiently (though it will need maintenance from time to time).

As explained in Chapter 10, the writing curriculum offered in focus lessons is most often in the form of a strategy (a way to do something), a technique (a way to fashion something), a question (a way to think about something), a relationship (a way to connect things), or a convention (a way to expect something). The lessons are necessarily short (five to ten minutes) because students need to get going on their own writing work. Teachers in writing workshops believe the lessons only matter as much as they help students do that work and understand that work *better.*

Setting the Tone

The tone of these lessons is very direct and has the sound of one writer talking to other writers. As we discussed in Chapter 4, the teaching of writing is very powerful when students see their teacher as both a writing mentor and a fellow writer, not as the "person who is going to tell us everything to do now." The teacher is showing students how to do things and how to think about things that he does and thinks about as a writer. Often, the teacher shares his own learning as a writer, letting students see what he is struggling with in his writing. This just feels so different from the traditional teacher delivery systems where teachers ask students to do things that seem so separate from anything the teachers themselves would ever do. So the feeling of "we are all people who write in here" dramatically changes the tone of the lessons.

We need to listen to the sound of our voices in our lessons. We want to make sure that our tone sounds as if we are talking to other writers, not to children, when we teach our focus lessons. We talk "across" to them rather than "down" to them. In the example lesson above, notice comments like, "I really like what I'm getting at here. I still want to do a lot of work on this . . ." where students actually get to hear me thinking aloud as a writer during the lesson.

When we plan for focus lessons in the writing workshop, we don't have to have some big "anticipatory set" to start the lesson or some catchy way of getting attention. Gimmicks "to get their attention" assume that students have no reason to be interested in what we are getting ready to say. But if we have set the workshop up well, and students are interested in what they are working on as writers, then they have real reasons to be interested in what we are saying in our focus lessons. This is actually one of my main teaching goals. I want students to be interested in my lessons because they have their own reasons (as writers) to be interested in them, and although I stab around at the extent to which I'm successful at that with different students, I still maintain that as a goal.

The example lesson above began just as it's quoted here. I launched right into it. We were in the middle of a poetry genre study, and I knew many of them were searching their notebook material for poetry possibilities just as I was. Because I had a good handle on what kinds of things were happening in the room, I knew students had reasons to be interested in this strategy I was about to show them. In many ways, I suppose, the workshop itself and the work students have going on there serves as a year-long "anticipatory set" for all our lessons.

"Show and Tell" Your Objective

A good focus lesson has a very clear objective. Sometimes these are "behavioral objectives" where we are actually showing students how to do something, but sometimes the objectives are more cognitive, ones that simply try to explain an important understanding about writing. Either way, it is important for us to be able to answer the question, "What's the point of this lesson? What do I want students to get out of this?" The answer to this question will help keep us focused on the lesson, and it will help us later in assessment as we look to see how the lesson is influencing our students' work.

Just as it's a good writing lesson when we teach students to "show and not tell" things, it's a good lesson for our teaching too. But focus lessons need to "show *and* tell" things. Explanations need to be accompanied by something that "shows" students what we are talking about, something that gives the lesson a concreteness. Now, this showing can happen in many ways. For example, the "showing" part of the lesson might be:

- a *quote of advice* from a professional writer that helps explain some idea about the process or products of writing;
- an *example from a published text* that shows how some crafting technique works or some conventional use of language;
- a *piece of student writing* that helps explain some idea about the process or products of writing;
- a *piece of the teacher's writing* that helps explain some idea about the process or products of writing;
- a *story or a metaphor* that illustrates and helps students understand something about writing;
- a *report on a conference* the teacher had with one student that will help other students understand something about writing;
- some *public writing* the teacher does, on the spot, that demonstrates a strategy or technique for writing.

The key is for us to decide exactly what it is we are going to teach in a lesson (the objective), think of some good way to "show" this to students, and then think through how we will explain (tell) what we are showing them so that we clearly get at our objective. When teachers are new to this kind of teaching, thinking through the explanation is a place where many falter. They know what they are going to teach, they have their something to show, but they haven't thought out in enough detail how they are going to explain it. In the middle of the lesson, they realize they don't really know what to say, exactly. To those who are new to this way of teaching and talking about writing, I suggest actually "talking out" your focus lessons before you teach them so you can work on what the exact language of the explanations will be.

In the lesson above, there were several layers to my teaching intentions. My curriculum objective was really twofold: one, I wanted to get in the idea that there may be poems "hidden" inside notebook entries where we really might not expect to find them (an understanding); and two, I wanted to show students how to find lines in these entries that could be pulled out to become the beginning drafts of poems (strategy). The "showing" part of the lesson was in my writer's notebook, which I actually physically showed them, and the "telling" part was in the explanation around that, which you see scripted in the example.

Notice that my explanation is fairly simple and straightforward. I don't worry (and neither do I expect) that in one focus lesson students will leave knowing all they need to know about what I'm teaching. I want to give them just enough explanation so that they can get started trying this strategy or technique, or thinking about this issue in their own writing—which is where the real learning will take place. I also know that the really big curriculum ideas will be woven in and out of lessons and conferences all year long, and students will "learn their way into these concepts" over the course of their whole writing lives. I simply think of each focus lesson as planting a new possibility in the room.

I often have ulterior motives when I choose examples to help me with an explanation in a focus lesson, and I had one when I selected the entry about my overalls in the dryer. I was battling the predictable battle against the big life topics—love, dreams, nature, wishes, and so on—that we have in most any poetry genre study. My students were trying to take on these giant issues in their poems and didn't have a lot of faith in the small things in life that illuminate these issues. They were trying to write about nature—all of it—instead of the miracle of one small leaf. So I choose an entry about the most ordinary, mundane kind of thing—a pair of overalls banging around in the dryer. And even though having faith in the ordinary (to illuminate the extraordinary) wasn't part of the overt curriculum of the lesson, it certainly was part of the curriculum underneath. I often choose what I will show in a focus lesson with an eye toward it being an example of the *kind of thing* I hope my students will write, providing a consistent layer of teaching that "goes without saying" but happens by showing.

Being Teacher Centered

One of the things that often surprises teachers who are new to workshop teaching and focus lessons is how teacher centered the lessons usually are. Many focus lessons have no student input in them at all. The teacher simply talks, shows, and explains the lesson, and students watch and listen. Now, you may be thinking, "But I thought good teaching always got students involved in the lesson." And what we have to remember is this: Students will be intimately "involved" during writing workshop when they move out to do a huge chunk of independent writing time after our very short, very focused lessons with them. Students have ongoing, day-to-day involvement with our lessons simply by participating in the workshop itself. So it is OK for us to do all the talking in the focus lesson—that's one of the best ways to keep it focused. We all know how easily five minutes can turn into twenty-five minutes when we ask for student input. We're not counting them out; their input in the lesson will come as they go out to do their writing and we go out to confer.

In the example lesson, for instance, I could have started by asking the students,

> How many of you have ever been reading through your notebook and have come across an entry where you found a poem hidden inside? Part of it just sounded like a poem?

And undoubtedly, some of them would have had a response to this, and we would have heard from them and it might have been quite interesting. It would also likely be at least ten minutes later before I started the actual text of my lesson. A better plan is for me to think about finding out the answer to this question during other structured times of the workshop: during conferences, during a share time, or in a reflective assessment I might ask them to do. In the focus lesson, I plant the curriculum possibility in the room, one that some of them may already be exploring on their own, and during other times, we see how that possibility is becoming a reality.

Although I'm quite comfortable doing all the talking in the focus lesson, one way I draw children into what I'm saying is to mention them and their work a lot as I'm talking in the focus lesson. I did this in the example lesson when I said, "Douglas, I was thinking that you might find some for sure in all those entries you wrote about Boy Scout camp!" Just a simple mention—sometimes I'll say two or three things like this in one lesson. I look through works-in-progress folders frequently, just to keep a better handle on what kinds of things students are working on so that I can do this very thing—mention their work specifically, often in focus lessons. I also draw from what I'm learning about their work during conferences to help me know what to mention.

Using my students' names and references to their work in my explanations in focus lessons does two things. First, it forces me to think about how the content of my teaching will really manifest itself in the work of my students. Thinking this through (whose work I might mention in a focus lesson) often helps me explain things in ways they understand better. The second thing it does is to make the students feel like this teaching is really very connected to them and their work, like I'm not just throwing stuff out there. They feel like I'm really in there with them and that I know what's going on with them as writers when I do this. So, while we will do most (if not all) of the talking during the focus lesson, we want to be sure to embed comments about our students and their work as we show, tell, and explain.

Getting Students Involved in the Lesson

Now, having said all this about how we should do most of the talking and stay focused in the lesson, sometimes there may be real reasons to have *some* student talk or work in the lesson. The key to using student involvement (other than listening) in the actual focus lesson is *time*. We must stay focused and timely when we solicit student talk or we will easily fall into the trap of spending too much time in this whole class gathering.

One way to get student input in a timely manner is to ask students to share a single line that matches some criteria we are getting at in our lesson. In a lesson on some form of revision strategy, for example, it may be a line from a draft that just doesn't sound right. In a lesson on asking questions in notebook entries, it may be a single question that could be asked about an entry that is already there in the notebook. Anything that lends itself well to students finding just a line—or even just a word—to contribute could be used as input in the lesson. We can ask students to read these single lines one after another, moving quickly around students on the carpet so that we simply get to hear a sampling of what they found as they looked for these lines that matched the lesson. We want to make sure, though, that we have some good reason for the sampling to be a part of the lesson itself—maybe we think the range of student contributions will help others imagine new possibilities, for example. Time is precious in the workshop and every moment *matters*. We don't want to waste any of them.

Another quick way to use student talk in the focus lesson is to have students talk in twos and threes as part of the lesson: "Turn to the person sitting next to you and tell that person a little about what you've been collecting in your notebook outside of class." This might be preceded by a very quick reminder lesson on how the really powerful stuff that goes into the notebook comes from the world outside, not from stuff you imagine out of thin air while you are sitting at your desk in the workshop. We can use this "talk to your neighbor" strategy when the most important thing we want is for students to have to articulate something, not for them to be exposed to a wide range of what others are doing and saying.

Do we ever have students actually do something other than talk as part of the focus lesson? Sometimes, yes. Remember that one of the biggest differences between focus lessons and the more traditional, direct instruction that happens in a classroom is that the focus lesson doesn't have to set up any work for students (see Chapter 11 for a discussion of this idea). The plan for the lesson doesn't need to include some kind of work or "guided practice" for students to do afterward; they already have that work going. The focus lesson just needs to show students how to do something—some idea that they will do when it makes sense for them to do—or to give them a way to think about something that will deepen their understanding of writing and writers.

Now, having said that, *some* focus lessons may have a "Try it" exercise as a part of the lesson, where students actually try a strategy or technique very quickly. For example, in a focus lesson on the technique of using strong verbs, we might, after showing and telling what we mean by strong verbs, ask students to look quickly for a sentence in their notebooks where they could use a stronger verb and to try rewriting that sentence. Usually with "Try its" like these, students do them while gathered, as a part of the lesson. We might ask students to read quickly around the circle or show their neighbors the new verb phrases they've tried, but we don't have to. We could just ask them later in conferences to show us what they've tried.

Some focus lessons may ask students to try something or keep something in mind during their independent work for that day. For example, after a focus lesson that explains a notebook strategy of finding two entries that seem to be connected and then writing about the connections, a request might be made for all students to try this strategy, either that day or sometime in the next few days. A lesson on a conventional use for commas might be followed by a request for students to look very specifically at how they are using commas as part of their independent work over the next few days, with a plan to talk about what they've found, say, three days later. Or a lesson that introduces a question such as, "What am I struggling with as a writer?" might be followed with a request for students to think about that during their work that day, and to make a plan to talk about it in small groups during share time at the end of the workshop. So, while some focus lessons will *frame* a way for students to go about their work, the lessons don't set up the actual day's work in specific ways.

The important thing for us to remember is that students don't need us to ask them to try things. If they have work going as writers, then they have things to "try" already. We need to have good reasons for requiring everyone to try something, especially as a part of their independent work. In the overall balance of our teaching, we need to *suggest* more things for them to try than to *require* things for them to try. The only way we really know for sure if students are "getting" things as writers is if we see them doing them on their own. So we use our teaching to fill the room up with things they might try, and then see what happens.

This "see what happens" mentality about teaching writing sometimes seems not quite rigorous enough for us. We have this checksheet-driven need inside us (because of our history in schools) to see if students can do what we've shown them how to do. We want them all to "practice" things until we're sure they've got it. But we have to remember that the actual act of writing, the thing we are trying to teach students to do, to *write*, is a continuous process of decision making about how a person will get the writing done. The decisions writers make during this process come from their repertoires of things they know how to do as writers. Our teaching is meant to broaden students' repertoires as writers, yes; but the things we show them how to do aren't the point. They are important, but they are not the point. The point, the "end result" of the teaching that we want to see, is for students to know when they need to do these things and then *to decide* to do them on their own in order to get their writing done. So when we are out there and we see students actually using some technique or strategy we have shown in a focus lesson, then we know with certainty—and with all the rigor in the world—that our teaching has been successful.

It seems prudent to mention here that many teachers in writing workshops ask students to show evidence—often in a section of a portfolio, but sometimes just during a conference—of how they are using the teaching in the room to grow as writers. So while there is a clear expectation that students will be using the focus lessons to try new things as writers, the specifics of how they will do that are left up to their own decision making as they write.

Ending the Focus Lesson

Most every focus lesson I teach ends in the same way. First, I say in a nutshell what I was trying to teach in the lesson:

> Anyway, if you find one you like, you might read it aloud like I did and listen for the lines and phrases you could pull out for a poem. Mark those somehow and then try them out in a draft.

I give a final, short version of the content of the lesson—I call it the *Reader's Digest* version. If it is a strategy, a technique, or a convention I am teaching, as this lesson was (a strategy), I try to say it so that they can actually picture themselves doing it; I say it with the actual steps involved. If, instead, the lesson was just something for them to think about as writers (a question or a relationship), then I end with my nutshell saying of exactly what it is I want them to think about.

The second part of my ending is to offer an invitation for students to try what I have shown them or to think about what I have explained. In the example lesson, I said it this way:

> So I know a lot of you are right in the middle of stuff you're working on, but if anyone wants or needs to try this strategy, let me know how it goes for you. I'd love to find out how you "found poems" of your own.

When I do this, I am stretching the teaching out into our future together, helping students to imagine this time when we will talk together as writers about this thing we have in common. When we think about it this way, we see that this kind of teaching is really an invitation to our students to live this kind of life with us, this writing life. This approach may feel very different than any teaching we have ever known, so we'll want to give ourselves time to grow into both our comfort with it and our understanding of it.

If I were to summarize all this in a short, bulleted list of things to remember about focus lessons—and somehow it seems prudent to do so—it would look like this:

We need to . . .

- make sure the focus lesson is focused—five to ten minutes max;
- make sure we know what we are teaching and why we are teaching it; it should fit into a larger unit of study;
- make sure our lesson has both showing and telling;
- make sure the tone is right: one writer talking to a group of writers;
- make sure we try to connect the lesson to the work students are doing in the workshop;
- make sure we look for evidence in students' work of their using the possibilities we are teaching them.

14

Conferring: The Essential Teaching Act

Conferring can be so hard.

Like any uniquely human interaction, in a conference there is always the possibility that something totally unexpected might happen. I mean, we have no idea what children might say in response to, "Tell me about how your writing is going." And because a conference is teaching we do *in response* to what individual children tell us and show us, we can't plan ahead for what we will say and we have to be ready to respond to *anything*. We don't like to be caught off guard as teachers—it's not in our nature—but we set ourselves up for it every time we sit down next to students and invite them to tell us all about how it's going with them as writers.

But conferring can also be so much fun, so satisfying.

As hard as it is, I still find that my favorite part of the writing workshop is when I'm out there having conferences with individual students. I love the side-by-side feeling of the conferences that helps me build such important learning relationships with my students. I love being able to help a student very specifically with some aspect of writing. I even love the challenge of the unknown in a conference. The same thing that makes conferring hard, namely, not knowing what students will say, also makes it very interesting. It is very boring to go into every teaching day knowing exactly what will happen every minute of that day, having the whole thing planned out ahead of time. That's what leads so many teachers to burn out too quickly. When we confer each day, we know we will be teaching, but we don't know what that teaching will be until we have to do it. I enjoy that. The promise of it is very interesting to me.

A conference in a writing workshop occurs when the teacher sits down beside a student (sit, don't squat or kneel—it will ruin your knees), finds out how the student's writing is going, and then in a very direct but conversational way, teaches (or tries to teach) the student something that makes sense at this time. I added in the "tries to teach" because those of us who have conferred have come away from conferences at times feeling as though we didn't teach very much or very well. We feel that way a lot when we first start, and we worry that it's just terrible for our students. But it's not. Even if we feel our teaching falls short of what we wish it could be in a conference, it is still *so significant* that we sit down and talk to a child about his or her writing. No one ever did that with me when I was in school. And we *teach* just by sitting down and asking about the writing. We teach students that we think of them as writers and that we take their work seriously, if nothing else. So when we are first learning to confer, we have to give ourselves plenty of growing room to have conferences that aren't so good. Even if we're not helping our students as much as we would like at first, at least we're not harming them if we have thoughtful, respectful conversations with them about writing.

Conferences are "the essential act" in workshop teaching because of their individualized nature. Because we invite students to do different kinds of things with writing, and because they are at many different places in their experiences as writers, they need different kinds of teaching to support that very individual work. We also need conferences to help us keep our fingers on the pulse of our classrooms. Conferences help us know a lot about what's really going on "out there" as our students are working.

Teachers confer during independent writing time in the workshop. The minute the focus lesson is over, the teacher moves out and starts meeting with individuals (and sometimes small groups). "Moving out" can be very important. Many writing teachers feel that if they go out to students, rather than having students come to them, it helps a lot with management. Students know that we are serious about their work when we are out there with them while they are doing it. Moving out to students also serves as a sort of spatial metaphor too, much like bringing students together for the focus lesson. It lets them know that we want to catch them in the act of doing their work.

Conferring Is Teaching, Not Troubleshooting

Conferring may look like the "troubleshooting" we know from traditional teaching, where students raise their hands when they need help and we go to them, but it's not. Not at all. Conferring is a much more deliberate, methodical kind of teaching. Most teachers have some sort of record-keeping system simply for knowing what students they have conferred with and when. They use this record to decide who will have conferences on a given day, their goal being to give students an approximately equal amount of teaching attention—to get around to all their writers routinely. We don't want to set the conferencing agenda for the day by saying, "Who needs help?" or by going to students with their hands raised. Although we will "help" many writers in conferences, the purpose of a conference is not to help. The purpose is to teach, and everyone needs teaching (whether they need help or not). Also, we don't want students to become dependent on our help to get them out of binds. As writers, they need to learn that they will encounter difficulties that they have to figure out. So we let our students know from the start that we will be "making our rounds" in conferences and that if they run into difficulties, they will just have to solve them on their own.

Early on in the workshop, I always have students who come up to me while I'm conferring with other students. What I say to them is, "Is this something you can take care of yourself? Because I really need you to do that." And almost always, they hesitate for a moment and then shake their heads "yes" and move on. I usually explain to the whole class at some point why I am doing this, and, before long, students learn to take care of their own problems during the workshop and not to come to me for everything. I also explain to them that I do not want them interrupting my conferences except in a very extreme situation that simply demands my attention (something's on fire, the Publishers Clearing House guys are here looking for me, etc.).

Although as a general rule, teachers set the conferencing agenda for the day, in some workshops teachers do allow a select number of students (two or three) to sign up for conferences because they *really need them*. They then balance these "as-needed" conferences with the regular-agenda conferences. When students are allowed to sign up for conferences, we want to watch this carefully to make sure that they are using this structure in productive ways and are not becoming dependent on us for all their problem solving. Some students will want our attention and validation daily, and so they will sign up all the time. If we realize this, we have to deal with them about this issue.

KEEP THE CONFERENCE SHORT

Conferences need to be kept short, not necessarily because that's the best way to teach an individual, but because we have lots of individuals to teach. A good conference lasts anywhere from about two to seven minutes. This would mean that on a good day in a forty-minute independent segment of the workshop, we would have six to eight conferences. At this rate in a daily writing workshop, most of us would see all of our students at least once a week. Now, some days are better than others. All kinds of things can happen, and sometimes our students are engaged in inquiry that we don't want to interrupt during independent writing time, and so those numbers are very approximate. But on any given day, our goal should be to have as many quality conferences as we can with as many students as we can.

Whenever I'm feeling like I'm not getting to my students often enough in conferences, I have to remind myself of two things. First, I have to remember that if I've only had three conferences with Sara during the past five weeks, that's three more conferences than I ever had in my *whole life* as a student. That helps me remember how significant it is that I'm having them with her at all. Second, I have to remember that I want my students to learn to do just fine without me; I want them eventually to feel like they don't

WRITERS' VOICES ON . . .

improving writing through conferring

> I wrote this story . . . *Leo Cockroach . . . Toy Tester,* and initially I wrote it like Robert Benchley, sophisticated and talking to the audience. The editor said, "I love this story but maybe you can pare it down," I said okay, and I tried. She said, "But maybe you could pare it down some more." I said, "Okay, you're probably right." I began to like it more as it played out as a straighter story without so much "nudge-nudge-wink-wink." The editor had strong suggestions and she made it a better book. (Kevin O'Malley, in Anna Olswanger, *BookLinks,* 27)

Similarly, Karen Hesse comments,

> Occasionally, I go astray. Either I can't hear the voice clearly in the beginning (*Letters from Rifka, Phoenix Rising*), and I have to struggle to find my stride in the book, or I write what I think is a picture book (*Wish on a Unicorn, A Time of Angels*), only to discover I have much more to say on the subject than can be handled in that format. This, among other things, is why I so appreciate the assistance of a perceptive editor to help me find my way. I have been blessed to work with editors who guide me toward the realization of the potential of each book. (in Judy O'Malley, *BookLinks,* 54–57)

Brian and Andrea Davis Pinkney confer with each other when they aren't collaborating on a project: "She always has a fresh eye in looking at my artwork. . . . She's very good at details, in noticing the details in the artwork that I sometimes miss, only because I'm looking at the bigger picture so much." Brian also confers with his father (Jerry Pinkney) when he is illustrating. When he is writing, however, in addition to conferring with Andrea, Brian also confers with his mother (Gloria Jean Pinkney). "Sometimes she will call him and tell him about something she is writing and read it to him and ask for his opinion. When he writes something he shows it to her for her opinion, as well." Likewise, Andrea, who works as an editor, says "whenever she writes anything that she is going to submit to an editor for consideration or when revising something at every stage, it does not leave the house until Brian has read it" (in Betty Roe and Mike Roe, *Tennessee Reading Teacher,* 20–24).

So writers don't sit in schoolrooms and editors don't pull up chairs and sit alongside them, but in a writer's life the interactions between editor and writer are perhaps most like those between teacher and student during conferring. There are important differences to note, however. An editor, in working with a writer, is primarily concerned with making the piece of writing the best it can be. The editor's responsibility is to the publisher, and the investment of time is to make better *writing.* A teacher, on the other hand, in conferring with a student, is most concerned with developing the student as a writer. The emphasis during conferring is on *teaching* the student to write well. The teacher's responsibility is to the student, and we have to make sure our work makes them better *writers.*

Olswanger, Anna. 1999. "Talking with . . . Kevin O'Malley." *BookLinks* 8, no. 6 (July): 27.

O'Malley, Judy. 1999. "Talking with . . . Karen Hesse." *BookLinks* 9, no. 1 (September): 54–57.

Roe, Betty, and Mike Roe. 1997. "Meet the Author/Illustrator . . . Brian and Andrea Davis Pinkney." *Tennessee Reading Teacher* (Fall): 20–24.

need me at all. They will never get that feeling if I am in their faces too often. So I've got to let my teaching in conferences surround their work as writers, but not take it over or keep it going.

THE FOUR PARTS OF A WRITING CONFERENCE

Conferences are short, focused sessions with individual students, and we get as many of them in as we can each day. Let's think through now what happens in a conference. In her book *The Art of Teaching Writing* (1994), Lucy Calkins explains that a conference is made up of three parts: *research, decide, teach.* I would add to those three a fourth component: *make a record.* Thinking of conferences in this way can really help us refine the teaching that we do with individual students. Defining these terms briefly, they mean essentially this: *Research* means that we find out how the student's writing is going first. Then, based on how it's going, we *decide* what would make sense to *teach* the student, and once we do that, we teach it to him or her in an individualized, on-the-spot focus lesson. When we're finished, either the student or the teacher (or both) *makes a record* of the conference by jotting down its essential content.

Research

The research part of the conference is an assessment that happens at the beginning. It involves trying to get a handle on how things are going for this writer, and a feeling for what the writer is doing and trying at this point. What we learn during this part of the conference will help us decide what to teach. We generally open this part of the conference with an inquiry of the writer. This inquiry may be as general as, "Tell me about how your writing is going." or as specific as, "Tell me about what kinds of crafting techniques you are trying in your writing." When we ask a specific question like that, it's usually because we are following the whole-class unit of study through the processes of individual writers, or because we are following an agenda particular to that writer. Sometimes we ask students to tell us about how something has been going that we worked on with them in our last conference.

As with any opening inquiry, our goal at the beginning of a conference is to get the student talking. This is why I preface almost every question with the three words, "Tell me about . . ." At the least, this sends the message that I want more than a one-word answer. Think about the difference between, "Tell me about how your writing is going" and "How's your writing going?" The second can and usually will be answered with one word: "fine" or "horrible" or "OK." And, of course, even if you ask the first one, some will still answer with, "It's going fine." Then you have to say again, "Well, tell me a little about it." And you wait—don't keep asking questions. You have to try to wait those students out because you really need to get them talking. Contained in their talk will be the information you need in order to know what to teach them.

In my writing workshop this past summer with third and fourth graders, the observing teachers noticed that after the first week, I often didn't have to ask a question to start the conference; the children would just start telling me about their writing when I pulled alongside them. The students had seen and heard enough conferences all around them to know that's what I expected them to do, and they went about their writing with this consciousness that made them ready to explain that work whenever I came their way. In this way, the structure of conferring in the room, the every-day anticipation of it, invites children to be metacognitive (thinking about their writing processes), even when we aren't conferring with them. Because they have to engage in conferences so often, they come to live with this sense of needing to explain their work. This helps them to think about it in such powerful ways, even when we're not right there asking them about it.

Now, some students will just want to hand us something to read. We ask them to tell us about how their writing is going, and they hand us their notebooks. We need to hand these back and say to the students, "Tell me about this first." We may look at them later in the conference, but students are opting out of their responsibility to help us know how things are going if they just want us to "read and find out." We could probably find something to teach by just looking at their writing, but they've taken themselves out of that transaction—and they are a very important part of it. You see, one of the best ways to help students develop a writing process that works for them (one of our teaching goals) is to help them become articulate about their processes. We really have to force the issue in getting students to talk to us *about* their writing.

Some students will just say very, very little in a conference. There's not a single answer to "How do I get them to talk?" As we've already mentioned, there are some things we can do to help—such as asking more open-ended questions, waiting longer for their responses, and insisting that they talk about their writing rather than having us read their writing. But we are still going to have reluctant talkers that we just have to deal with on an individual basis. We need to try to understand why they're not talking, and then decide how to handle the conferences with them based on that. Here are some things to think about with the "no-talkers."

- Some are shy at first and will warm up to talking to us as they get more comfortable with us. We may have to do more of the talking at first to get them comfortable, and we want to be sure to work with *anything* they give us in the way of talk by letting them know how valuable every word they say is to us.

- Some normally talkative students just have no experience with this kind of talk with a teacher and are very uneasy about what we really expect from them in this interaction. They too will get more comfortable with time as they have conferences with us and listen in on our conferences with other students. But at first, we have to handle them as we would the very shy students.

- Some students who normally talk easily in conferences may have days when they say very little because they are just having a bad day or because something they are writing about is upsetting to them. If either of these is the case, we can give the student room to talk about that—about what's bothering him or her—instead of talking about writing at first. We need to recognize and value this very human side of writing. Often talking about something that's bothering students will help them deal with the issue and get redirected in their work as writers.

- Many times when students are really struggling with something in writing, they will throw up their hands and say, "I don't know," in response to everything. In this case, we want to get them to tell us about what they don't know, about the struggle itself. We let them know that it's OK if their response to "Tell me about how your writing is going" is rambling, inarticulate, and uncertain. We can help them work that out *if* they will just talk about it.

- Occasionally, we will have students who are just butting heads with us, as they will on many things, testing us to see if we are going to "make" them do this. If we really believe this is the case, then we will have to handle it just as we would if a student chose not to do something else that was required of him or her in our classroom. In a writing workshop, working with the teacher in conferences is not one of the options students have. It is a requirement.

The answer to "How do I get this child to talk" is always found in the story of that child. We have to find out that story and then work from there.

Now, for many students, talking won't be a problem at all. No sirreee. They will talk all day if we sit there and listen! But we can't, of course, so we have to become comfortable saying to these students, "Excuse me. Let me stop you for just a moment. I want to go back to what you said a minute ago . . ." Once we have heard something in the student's talk that gives us a teaching direction we want to follow, we have to interrupt and go in that direction. It's hard at first to get comfortable doing this. We think that if the student keeps talking, we will find something better to teach—and we probably would find something better. But what makes a conference a powerful teaching interaction is not finding the best thing in the world to teach this student; it's in teaching in *direct response* to something the student has told us or shown us about his or her work as a writer. So as soon as we see a way to go with the teaching, we head in that direction. That's the decision-making part of the conference. We'll open it up next.

Decide

When you watch a really good teacher confer, you can't observe the decision-making part of the conference. You can sometimes see it in the teacher's eyes when you know she is making a decision, but you can't see the decision itself. Basically, the teacher has to get the student talking about his or her writing, has to listen very closely to what the student is saying, and, alongside that, has to think, *"What do I know about writing* that I could say in response to *this* that would teach *this writer* something?" We are making a curriculum decision here, a "what-does-this-student-need-to-know" decision. Now, there are two key parts (highlighted above) to that decision-making question. You see, a writing conference is a meeting of a teacher's knowledge base about writing with a student's work as a writer. Those two have to come together to help us make our decision about what we will teach. We should help that student either think about something or do something that he or she could not do if we weren't sitting there.

When we sit down next to a student, we bring with us what I call a "fistful" of knowledge about writing that we draw from to teach this writer. And in a conference, we can't teach what we don't know. We can teach what we don't know in a lesson we plan for next Friday because we can read up on it and get to know it. But in a conference, all we've got to go on is what's already in our fist because we have to do it right there on the spot. When we first start teaching writing, we have only a few things in our fist; it's a very small fist, so we teach the same things over and over, all around the room. And we must know that that's OK! It's still very powerful teaching because we have explained it to each child in the context of his or her work. I tell my students who are going to be teachers soon not to let their small fists stop them from conferring. If we know only two things about, say, crafting writing, then we teach those two things to everybody—as if our lives depended on it—until we can learn two more things.

I'm being a little flippant here, but only a very little. The truth is, we have to decide what thing about writing we want to teach a student from the fistful of things we know. And we won't know as much now as we will three years from now or fifteen years from now. But we will start anyway, and we will develop our fists as we go. To help writers who are at many different places, we will need fistfuls of knowledge about all the kinds of things they will be engaged in while in our writing workshops—things such as:

- living the life of a writer, keeping a writing notebook, and choosing writing projects to pursue;
- planning for published pieces of writing: collecting and developing ideas; being aware of genre, structure, purpose, audience, and so on;
- drafting pieces of writing;
- revising writing and crafting writing for an audience;
- getting and giving responses to writing;
- editing, proofreading, and knowing conventions of grammar and usage;
- publishing.

How big is your fist in each of these areas? What do you already know about these different aspects of a writer's work that you can use in your teaching? The knowledge in our fists can come from our own writing experiences, from the experiences of our students, from texts that we have read as writers (for craft especially), from books that we have read about how to write, or from authors we have heard speak about their processes. Our conferring will get better and better as we make the size of our teaching fists bigger. Developing our knowledge base gives us a much broader selection of curriculum we can offer students who will have a wide range of needs.

So part of our decision about what to teach is made based on what we know, and part of our decision about what to teach comes from our thinking about the student with whom we are conferring. A conference is individualized instruction, and we never want to lose the individual in the decision-making process. If there are two or three things we can think of to teach in a conference, we might ask questions like these to help us make a decision and stay focused on the student:

- **What would help most at this time?** For example, suppose a student is working on fiction for the first time. He tells us about a conference he had with a peer, and we hear in what he says that he needs a better strategy for getting help from a peer. We also hear that he is struggling to develop his plot and needs help with that. *At this time*, we should probably decide to give him a strategy for developing plot and let the other help he needs with peer response come later. The peer issue will be there in the future of his writing, whereas the fiction help is much more immediate.
- **What would bring quick success?** We might want to ask this question if a student has really been struggling a lot as a writer and needs something to go well. To put it simply, we might teach the thing we feel will be easiest for the student because we believe she *needs* success right now.
- **What would be a stretch, a risk, or a challenge?** We may feel that it's time for a student to be really stretched as a writer, and so we choose to teach her the thing we think would challenge her the most. This is the "step-up-to-the-plate" teaching that helps students really outgrow themselves.
- **What is not likely to come up in whole-class instruction?** If we are deciding what we need to teach a student, and one of the things we

think of will probably never come up in any whole-class teaching, we might decide to teach it to this student for just that reason. "I can see that this student needs to know about this and he's not going to get it anywhere else," we think. Sometimes this is something everyone else basically "has"—as with convention teaching—but sometimes it's very specific to that writer, so specific that no one else is likely to need it.

- **Is this something I need to reteach or extend?** As we are making our teaching decision, we might listen as the student talks for evidence that past teaching may still need work or extension. If we can see that a student still needs to develop some understandings in an area that we've already worked on, it might make sense to go back to that, rather than moving on to something new.

- **What is the balance of curriculum I have offered this student?** There is a danger in offering some students the same kinds of curriculum over and over. The struggling writer gets nineteen conferences that teach him about convention and one that helps him write more interesting things in the notebook. The gifted writer has bunches of conferences where we confirm her growing sense of self as a writer and hardly any that stretch her knowledge of technique in writing. We want to offer every student a good balance of teaching that helps him or her grow in all areas as writers.

- **What kind of teaching would this student like me to offer?** If a student says to us, "What I really need help with right now is . . ." then we should honor that with some teaching. This may show that the student has a good sense of self and that he knows where some redirection in his writing life and process is needed. And don't worry. Sitting down next to a writer who can tell us what kind of help he needs is not the same thing as having a writer constantly raise his hand for help. The one has been carrying on without our help until we come to him; the other is paralyzed without it and sits there waiting for us. The one sees our help for what it is—teaching support for his writing; the other depends on us to keep him going.

So any one or any number of these questions can help us decide, from all we know, what one thing to teach a student in this conference. Sometimes this seems almost overwhelming. We think, "And I'm supposed to think all this through in a two- to seven-minute conference?" Yes, we are. We won't do it very well at first, remember that. But we give ourselves time and experience to become proficient at conferring. One thing I tell my students who will soon be teachers is, when you are trying to make your decision in a conference about what to teach, it's OK to stop a student's talking and ask, "Would you give me just a minute to think?" before you begin your teaching. As a matter of fact, if we do this, it will help us listen to that child better because we're not distracted. We know we will take a pause to make our decision. Children are pretty amazed when they sit there and watch us thinking about what they have been saying. Imagine how significant that is—for a teacher to be sitting there thinking hard about only you and what he or she will say to you. It's an amazing part of the interaction. At times, I have even had to ask students if I could get back to them tomorrow because I needed to think a little bit more about what they were saying and how to teach them.

So we can take some thinking time before we teach, but believe it or not, knowing what to teach in a conference really does become easier and easier over time. Talk to anyone who's been conferring for a while, and they'll tell you that. Our history of having conferences will help us know better how to make decisions based on student needs, and, of course, letting our fists (knowledge base) get bigger helps too. Remember that as I was explaining this, I was explaining in detail a thought process. By definition, that's going to be complex because all thought is complex. But we are very used to thinking, and the more experience we get with this *kind* of thinking, the easier it will be for us to have good conferences.

Teach

Once we have decided what we want to say to a child in a conference, we fall very much into our focus-lesson, direct-instruction mode. Either we explain to the student how to do something, or we help him or her understand something better. We teach all the same kinds of things we do in focus lessons: strategies, techniques, questions, relationships, and conventions (only one in a conference, of course). Also, just as in focus lessons, we try to "show and tell" in conferences as much as we can—by grabbing a book to illustrate a crafting technique, by showing an entry from our notebooks that is an example of a collection strategy, or by writing a quick example that shows how a convention works, for example.

Often in a conference, when we teach a child something, we are teaching this child something *new*, extending his "fistful" of knowledge about writing, for example, a new way to use the notebook, or a new way to think about revision. Sometimes, though, a conference confirms something during teaching rather than extending it. If, in our research, we realize a student is doing something really smart that she may not realize is a smart thing to do, then our teaching might be to name that thing for the student and to confirm that it is smart.

For example, if Julie shows me an entry in her notebook where she has written about what her cat might say to her when he is grouchy, I might say, "Julie, you *shifted perspectives* here," and give her a name for what she is doing. And then I would talk to her about how writers can do that—write something from a different perspective. I might try to help her think of other places where she might use this writing technique that she did without really realizing (in an articulate way) what she was doing. So the teaching in a conference can be either an extension of what the child knows, or a confirmation and naming of something that the child is already doing that is smart.

Often, after I have finished my teaching in a conference, I will ask the student to "Say back to me what I just talked to you about." This is a better request than asking, "Do you have any questions?" or "Did that make sense?" I can get a better handle on what the student understood about the teaching by listening to the "say back," and the student gets a chance to articulate what he or she has heard from me. I'm not hoping for an exact, detailed rendering of my teaching. I know that a lot of my teaching in conferences will make more sense after a while, when the student has had time to think about this strategy, technique, or convention and to try it out. I'm just listening for a general understanding of the content of my teaching. I try to clear up any really big misunderstandings right then, and I make notes to return to ideas in later conferences if I just feel that the student is going to need time to grow into what I've taught.

Make a Record

At the conclusion of a conference, I almost always say to a student, "OK, so what I'm going to write down is . . . ," and I proceed to tell that student the summary of our conference that I'm going to write in my notes: "I'm going to write down that we talked about how to write a fast and long entry," for example. This summary statement is the "lesson" of the conference in a nutshell; it lets the student know what I am writing about him or her.

Records of what we teach in each conference—the tracks of our teaching—are absolutely essential. They serve so many important purposes. They help us with our own accountability because we can show others what we are teaching. They are like "lesson plans" that we make after we've taught the lesson. They help make our students accountable because they show what's been explained to each one of them (and we expect them to attend to that). They help us think about our future teaching with each student, because they let us see the balance of curriculum we've given each individual. They help us with assessment, both for individuals and for the whole class. We can look across student records of conferences and see patterns of things we've been teaching students. Often, these patterns help us plan units of study. We can use them as one source of information in evaluations, as we make judgments about the quality of students' work in the workshop.

Close to an extra minute is added to each conference when we stop to record it, but it is worth the investment. Over time, we will develop a system for making conference records that is efficient. Teachers, it seems, have many different variations of these systems, because they have to find one that feels comfortable for them or they won't use it. One thing a conference recording system needs is a way to divide records easily by individual students. We need to be able to see all of the recorded conferences we've had with William, for example, in one place. Our system needs to help us make the record quickly, so we devise codes and cryptic ways of noting what we've taught. It needs to be easy to carry around; we move a lot as we confer, and we need to be able to take it with us easily.

Figure 14.1 shows a sample of my current conference note system.

Getting Better at Conferring

When I worked for two years as a staff developer doing demonstration teaching in the New York City Public Schools, I conferred with hundreds of students at all different grade levels in all different kinds of writing workshops. And every time I had one of these conferences, I had to step away from it and explain it to the other teachers who were watching. Needless to say, I

FIGURE 14.1 Conference Notes

Cori	Logan * 7/13 revising by the sounds of words. * 7/15 using notebook for revision	Grace 7/9 - likes poetry that doesn't rhyme 7/12 - Try write-offs from entries 7/13 - working with words & phrases in entries 7/14 - rhyming strategies; not let the rhyme mess up tone	Janelle 7/12 try writing a long entry short like a poem; a poem entry like a long reflection - sort of tried that	Mandy 7/12 Try fast & long writing —
Courtney 7/12 use notebook to listen to 3 year old sister; going to try the atlas strategy - Tried this!! - going to turn into a poem 7/15 has an anthology of weather poems - going to work on this	Brittany 7/10 - has an entry from Walmart I going to try writing off words. 7/13 ready to revise some 7/14 added to draft; playing in notebook	Rachel 7/4 - Choose book based on animals; copying one in [illegible] 7/13 needs more Rachel entries; try writing fast & long about animals	Douglas 7/12 mom has a notebook; list keeper; study Slam Dunk for Shape 7/14 poem digging	Cayla 7/13 write fast & long about dogs 7/15 difference between draft & entry
Bryan 7/13 - started with rhyming words; try writing fast & long and the reconsider your draft.	Anthony 7/12 - Not to worry about it not sounding good 7/13 Keep getting it down. I'll help with the editing 7/15 working on line breaks	Alder	Julie 7/12 * write using similes; going to use photos of cats to write 7/14 trying from cat's perspective	Natalie 7/12 try fast writing to the bottom 7/14 collecting lines you like from poems to make a new poem - going to try rearranging
Marie 7/12 - try writing off of pictures at home - did this & it worked 7/14 Keep working on Katie poems 7/18 worked on reordering the shape of a piece				

became very reflective and very articulate about my conferring during those two years, and I grew and grew as a teacher in this way. I have found that now, even when I'm not demonstrating teaching to others, even when it's just me and a group of student writers working together, it helps me to step away from my conferences and act as if someone is still there wanting to know exactly what I did and why I did it.

I take time routinely to look at various conferences I am having with students and to ask myself three questions about them. One question is, "What, exactly, did I teach in that conference?" This helps me get at my teaching objectives, and it helps me remember that I need to teach *something*, that my lesson in the conference needs an objective. The second question I ask is, "Why did I decide to teach that?" This question helps me continue to be intentional about letting what I decide to teach come from what the student needs as a writer. The third question is, "How does the student seem to feel about the conference?" This helps me develop a sensitivity toward my students' feelings about this very personal kind of teaching. I want to leave students with an energy for their work after a conference, and I watch for the signs of that in my teaching.

If you can work with two or three supportive colleagues to study your conferring in this way, it really helps. Visit in each other's classrooms, if you can; observe conferences and then talk them through together. If you can't, get together to share your conference records and your reflections on what kinds of things you are teaching and why. In addition to adding to your knowledge base for teaching, studying your own teaching is one of the best things you can do to get better at it. You might also read Carl Anderson's book, *How's It Going?* (2000), which is very specifically about conferring, with a study group of other teachers interested in conferring. Conferring is very challenging, and you will probably struggle with it for quite some time before you begin to feel at ease. But most really good things in teaching—as in all of life—are like that, aren't they?

References

Anderson, Carl. 2000. *How's It Going? A Practical Guide to Conferring with Student Writers.* Portsmouth, N.H.: Heinemann.

Calkins, Lucy McCormick. 1994. *The Art of Teaching.* 2nd ed. Portsmouth, N.H.: Heinemann.

15

Making Share Time a Better Time

My friend and fellow writing teacher Isoke Nia likes to talk. Everyone who knows her, knows *that*. So the first time I heard her say, "Without lots of talk, your workshop will fall apart," I probably thought—along with everyone else who heard her say it—"Well, of course *she* would say *that*." And those of us who are a little quieter (and I'm only a tiny bit quieter) might have thought we didn't need as much talk in our workshops as Isoke needs. But we would have been thinking wrong, I can tell you from experience. Isoke is right about that, like she is about so many things when it comes to teaching writing. Talk is essential to the healthy maintenance of any writing workshop.

Talk reverberates throughout the workshop. In the focus lesson, there is mostly teacher talk. During independent writing time, there is teacher-student talk during conferences, and there is much casual talk among writers as they carry on with the writing for the day. Students in most writing workshops know how to seek out an official conference with a peer during independent writing time if one is needed (they learn to confer with each other from the demonstrations we provide on how to confer), and sometimes small response groups of students will meet for a portion of independent writing time to talk about their writing. In some classrooms, these peer response groups are actually organized and do actually meet on regularly scheduled days. But it is the predictable time we plan to bring everyone together for *just talk* about writing, known as "share time," that sends the message of a daily structure: This is important enough that we'll do it every day.

The share time when we talk about our writing usually lasts from five to ten minutes a day. It may come at any point during the workshop, but it often happens at the end because it is a good way to process the work of the day and make a transition into something else. If share time gets moved up front in the workshop, it's usually because students need to do some kind of talk that sets them up for their independent writing time. In a genre study, for example, when many students might be revising pieces in the genre at the same time, we may have them start the workshop with a share time when they get responses to one revision question they have about their drafts.

WHY DO WE NEED TALK?

Just as the teacher is responsible for most of the talk in a focus lesson, students are responsible for the talk during the share time. We plan for having this regular time when students talk about their writing for two main reasons. First, for many of our writers, talk is essential because when they are writing every single day, they just need to get some regular feedback to keep their momentum going. They need someone to laugh or smile or say, "Oh, disgusting!" about what they are writing. This kind of feedback helps them know they are on the right track—the track that will move readers to respond to their writing in certain ways. These students write with this anticipation, this knowing that they will get to try out what they have written on readers, and that anticipation is a driving force in writing for most of them. And learning the role of audience—of readers' responses—is the first important move in the whole process of publishing. The share time provides a forum for students to learn this, a place where they can begin to feel what it's like to have one's ideas "go public."

Second, we value the regular share time because, as teachers, we see it as important curriculum time. Students can learn so much from each other during this time. Remember that the writing workshop is a place where students learn how to live as writers and how to do what writers do. If we've got twenty-eight people in the room writing, that's twenty-eight ongoing demonstrations of how one might go about that, and students can learn from all of those demonstrations. They may learn things they want to do in their writing lives as well as things they don't want to do, but they can learn from anyone. So we expect students to live these writing lives, and we ask them to share in talk about their lives so that they make their individual writing moves public and available for others' learning.

For me as a teacher, share time really gets at a value that is bigger than writing itself. It's a value I have about *learning communities*, and a writing workshop is a learning community. It is a place that I create where we learn *together* and where we support each other in that learning in important ways. Some of my students (not many, but some) would probably rather not talk about their writing. Either these students don't need constant reinforcement, or they are just more shy about their writing. Some professional writers will tell you that they work in this more isolated way, preferring not to let anyone know or see what they are working on until they feel it is basically finished. These are the writers who don't have response groups or never apply for fellowships to writers' colonies. But I don't really give my students that option, because I believe it is important for them to participate in the exchange of learning demonstrations in the workshop. So while these students who don't want or don't need as much response to their writing will find ways to engage in it less than others—not seeking out response during independent writing time, for example—I do expect them to take part in the regular share time each day

Now, requiring students to share in talk about their writing may seem like an oxymoron. Is it really *sharing* if I require someone to do it? Or is it more like what I was doing when my mother used to make me share when I was a child (when it was really the last thing I wanted to do with my chocolate bar), when I was too young to understand the value of that concept? Maybe, since it is required, there is a better word than "share" to capture this daily structure in the workshop. We could call it "talk time" or "writing chat time" or even "response time." But I think that what I call it is probably less important than that I capture the spirit of what I want, and, for me at least, "sharing" is the spirit I want. I try my best to demonstrate a spirit of sharing in all the talk around writing that happens in the workshop. I share from my own writing, and I delight in listening to writing ideas that students have, accepting what I hear in the spirit of sharing, whether it was offered that way or not. I want students to develop the confidence that comes from offering up one's ideas to an audience and having the experience of seeing oneself among others in that way.

WRITER'S VOICES ON . . .

reading their drafts aloud

> It is important to read aloud what you write. In writing groups, I ask people to write and then immediately afterward ask them to read it to either the large group, a smaller group, or to a person sitting next to them. It is part of the writing process, like bending down to touch your toes and then standing up again. Write, read, write, read. You become less attached to whether it is good or bad. . . . If you don't read aloud, the writing tends to fester like an infected wound in your notebook. I cannot say why, but the simple act of reading it aloud allows you to let go of it. . . . I don't know quite what this reading aloud is about, but we tend to get swampy, thick with sludge, when we write. We listen too much to monkey mind. Reading aloud gives us an airing. (Natalie Goldberg, *Wild Mind,* 81–82)

Writers need feedback from trusted others. We need to hear from that objective, outside-the-story voice in order to help us gain perspective and to see where to cut, add, or redirect. Anne Lamott suggests that

> You may need someone else to bounce your material off of, probably a friend or a mate, someone who can tell you if the seams show, or if you've lurched off track, or even that it is not as bad as you thought and that the first one hundred pages do in fact hold up. But by all means let someone else take a look at your work. It's too hard always to have to be the executioner. Also, you may not be able to see the problems, because in finding your characters and their story, you are trying to describe something by feel and not by sight. So find someone who can bring a colder eye and a certain detachment to the project. (*Bird by Bird,* 57)

Sharing our words—going public—is essential to moving forward in the work of a writer. Goldberg and Lamott encourage us to gain a sense of distance and perspective by moving from marks on the page to sounds in the air. Hearing our words helps us to both see and hear the rhythms of our writing. It gives us the opportunity to test the reactions of audience and to explore whether we have lived up to our intentions.

Goldberg, Natalie. 1990. *Wild Mind: Living the Writer's Life.* New York: Bantam.

Lamott, Anne. 1995. *Bird by Bird: Some Instructions on Writing and Life.* New York: Anchor Books.

Looking Closely at Kinds of Shares

If we take the two big reasons above for having share time—so writers can get responses and so students can learn from each other—then we can move from there into thinking about what kinds of things should happen during this window of time each day. First, let's think about four particular kinds of shares:

1. simple response share
2. survey share
3. focused share
4. student-as-teacher share

Remember that the characteristic that is true of all kinds of shares is that students take the major responsibility for the talk during this time.

Simple Response Share

This is a share time when students simply share from the writing they are doing in their notebooks or from the drafting process they are doing for their writing projects. During these shares, students may read actual notebook entries or drafts to listeners. They may simply talk "about" what they are writing rather than read it. Or they may do some combination of both. The purpose of the share is just to let students have an audience for their ongoing writing work.

As we think about this kind of share, let's start with one thing that should probably not happen. This kind of share—individuals just getting responses to what they have written—should probably not be done as a whole class. Now, I know that when we all started our writing workshops, we did a lot of this. As a matter of fact, that's mostly what share time was—a time for a select few students to read something they'd been working on to the class. After the students had read their entries or pieces, they called on other students to give them responses, or they solicited particular kinds of feedback. We went at share time this way for some time, but we've learned some things with experience that have helped us refine this time.

For one thing, we've learned that if students read something to the whole class, we often see that they don't have much energy to return to the piece after that. You see, everyone's already heard the piece. In a very real way, reading something in its entirety to the whole class is like publishing. It's certainly going very public with something in the room, and so you get that anticipated readers' response to it. Once you've had that, that driving force of future readers who will laugh, cry, shout, or sigh is greatly diminished or gone altogether, because everyone has already heard the idea from the notebook or the draft of the piece.

Happily, this "already-published-during-share-time" dilemma is not the case in classrooms where students routinely take their writing to audiences out in the world. If the class has heard it, there is still that other "worldly" audience waiting. So that gets rid of the "only-audience-has-already-heard-it" problem. But still, there are other issues that give us trouble with this kind of share. If the point of sharing the piece is to get a reader's response to our ongoing writing (one of our purposes for share time), then really only one or two writers are going to get the benefit of that when we do whole-class sharing. You can up the number of children engaged in getting and giving responses to writing by one hundred percent simply by having students do this in twos. Sharing from their writing in two's, or in small response groups of three or four children—what a simple solution! Reconfiguring sharing in this way accomplishes our purpose for so many more children, and it eliminates the problem of "everyone's already heard this." Only a select few students have heard it, helped the writer with it, and can anticipate along with him or her the response of other readers when the piece is finished sometime in the future.

So if the purpose of our share time is a very wide-open, simple, "get-some-responses-and-let-them-be-heard" time for our writers, we can maximize this time by getting lots of students engaged in the share at once. We might want to have regular partners or small groups that get together when we say, "Today for share time, let's just get together with our partners (groups) and share what we've been doing with our writing." Having a structure like this can cut down on setup time, when everyone is trying to find some other person to join.

Survey Share

> I want all of you to find a line in your drafts that you think is particularly well crafted, and today for share time, we are just going to go around the room and read that single line to the whole class. Let's listen for how we are defining good craft through these examples from our writing.

These instructions would set up a survey share where every student contributes something concise that is shared with the whole class. Sometimes what we need most from share time is for students to hear a wide variety of responses to something. We might think the variety of responses will broaden the students' ideas of what's possible and give them alternative ways to think about things, or we might think the sampling of responses will simply help boost interest in what's going on with different writers around the room.

In a share like this, we move quickly from student to student, without talk in between their responses. We are simply trying to survey the room, to hear from everyone, so that we create this single "text" made up of all our different responses. Sometimes, especially when we are reading single, well-crafted lines from our drafts, we are amazed at how much the shared text we create sounds like a poem. The trick is to get students to follow one after another once we start sharing so that everyone who is listening hears what sounds like individual responses flowing into a single river of response from the class. It helps to sit in a circle when we are doing this so that it's easy to tell who follows whom as we go.

This "text" we are making from a survey of our responses is framed in some way, as the one above was framed by asking students to look for a particular kind of line in their drafts, one that is well-crafted. The frames we choose for this share are important because they communicate important values about what is worth thinking about and sharing as writers. Here are just a few examples of other kinds of "frames" we might have for a survey share:

- Share a line or a phrase from your writer's notebook that you collected while you were outside of class.

- From your draft, share a single striking word that you really like.
- Share with us an insight you've had over the last week about writing.
- Share with us what your plans are for tomorrow in writing workshop.
- Share with us the one thing you really want to work on as you revise.
- Share with us a crafting technique you are going to try.
- Share with us the name of an author you are learning from as a writer.
- Share with us the seed idea for your writing project.
- Share with us one thing you've learned from another writer in the room.
- Share with us something that you are struggling with as a writer
- Complete the statement, "As a writer right now I . . ." and share with us your completion.

Sometimes these shares relate directly to something we have explained in the focus lesson and that we have asked students to think about during their work that day, but sometimes they are simply things we think will be beneficial for us all to hear. Often, we return to the same frames for these shares over and over again during the year. If we want students to contribute something that we haven't thought about before in another share or a focus lesson, then we quickly need to give students a sample response or two as we explain what we want them to share. For example, let's say that we want them to share something they are struggling with as writers. We might explain it this way:

> We are four months into our writing workshop and heavy into all kinds of projects. I know that some things come easily from some of us, and some things are really hard for others of us. But we all have our own struggles. That's just part of being writers. Some of you may struggle with keeping your notebook with you. Others of you may struggle with volume in your writing life. Some of you may think you're not publishing enough. Or some of you may feel your biggest struggle is with all the mechanical aspects of writing. There are many, many struggles a writer can have. It's important for us to know what these are so that we can deal with them ourselves and help each other.

> If you will, think for just a minute about what you feel your biggest struggle as a writer is just now. Jot down a sentence about it, and then we'll do a read-around of these just to see where we are with our struggles.

In a way, instructions like these for finding the share material are tiny focus lessons in themselves. But we're going to keep them very tiny because we already know that some students will name as their own one of the very struggles we gave as an example, not because it is their struggle, but because they really aren't quite ready to think this through yet. We also know that some other students *will* be ready to think about this question and will offer some important demonstrations to their classmates. We know that we will contribute to the share by offering our own demonstrations of what's possible. And we know that, above all else, this will be the first of many times students will be asked to think about the question, "What are you struggling with as a writer?" As with all our teaching, we know that this ten minutes of sharing we'll do together is but one fine thread in the huge woven tapestry of teaching we'll do throughout the year.

If I am asking students to share with us something that is not already written (not as a line from a notebook or draft is written) like an insight or a question, I usually ask them to jot this down quickly in a sentence that they will read to us. This forces students to use writing to get hold of what they want to say, and it expedites the sharing process because everyone knows exactly what he or she will be contributing once we start surveying the room.

Sometimes, at the end of a survey share, we might discuss a little about what we've heard. I have one question I use over and over when we do this. After the last person has finished, I say, "What did you guys notice about our responses?" Often, the first time I ask this, my students don't have a whole lot to say because they aren't quite sure what I'm asking. "What do you mean what did I notice?" But that's OK. I let them answer not so brilliantly at first because I know that, over time, they will come to understand this question as one of connections and relationships. If I keep asking, over and over, "So, what did you notice?" they will start to anticipate that question and begin to listen differently to each other and across each other's responses because of it. Before long, we will have these rich, generative discussions that take flight from these kinds of shares.

Focused Share

A focused share is similar to a survey share in that it has some kind of frame, some kind of focus. The difference is that students talk with their partners or with members of their small response groups about the frame or the focus for that share. So we use the same partnering or grouping structure that we use for the simple get-some-responses-and-let-them-be-heard share, and we use the same kinds of frames we use for a survey share.

For example, at the end of a week where we have offered several focus lessons on how writers get ideas and material from the world around them—overheard conversations, close observations, fleeting thoughts—we might ask students to have a focused share with a group where they talk about notebook entries they have gathered outside of class. Usually, when I ask students to have a conversation like this, I tell them, "Be sure to listen for things that others are doing that you might want to try yourself. Learn from each other." And this is really the whole reason for having these conversations. We may close out the focus share with some whole-class talk or some written reflections about what students have learned from each other. We want to make it very clear that we expect this sharing to help students think of new possibilities for themselves as writers.

Student-as-Teacher Share

As I move about the room conferring, I often learn about very smart things that various students are doing with their writing. I want everyone to know about these things, and the share time can be a time both to "celebrate the smartness" and to spread it around. So occasionally I will ask one or two students to share with us about something they are doing or something we talked about in a conference. I am often a part of this sharing; I ask questions and help the students develop their comments in ways that are meaningful for listeners.

For example, one day this past summer, in my poetry workshop for third and fourth graders, I came across Bryan doing this very interesting thing with scissors. You see, we had this magnetic poetry board in the room—the kind with lots of different words that you can arrange and rearrange into poems. The students loved it. But what Bryan had figured out was that he could use that same process as a revision tool for his own poetry. He had taken a single draft of a poem he'd written, cut out each of the words separately, and was toying with the arrangement of them in the same way he had done with the "magnetic poems." He explained to me that once he had an arrangement that sounded good and looked good (in terms of line breaks), he was going to copy it down as a new draft. I loved the way the revision tool he had developed caused him to think very specifically about single words and their relationship to the other words around them. I asked Bryan to show the other students what he was doing and to explain his process to them during share time that day. He was being smart and resourceful, and I wanted the other students to know about that, so I gave over some share time to him so he could teach others.

Over time, as different students are asked to share smart work they are doing in the workshop, there comes to be an understanding in the room that smart work *matters,* that smart work is valued here. When this understanding is in place, we usually see that students begin to raise the level of their work because they want to contribute to the pool of smartness. It's almost combustible, the way one smart thing leads to another and another and another. We make students "experts" on various strategies and techniques when we share them in this way, directing other students to see them for advice on using these writing moves in their own work.

When using share time in this way, there are several things to keep in mind. One is that this kind of share will be successful only if we also learn to celebrate the times when someone does the *exact same thing* that someone else has shared. Think about that. The whole point of getting smart writing moves into the room is so the repertoire of what *everyone* knows how to do as writers is increased. So we have to make as big a deal about it when someone *copies* Bryan's process, as we did when he tried it in the first place. We may really be "bucking a norm" when we communicate our values about this. Many of us and many of our students have learned that school is a place where you should never "copy" someone else, and yet in the workshop that's exactly what we want students doing—trying things that others are trying.

We want to maintain that sometimes-delicate balance between celebrating new strategies and techniques that students are inventing for their writing work, and celebrating students' attempts to learn from others in the workshop. One of the toughest challenges will be helping the writer who has a strong sense of self but who doesn't want to learn anything from anyone else. For this reason, I think an important assessment and evaluation question to ask students is, "What things have you been learning and trying from other students in the class?"

A second challenge is to have the eyes to see smartness in the work of *all* our writers. It is easy to fall into the trap of celebrating the smart writing moves of the few students who are *always* doing something new and clever in their work. But can we see the smart things our struggling writers are doing? Remember, if writing is a struggle for some of our students, then it's likely that they are having to be much more resourceful in figuring out ways to get it done. What can we see in their resourcefulness?

My favorite story related to resourcefulness happened once in a kindergarten classroom. The thoughtful, sensitive teacher of writing in this room was watching and listening with an eye toward smartness on the morning that Manuel announced to her as he came into class, "While I was on the bus, I was thinking about what I was going to write in writing workshop today!"

"Manuel," she said, "You were prewriting! How smart! We need to tell all the other kids about this!" And she had Manuel talk to the other children that day about how he had done this very smart thing—prewriting (this thing he'd never heard of before!). She told them that if any of them had any questions about it, they should ask Manuel and he could help them. Now the thing is, Manuel was developmentally in a very different place with writing than most of his kindergarten classmates. He was still quite unsure about both letters and drawings in his writing, and there was very little convention showing up (yet) in either one. But on this day, none of that mattered, because his teacher had the eyes to see what he was doing that was smart, and she celebrated this by naming him the "expert." As we think about using share time in this way, we need to be sure to think about developing our own vision for seeing smartness in the work of all our students.

Another thing we have to remember is that with this kind of share, we have necessarily limited the sharing—the talk—to only one student. We expect the other students to be listening, and we can make that listening more active if they know we expect them to be trying some things they are learning from other students, and if we allow them to ask the "student-teacher" questions. But still, only one student is really responsible for the talking. In many ways, this type of share is really a lot more like a focus lesson. It can, in fact, be done as a focus lesson instead of as share time. But if we choose to use share time in this way, we want to be careful to have a good balance of share times when lots of students are talking, as well as ones like this where only a student or two is responsible for the talking. Our old traditional selves will sometimes pull at us to do share times like this one more often because we really prefer to have only one student talking at a time, so we have to watch out for that.

So there we have it: four routines for talk that can be used again and again in so many different ways to fill the writing workshop with productive talk and active listening. It is probably important to mention at this point that these routines are not the only routines possible; they are simply four that I have found to be useful in many different settings. Like so many other things about this kind of teaching, *how* you choose to structure the talk in your writing workshop is probably less important than *that* it be structured. Talk about writing needs to be an essential part of the work of writing *workshop,* and you really don't want to make up new routines for it over and over again. You'll want to find a few ways of talking that seem to work for your community of learners and stick with them the whole year. The predictable formats you create will allow for wonderful, unpredictable kinds of talk to happen.

16

The Writing Workshop Teacher's Plan Book

OK, I just have one question," a student in my teaching of writing course wrote to me recently in a weekly thinking paper. "I'm not sure how I would write lesson plans for the writing workshop. What would they look like?"

Well, if she's got only one question, that's a good one to have. What this student was coming to realize was that planning for the writing workshop was this really complex process that didn't fit very well with what she'd learned about lesson planning in her early general methods courses: six-point lesson plans, anticipatory sets, independent practice, and so on. And knowing that, as a new teacher, she would have to show evidence of her extensive planning, she was beginning to worry about what shape and form this planning would take.

As we have developed our writing workshop teaching over the years, we have had to develop alongside this teaching new ways of thinking about and enacting "lesson plans." Certainly, we can no longer fit our planning into the daily little boxes that published plan books would have us use. Whenever I see these little plan book boxes, I'm always reminded of Kate, the passionate narrator of Jean Little's book *Hey World, Here I Am!* (1990), who gives away her small pink diary with the little spaces for recording life. She gives it to her friend Lindsay Ross who, Kate says, "has a smaller life." The learning life that we plan for our students and with our students in a writing workshop is just too big to be held in such small boxes. It's not that we are against traditional lesson planning, it's just that, well, *we have bigger lives than that* in a writing workshop.

All of us, new teachers and experienced teachers alike, need to be articulate about how we plan for our teaching. When I think about this planning, I think about that wordless picture book that deals with perspective, *Zoom,* by Istvan Banyai (1995). The "gimmick" of this book is that you start out thinking you are looking at this complete picture, but then as you turn each successive page, you realize (as the camera zooms out) that you are seeing only a tiny part of a much larger picture. Each scene on each page is actually a part of something bigger that you cannot see until the "camera" pulls further away from it. The teaching we plan for in the writing workshop is a lot like this.

If we walk into a writing workshop on any given day and look at a single instance of teaching—in a focus lesson, a conference with one child or a small group, a share session, any instance of teaching—we are seeing just this tiny, very focused part of a much, much bigger picture. We would have to move farther and farther away from that one instance to really understand all the "planning" that has gone into that moment of teaching. There are so many layers of thinking that go into planning for the writing workshop. And, truly, we can't make any one of the small moments of teaching matter that much, regardless of how well-made our plan is, if we don't pull back that camera and start with the biggest picture of all, then work our way in. With our planning, we have to start at the end of Mr. Banyai's book *Zoom* and work our way to the front, from the biggest to the smallest plans of all, some of the best of them being made almost at the moment we enact them.

So let's do some of that now. Let's start with the biggest picture of all and work our way forward. And all along the way, let's think about what we need to have "to show for" this planning so that those outside our classrooms can understand the teaching they see there. Let's think about lesson plans.

Our Orchestrating Vision

The biggest picture of all in planning is the orchestrating vision we have for our teaching of writing. In Chapter 3, Teaching and the Development of Writing Identities, I outlined for you the vision I have that guides all of my teaching of writing, and I used that vision as a frame for discussion in several subsequent chapters. There's a reason for that. This vision evolved from my answering this question: "Over time, what and how do I hope to see my students developing in the writing workshop?" This vision guides every move I make when I teach writing, both planned moves and spontaneous ones alike. This vision guides me regardless of the national, or state, or district, or school (or even one of each) curriculum guides I am responsible for in my teaching. This vision represents my most essential beliefs about teaching writing and about what it means to write, and so I have to make my other curricular responsibilities fit with it, not the other way around. And this vision guides me, regardless of the students I teach. How it manifests itself may change a great deal depending on the students I teach, but the vision itself does not. It's my bottom line.

Now, other teachers may have a different bottom line from mine in their teaching, but *there needs to be one in place.* We have to work at understanding how we want our teaching leading students' development as writers, because we can't plan anything well until we know this. And I chose that expression "work at understanding" with intention. Good teachers of writing have thought deeply, read widely, written extensively, and listened intently in order to develop the understandings they have about the teaching of writing. I think we make a mistake when we don't acknowledge this—that there is no easy road to this teaching. I suspect that if there were one, we would have a lot more company on this journey of ours.

So the first layer of planning we have to do is to decide on some kind of vision for our teaching that will guide all our decision making—all the rest of the plans we will make from day to day. We need to spell this vision out. We need to write it down and paste it in as the first entry in our planning book, and to be ready to talk to someone about it at any time when they ask us to show evidence of our planning. If we have to turn lesson plans in regularly, we should turn in a copy of this vision with the plans *every single time*. We need to let everyone know that this part of the planning is always there.

PLANNING OUR STRUCTURES AND ROUTINES

If we zoom in a little closer to the next layer, we see that there is a lot of planning we have to do simply to make the workshop work. This is not specific curriculum planning; it's planning a predictable space and time during which the curriculum work will happen. Anytime we think about management issues, we must go back to our vision for teaching and think about what kinds of time and space and supplies our students need in order to grow into the vision that we have for them.

So basically, we use our vision to plan an outline for how most every day will go in the writing workshop. The day will have these components (focus lesson, writing time, share time) that will last about this long (an hour); students will use these materials (writer's notebooks, folders, dictionaries, etc.); we will do this (confer) while students do this (write); and on and on. We plan out how we want our days with students to go in writing workshop. I guess in a way, if we think about traditional planning, the structures and routines and management we plan for and that we put in place from the start are like planning all of our "guided and independent practice" times *for the whole year*. You know that time in the lesson when students are "practicing" what we've just taught? We don't plan and replan that for every lesson. We set it up at the beginning of the year and keep it going all the time. Independent writing time is the "guided practice" time in writing workshop.

Now, we know that our workshop teaching must set students up to work independently as writers, but maybe we hadn't thought about this as part of our planning, our *daily* lesson planning. We are setting this up for the days that come, and so it is daily lesson planning. Again, then, we need to spell this part of our planning out (how our days will go and how the room will work), write it down, paste it in our plan books, and turn it in anytime (and every time) someone wants to see our planning. If there is any day when we decide to break our routine, we will note this in our more specific plans. Otherwise, our daily structures and routines represent the specific "flow" we have planned for the "lesson" for the next 180 days.

Planning for Units of Study

Once we have our orchestrating vision and the structures and routines for the workshop planned, the next layer of planning is to decide on the units of study we will have during the year. Chapter 12 outlined possibilities for units of study that would support students' development as writers (in the context, once again, of our vision), and it suggested ways we might decide which studies we will undertake. As noted in that chapter, we probably don't want to plan out a whole year's worth of studies before we get to know our students. We'll leave some room to plan studies that our particular group of writers (that particular year) would be interested in studying.

So knowing that we don't want to map out the whole year, we still must begin planning in some specific ways. If someone were to come to us before the school year started, we should probably be able to answer these questions, for example:

- What unit of study in writing will you start the year with? How long do you think it will take? Where do you think you will most likely go after that with the next unit of study? How long do you think it will take?

  Note: Since we won't know our students at first, we will need to go ahead and plan how we will get started.

- What are some units of study you want to plan during the year? How long do you anticipate each of these studies being?

  Note: Again, we don't need to know when and where every one of these studies will fall, but we should have some idea of what they might be.

- When will you be studying narrative writing? (Fill in that blank with any kind of writing students will be tested on.)

  Note: A genre study of the type of writing students will be tested on is a responsible teaching decision. It should, however, be a *real genre study* of a type of writing (like any other in the writing workshop) and not a time to do practice tests and prompt writing. We can do that in a specific study of testing.

As with the previous two layers of planning, our answers to these questions should be spelled out, written down, and included as a document we update periodically in our plan books as we make more specific decisions. We can think of it as a "curriculum calendar," as my friend Isoke Nia calls it. We need to go ahead and think through time issues—how long we want to spend in different studies. Even though our estimates of how long something will take are sure to be off a lot of the time, it helps to think them through so we can plan for breadth in our studies across the year. We might call this document in our plan book "Planning across the Year," and we'll need to look at it often, always thinking, "Where does it make sense for us to go next in our studies?"

We should let any outside person who is interested in how we are planning know about what thinking we are doing as we make these year-long plans and decide where to go next in our teaching. We should have some kind of year-long outline of possibilities sketched out and pasted into the plan book. Beside each unit of study on the year-long outline, we should state specifically which part(s) of our curricular vision this study will be supporting. For example, if I were to have an author study of Patricia MacLachlan planned for March, it might look like this on my curriculum calendar entry:

March	***Author Study: Patricia MacLachlan***
	Main Objectives: To help students develop . . . • a sense of self as writers and personal writing processes that work for them; • ways of reading the world like writers, collecting ideas with variety, volume, and thoughtfulness; • ways of reading texts like writers, developing a sense of craft, genre, and form in writing.

In an author study, these are the parts of my curricular vision that I emphasize. Using the author under study as a writing mentor, we study her writing process, her ways of living in the world as a writer, and the particular crafting techniques she uses to write well. Most studies we plan will have "objective overlap" like this, meaning that we see an opportunity in the study to emphasize several parts of our curricular vision. And because of the dynamic nature of a unit of study, objectives that we haven't spelled out in our preliminary planning will often come up as well. For example, we may read about MacLachlan being a part of a writing group that meets routinely, and learn how she and the other group members give each other feedback on drafts. This knowledge will help my students develop their sense of what it means to be "members of a responsive, literate community," which is an important curriculum objective even though it is not one of the guiding objectives for the study.

We're zooming in closer. Once we have decided on the unit of study we will undertake in our workshop and on the guiding objectives for that study, then we begin to plan specifically with that study in mind. Let's think about that next.

Planning and Developing Curriculum for a Unit of Study

Remember that units of study deal with writing curriculum that is big enough and deep enough for students to be learning about this curriculum their whole lives. We cannot expect to "explain revision" in a single lesson, for example, or even expect to "cover it all" in a single unit of study on how writers really go at revision. We need to remember that our students will be learning about revision—and all the curriculum of writing—throughout their whole lives. So in a unit of study, we take what we know about writing, we take what we know about our students, and we plan a series of lessons that get students thinking about this area of writing in important ways. We go into the study knowing we will eventually leave it with the doors still wide open for students to learn more, but we have already made peace with this. "Coverage" just doesn't work as a concept for writing curriculum. "Depth" is the word we need in order to help us plan. We'll go deep, staying down as long as we can, but eventually we'll have to come back up for air.

We'll begin planning for a specific unit of study by gathering curriculum resources around the topic of the study. We will use many of the same resources we have made available to students in our workshop (see Chapter 9) in order to build up our curriculum knowledge for a unit of study. Basically, writing workshop teachers will be finding the curriculum they need for any unit of study—the content for the lessons they plan to teach, and the conferences they anticipate having—from the same kinds of sources they use to help them get smart about writing (Chapter 10):

WRITERS' VOICES ON . . .

revisiting the troubling issues of writing

So one thing I've learned to do is handle time, which is a very difficult thing to do. The other thing, writing this book [*Beach Music*], I've become much more comfortable with third person. Nan [editor at Doubleday] made me write this one in third person.

. . . But she had a point when I wrote the first couple of chapters. She thought the first person with me would always sound like Tom Wingo. And she said, "You've got to suppress that voice for a while." And I thought she was right. So these two thousand pages are all in third person. (Pat Conroy, in Dannye Romine Powell, *Parting the Curtains,* 74)

We should share with our students that writers, even very successful, proficient ones like Pat Conroy, are continuously learning their craft. One of our roles as teachers in writing classrooms is to help students learn to know themselves as writers. To know what they are especially good at and what they might need help with. As teachers, we provide them with instruction to guide that growth and to lead them to self-awareness.

Pat Conroy is aware of his strengths:

Dialogue is pretty easy for me. I thought they were giving me money for nothing when I started writing screenplays. I could write dia- ➤

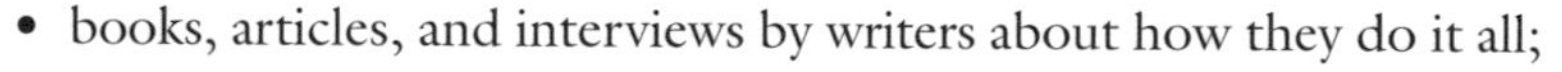

- books, articles, and interviews by writers about how they do it all;
- professional books, journals, and courses on the teaching of writing that offer lots of curriculum;
- personal writing experiences, and the experiences of former students;
- model texts (found from real-world writing) that are like the kind of writing they want their students to do;
- conversations with other teachers of writing;
- handbooks on writing style and convention;
- curriculum guides that accompany "writing programs" and textbooks. (Yes, used with a watchful eye and a *solid background in all the resources listed here,* a good teacher of writing can use these manuals for curriculum support.)

Many of the really good teachers I know keep curriculum notebooks or files of things such as quotes from writers, examples of writing, strategy ideas, and so on, organized by how they relate to various aspects of the writing life and writing process. When we first start teaching writing in this way, we just

> logue all day long. Give me a character. What do they like? I can tell you what they'll buy at the grocery store. The hard part for me is narrative. And that's what I suffer over, and that's what's difficult for me. (76)

As a writer, Pat Conroy also knows where he could use some help:

> I thought it [writing in third person] would teach me about point of view, but it didn't. I'm one of those novelists that you could explain what point of view is and I can't quite get it. My IQ does not go up that far. I've read everything anybody's written about point of view. It's still a mystery to me. . . . Here's what I understand: I was there. I saw it. This is what I'm saying about it, and this is what I'm thinking about it, and if you don't like it you can kiss by behind. I understand that point of view. It's when you got into these little things—Eddie Fluffalo gets his version, and Betty Fluffalo gets her version—then I get very confused by all that. (74–76)

There will be those things we teach over and over. There will be those students who need it again, whatever "it" may be. For Pat Conroy, "it" is point of view. Our students will have their own "its." As teachers we should not be frustrated with our teaching when it's clear our students need to revisit the big ideas of writing again and again.

Powell, Dannye Romine. 1995. *Parting the Curtains: Voices of the Great Southern Writers.* New York: Anchor Books.

have to spend lots of time doing our curriculum homework. With experience, we'll have lots more to pull from, but at the beginning, it's just a lot of work. The best thing to do is to find one or two good resources that can "get us through" the first time around: Georgia Heard's *For the Good of the Earth and Sun* (1989) in a poetry genre study, for example, or Donald Murray's *Shoptalk: Learning to Write with Writers* (1990) for a study on, well, anything. It's full of writers' quotes on all parts of the writing process.

The collection of "stuff" from which we pull curriculum in a unit of study is the next (very important) part of our planning document. At the beginning of a unit of study, we can take an inventory of what resources we have to support the study and then make a list of these that is pasted in the plan book. And why is a list of curriculum resources evidence of *planning*? Because we know we will need them. Because we know we can't plan ahead for all that will specifically come up in our students' writing work that is related to this study. Their work is too dynamic, too complex, to know exactly what we will need for the whole study. We *anticipate* our need for back-up curriculum resources, and so we have *planned* to have them ready when we need them. When we show our planning to an outside person, we need to be ready to explain how we will be using these resources to guide our teaching in the unit of study.

DETERMINING SCOPE AND SEQUENCE IN A UNIT OF STUDY

OK. This is a really hard part of planning: "Which lessons do I do and in what order?" We know that during a unit of study, all of the focus lessons and sharing times and many of the individual conferences relate in some way to the topic under study. With most writing curriculum, though, there is not a "scoped and sequenced" way that makes sense as an order or as an organization for the focus lessons. Sometimes there are places where it makes better sense to begin a study—often several of these places—but where we go next will have a lot to do with what we see our students understanding along the way and what we are learning along the way to support them.

Take, for example, a unit of study on learning to live the writing life. On our curriculum calendar, the study might look like this:

September	***Learning to Live the Writing Life***
	Main Objectives: To help students develop . . . • ways of reading the world like writers, collecting ideas with variety, volume, and thoughtfulness; • a sense of thoughtful, deliberate purpose about their work as writers, and a willingness to linger with those purposes.

In the four weeks of this study, we will plan and teach approximately twenty focus lessons on this topic of *learning to live the writing life*. Now, in our curriculum gathering for this study, we may have found thirty different notebook strategies that students could learn to use, and we may have a whole collection of over fifty quotes from writers about how they live their writing lives. Where will we start? We have to choose somewhere to start from all that we know, and we need to remember that we will most likely not use all we know in focus lessons during this unit of study. We may use more of it in conferences, but the focus lessons will represent just a selection of what we know. Our goal is to put together, over time, a series of lessons on the topic that "go deep" and ones that leave students with some important new understandings about this area of the writing life and the writing process that we are nurturing. The art of our teaching is in the selection of lessons we choose to do in any unit of study.

We need to plan for several of the focus lessons before the study even begins. We'll draw from what we know about the topic and use resources like those outlined above to help us plan these first lessons based on what we think would really get the topic going well in the room. In many studies, there is no one logical place to start (in terms of scope and sequence). A study of how authors revise their writing, for example, has no logical starting place. We might start right off with a strategy for revision, or we might start with a lesson that uses a metaphor to help students begin understanding what revision is. In most any study, I *like* to start with a few lessons that bring authors' voices into the room, so I'd be likely to start a revision study with focus lessons that share great quotes on revision from famous writers. But I'm starting there because I'd like to start there, not because that's a *beginning* place inherent to the study of revision.

Lots of writing study will be this way, without clear beginning, middle, and ending places in terms of content. We just have to choose somewhere to start and then keep choosing the next logical place to go. And how do we know what the next logical place is? We make this decision based on several combined factors. We can ask ourselves these kinds of questions as we decide what our next lessons will be:

- Is there another way to approach the content of today's lesson that would deepen or extend students' understanding?

  For example, in a study of peer conferring, it might be better to have several lessons in a row on just what kinds of questions to ask a peer, rather than one lesson on questions to ask, then one on making eye contact in a conference, then one on giving good feedback.

- From my conferring, what do I see that my students are understanding so far? What do they still have questions about?

  For example, in a study of revision techniques, I see that students are still thinking of revision as looking only for parts that need "fixing." So I decide to go back to the idea of revision as playing around with draft possibilities and teach several more lessons on this.

- What content would really match and support the work of these particular students?

  For example, during a study of how writers use punctuation marks to support and enhance meaning in their texts, I might decide to slow down and use several focus lessons just to look at alternatives for punctuating dialogue, because I have a lot of students who are writing stories filled with dialogue.

- What could I teach students in this study that is just really cool stuff?

  Don't ever leave out the cool stuff—always plan to get it in. For example, I once read an interview with a writer of horror fiction who said he would frequently take his notebook to unusual places—like underneath the dark stairs of his building—and write there just to get the feeling of places that are kind of creepy. I *always* teach this lesson in a study of ways to get material for writing fiction. It's just a cool idea.

- How much time do I have left in the study? How many more lessons can I teach?

  We always have to keep this question in mind as we are selecting from all we know in order to plan our next focus lessons in a study. Remember, it's likely that we won't teach all the things we know about a topic, so from all we know, "What would make the most sense for the time we have left?"

So the ongoing planning during a unit of study is an intricate weaving of planning ahead and planning in process, based on what we see happening in the room. Our plan book, then, will have the outline of a few daily lesson plans written down (discussed later), and then open spaces for the plans that we will make during the study. We need to be able to explain why there are open spaces there. We should help anyone who is interested in our planning to understand why we are waiting to see what happens on Monday and Tuesday and Wednesday before we decide exactly what we will teach on Thursday and Friday. We must be very articulate about this—about how we are planning in process based on what we see our students doing and understanding. We can share the frame that we use for thinking this through (outlined above), and we can show the list of curriculum resources that we are pulling from in order to let outsiders know that we have some idea of where we might be on those days, but that we are waiting to see what makes the most sense to teach at that time.

Planning in process is *very good teaching* that responds directly to the learning that's happening in the room. But this kind of planning is a challenge to the more traditional notion that the best teachers can tell you exactly what they will be doing, say, next Thursday at 1:20 PM. This is why it is important to show anyone interested in our planning all the layers of thinking we are doing that will take us to next Thursday at 1:20 PM, at which time we will know exactly what it is we are doing, and we will have a very, very good reason for why we are doing it: because it has grown out of what's been happening in the room.

Scope and Sequence of Genre and Author Studies

In at least two kinds of studies, however, there really are logical starting and moving-forward places in the organization of the curriculum we offer. In genre studies and author studies, there is often a "process-to-product" nature to the curriculum that can help us organize and order our lessons. For example, in any genre or author study, it has always made sense to me to start my series of focus lessons with ideas about how to live *this* kind of writing life. So at the beginning of the study, I teach lessons that help students think about these kinds of questions:

> How does a poet (or a memoirist, or fiction writer, or Gary Paulsen . . .) keep a notebook?
>
> Where does a poet (or a memoirist, or a fiction writer, or Gary Paulsen . . .) get ideas?
>
> How does a poet (or a memoirist, or a fiction writer, or Gary Paulsen . . .) live a writing life?

In other words, early in the study, as my students are immersing themselves in reading the genre or in reading works by the specific author during independent writing time, I'm using my focus lessons to get them thinking about the lives and the writing processes behind either the genre or the writer's life whose works they are reading. In a way, then, I start genre and author studies by looking at issues of *prewriting*.

As the study moves on, I plan lessons and inquiries that look at how to do this specific kind of writing well (if it's genre study), or how this writer uses crafting techniques to write well (if it's an author study). This plan supports students as they are drafting writing projects in the genre or under the influence of the author (Figure 16.1). Still later in the study, I plan lessons that look at how writers of this genre—or how this writer specifically—engages in revision. So in this way, the "scope and sequence" of focus lessons in genre and author studies can be roughly outlined to support students through the writing process. Knowing that I can plan these studies in this

FIGURE 16.1 A Frame for Organizing Genre and Author Studies

GENRE STUDY

Early in the study . . .

Focus lessons

- Looking at poets' (fiction writers', memorists', editorialists', etc.) *writing lives.* Helping students imagine possibilities for living this kind of writing life.
- Thinking about notebook work for this kind of writing.
- Helping students position themselves in relation to this genre: their reading and writing history with it, their existing knowledge, what they are beginning to see in their immersion, etc.

Independent writing

- Immersing students in reading the genre—both examples I have found and ones they are finding.
- Filling notebooks with material for this kind of writing and searching old notebooks for material possibilities.

Share time

- Sharing examples of the genre we like.
- Sharing ideas for how to use notebooks for this kind of writing.

Homework

- Living in the world with the notebook as a writer of this genre.
- Searching the world for more examples of the genre.

Middle of the study . . .

Focus lessons

- Setting up specific inquiries for our touchstone texts in the genre. Some of these will deal more generally with craft, such as ways with words or text structures, and some of them will be very genre-specific, such as looking at white space in poetry or where the point of argument comes in an editorial.

AUTHOR STUDY

Early in the study . . .

Focus lessons

- Looking at Cynthia Rylant's (Jacqueline Woodson's, Gary Paulsen's, etc.) *writing life.* Helping students imagine possibilities for their own writing lives from looking closely at this one author.
- Finding out or hypothesizing about how this author keeps a notebook.
- Helping students position themselves in relation to this author—their reading and writing history with the author, their existing knowledge of this author's work, what they are seeing in their immersion, etc.

Independent writing

- Immersing students in reading a wide variety of works by this author.
- Under the influence of this author, students will eventually draft projects in various genres. So at this point they are writing independently in notebooks toward a project of their choosing.

Share time

- Reading aloud favorite parts and sharing from what we find in the author's texts that we like.

Homework

- Living in the world with the notebook as we know or imagine this author to live.

Middle of the study . . .

Focus lessons

- Setting up specific inquiries of this author's texts. The range of what we might look at here is broad, depending on the author. We might study a few texts specifically for craft, look at leads or endings across many texts, study passages of description in a single text, etc.

FIGURE 16.1 (continued)

GENRE STUDY

Middle of the study, cont. . . .

Independent writing

- Using some of this time to do the specific inquiry into this kind of writing (set up in the minilessons).
- Continuing to develop notebook material for a specific seed idea that will be written in this genre.
- Beginning to use the notebook as a toolbox to try out some things we are seeing as we study the genre closely.

Share time

- Discussing the things we are finding as we closely study examples of the genre during independent writing time.
- Sharing things we are trying in the notebook "toolbox" for honing the craft of this genre.

Homework

- Doing any "world work" we need to do for the seed ideas we're developing.

Having a go . . .

Focus lessons

- Showing specific techniques (that haven't come up in inquiry) for writing well in the genre.
- Sharing what writers in the genre have to say about drafting and revision.

Independent writing

- Drafting and revising a writing project(s) in the genre under study.

Share time

- Sharing parts of drafts and helping each other with revision possibilities (that we have learned in the genre study).
- Sharing specific things we are trying (that we have learned from our study) as we draft.

Homework

- Getting feedback on drafts from readers outside our class.
- Continuing any "world work" that needs to be done in support of the project.
- Beginning to use the notebook as a toolbox to try out some things we are seeing as we study this author's work.

AUTHOR STUDY

Middle of the study, cont. . . .

Independent writing

- Using some of this time to do the specific inquiry into this kind of writing (set up in the mini lessons).
- Continuing to develop notebook material for a chosen seed idea (in any genre) that will be written under the influence of this author.

Share time

- Discussing the things we are finding as we closely study this author's work during independent writing time.
- Sharing things we have learned from this author that we are trying in the notebook "toolbox."

Homework

- Doing any "world work" we need to do for the seed ideas we're developing.

Having a go . . .

Focus lessons

- Showing specific techniques (that haven't come up in inquiry) this author uses to write well.
- Sharing what this writer has to say about drafting and revision.

Independent writing

- Drafting and revising projects (in different genres) under the influence of this author.

Sharing time

- Sharing parts of drafts and helping each other with revision possibilities (that we have learned from the author).
- Sharing specific things (from the author) we are trying as we draft.

Homework

- Getting feedback on drafts from readers outside our class.
- Continuing any "world work" that needs to be done in support of the project.

way helps me get started with the first few lessons, and it helps me keep the study moving forward with time. I will still use the in-process planning described above: watching students' writing and their inquiry to see which lessons make the most sense to teach. It's just that the nature of these studies gives me an overall frame for organizing as I move along in my planning.

PLANNING DAILY LESSONS

Regardless of the unit of study, we know that a "day" in the writing workshop is going to consist of three predictably structured components: the focus lesson, independent writing time, and share time. So in one sense, we don't have to plan for these to happen. They are there every day and have already been pasted into the plan book as structures and routines. Most of the materials that students and that we need for these three components of the day are already available in the room, and all of the management for students working in these three components of the day is already firmly in place. This takes a huge planning burden off of us because we don't have to "reinvent the room" every day or spell out how different work will go on through every bit of time devoted to instruction.

However, because there is instruction that will happen during each component of the writing workshop, there must be some planning for that instruction. As a matter of fact, the three components can serve as a nice plan book organizer. Some writing workshop teachers organize their daily lesson plans in this way each day (focus lesson, independent writing time, share time), and they have planning notes for each of these.

Date:
Focus Lesson:

Independent Writing Time:

Share Time:

As you might imagine, the detail of the notes varies from day to day and from component to component (the focus lesson obviously requiring more specific planning than the other components), but good teachers spend some time thinking about each one, each day of the writing workshop. They use their lesson planning to help them get an image of how that teaching day needs to go. So let's look at daily lesson planning now at those three levels.

Focus Lessons

When I write down a plan for a focus lesson, I simply make notes about it. I begin by saying in a nutshell what the specific objective and content of the lesson will be, then I make notes about how it will go. If you look back at the beginning of Chapter 13, you will see the text of an actual focus lesson I did in a poetry genre study. The plans for that lesson looked like this in my planning document:

July 13	***Focus Lesson: Strategy for Looking for Poems in Notebook Material ("Found Poems")***
	• Look for entries that have vivid images in them—words that sound like poetry. • Use my notebook entry on my overalls in the dryer to show how to do this, and explain it. • Be sure to emphasize that this is not an entry where I was trying to write something poetic—I just found poetry material in it. • Maybe mention Douglas' entries on camp as an example of a good place to start looking for found poems. • Ask them to spend some of their writing time looking to see what they've got in entries that might be used for poem drafts.

In my plans for this day, this is exactly what I had written. My lesson plans are just for me. I write whatever notes I need in order to think through the lesson in my head before I teach it. Now, there are two things to know about that. One is, I have a lot of experience teaching focus lessons, and the language and flow of the lessons comes very naturally to me now. I *used to* write more notes of things to remember in a lesson when I had less experience with this teaching. The key is to make enough notes so that they give you the confidence you need in order to teach the lesson—so that they give you a feeling that you know exactly what you are going to say. Remember, you will be doing most of the talking, and you need to think that talking through. When you are inexperienced in writing workshop teaching, you may want to try looking over your notes and then actually role-play teaching the lesson. See how it goes. If you need more reminders, put them in.

The second thing to think about is this. I didn't have anyone checking these lesson plans, but if that were required in my teaching situation, I could certainly add to the plan if other information were requested. I know more about this lesson, in other words, than I've written down. For example, I could write out a rationale for the lesson that would explain why I am teaching it at this point. If I did, it would go something like this:

> I've noticed that students seem to think that they have to set out to "write poems" to begin a draft for a poem. This lesson is to help them realize that there are other ways to begin the draft of a poem, namely, to look for material that's already in the notebook that is poetry-like.

Regardless of whether I have to write this out as part of my plan or not, I should be able to explain it to someone who is interested in my teaching. It might be that I am required to have a list of materials for the lesson. If that's true, then I would need to write into this plan that I need "my writer's notebook." That's all for this one. Sometimes it helps to do that even if it's not required so that you are sure to have what you need before you start the lesson. There is nothing worse than a lesson that gets underway and then the teacher has to get up to go find something he or she forgot that is needed for the teaching. The point is, I can write out as much as I need to write in order to meet the planning requirements of my school. If what I write for plans is left up to me, I write only what I need to write that will help me teach the lesson well and that will provide a good record of the teaching I am doing during the study.

Now, I have heard some administrators say that a teacher's daily lesson plans should be written in enough detail that someone else could come in and teach the lesson if the teacher were absent. To this I say, "Poppycock." I would have to write a whole book to explain what someone would need to know to teach most of my writing lessons. I don't think just any warm body off the street—or even a very experienced substitute teacher for that matter—can just walk into my writing workshop and teach the focus lesson I would teach if I were there. The teaching that happens in the workshop is a very personal interaction between my students and me. Any single focus lesson is part of a months-long ongoing conversation about writing between me and my students that a substitute just can't jump in and join in a day in any meaningful way. For the curriculum explanations offered in focus lessons to make sense, the teacher must have a very solid understanding of the content, and quite frankly, I know that many people don't have the proper training in writing to teach lessons in the workshop. The bottom line is, the teaching we do in a writing workshop is just way too sophisticated, way too complex, to think that anyone can just step in and "do the lesson" in our place.

So how do we keep ourselves responsible for plans to cover us when we are out unexpectedly? My suggestion would be to have anywhere from one to as much as a week's worth of lesson plans written that a substitute teacher could enact in our absence at any time during the year. You may have him or her work with students on some things you think would be easy to handle, or you may simply plan for the independent writing time to happen with no focus lessons in your absence. Either way, it likely means there will be an interruption of the unit of study, but that is just a necessary part of doing this highly sophisticated kind of teaching. Your students can continue to grow as writers by carrying on with their own projects until you get back. If your absence is one you know about and can plan ahead for, then you might have a student or two assigned to do the focus lesson for you from some of their individual work in the unit of study.

Independent Writing Time

I plan, every single day, to have writing conferences during the time that students are writing independently. If someone wants to see my planning, I can include copies of my conference records with open spaces on them that show where I *plan* to write notes from the conferences that I will have during the week. The empty boxes themselves show that I am planning to have these conferences.

In addition to this, however, I often have some idea of what kinds of conferences I want to have with students on a given day. When this is the case, I make a note in my daily plans to focus my conferences on a certain topic or question. For example, on July 13 when I taught the lesson on "found poetry," I made this note for independent writing time: "Continue to find out how students are starting drafts of poems." This was something that I had been investigating for several days; In fact, this lesson came from what I was finding out as I talked to students about their drafts. I wanted to continue to look at their drafting processes on this day in my conferring, so I noted it both as a plan for the day and a record for the day. So if there is any particular thing we want to be working on with the class in individual conferences, we make a note of this in our lesson plans under the heading "independent writing time." If we aren't working on anything specific to the class, then we simply write, "conferences on topics as needed."

I also note in my plans for independent writing time any specific things other than the routine carrying-on with writing projects that students will be doing. For example, early on in a genre study I will have several days' worth of plans for independent writing time where I have noted, "Continue reading immersion." This means I need to have the texts available and that students will spend some of the writing time reading examples of the genre under study. If, in the focus lesson, I ask for students to think about something or to do something during their independent writing time, as I did in the July 13 lesson when I asked them to search their entries for poetry possibilities, I also make a note of this in my plans under independent writing time. Now, I don't have to have a plan for anything other than working on writing in general in this space, and many days I won't have anything but that, but I'm sure to note it if there is something I envision students doing during this time in addition to their routine work.

Share Time

Share time is a little trickier in terms of planning. I always know we will have this time in the workshop when we come together to just talk about what we're doing, but the truth is, I don't always decide ahead of time what we'll talk about. *Sometimes* I know ahead of time, and when I do, I write this into my plans. For example, on the day I taught the poetry focus lesson, I knew that I was going to have students talk with their partners during share time about what they had found as they searched their notebook entries for poetry possibilities. So underneath "share time" in my plans, I made a note of this intention.

A lot of times, though, I base what we talk about during share time on what has happened during independent writing time. I might use share time to report on an interesting conference or two from the day's work. Or if students have seemed really into their writing, I might decide to lengthen writing time a little and then have a quick survey share from "a line you wrote today that surprised you." The truth is, I like for there to be some spontaneity to this part of the workshop, so I often "plan" it right on the spot, or at the last minute I change what I had planned for us to share because something else seems more logical or more important based on what has happened that day. Personally, I think leaving some room to decide this is good teaching. It's teaching that is in response to what happens in the room. Now, this is where having a few predictable structures in place for share time really helps (as described in Chapter 15). When students know *how* to share, it means we can make an on-the-spot decision about *what* to share because we don't have to think through all that how-to stuff.

So, we may have a definite note written down ahead of time in our plans of what we want students to share that day; we may have several possibilities noted down, or we may simply have the space there showing we plan to share but that we will decide what to share when we get there. If we do it this last way, we need to be sure to go back and make a note of what we did during share time, since lesson plans are also important records of our teaching.

Using Reflections in Future Planning

The final layer of lesson planning is to look over the plan after the writing workshop is complete and write any notes of reflection or observation that seem important to remember or that might help as we make future plans. We should already have notes from all our conferences for that day, so really we are just thinking back on the focus lesson and the share time, as well as any observations outside of conferences we might have made during independent writing time. Some kinds of things we might note in these reflections include:

- students' verbal and nonverbal responses to the focus lesson;
- our own feelings about how well we communicated in the focus lesson;
- ideas for what we might have said but didn't say;
- observations of students' engagement in independent work;
- questions or insights we have about the impact of the lesson in students' work;
- notes on interesting things that came up or that we noticed during the share time—we want to try to capture the richness of this talk in our reflective notes.

I mostly leave wide-open margins around my word-processed lesson plans so that I can add layers of handwritten reflections whenever I need them. In many ways, our reflections on our teaching are also planning. We look back because it helps us look forward more thoughtfully. We must be sure that anyone interested in our planning understands how it is we use our reflections from one lesson to help us plan future lessons.

Creating a Planning Document

What it all boils down to is this: Planning for the writing workshop is a sophisticated, complex web of planning that has a number of different layers to it. Anyone interested in our planning needs to be shown *all of these* layers to get a clear picture of how we are planning for our teaching. To summarize, then, our planning document could have the following things in it:

- a list of the orchestrating vision for our teaching—our overall objectives for everything we plan in the writing workshop;
- an outline of the structures and routines that manage the daily work in the workshop;
- a calendar outline of units of study that we are planning throughout the school year;

- a list of curriculum resources that we are using to support the current unit of study in the workshop;
- a few days' worth of daily lesson plans in the unit of study, including plans for the focus lesson, independent writing time, and share time;
- a sheet for recording individual conferences that we are planning to have;
- reflections on the teaching in each day's workshop.

Perhaps more important than anything we will ever write as lesson plans, however, is our ability to be articulate about how we are planning for our teaching. This will not only help us explain ourselves better to others, but also help all our teaching moves be better when we have a good sense of what we are doing and why we are doing it. Time spent planning and thinking about how we want our teaching to go is never wasted time. It is the most worthwhile investment in excellent teaching we can make.

References

Banyai, Istvan. 1995. *Zoom!* New York: Viking.

Heard, Georgia. 1989. *For the Good of the Earth and Sun: Teaching Poetry.* Portsmouth, N.H.: Heinemann.

Little, Jean. 1990. *Hey World, Here I Am!* New York: Harper Trophy.

Murray, Donald M. 1990. *Shoptalk: Learning to Write with Writers.* Portsmouth, N.H.: Heinemann.

17

Assessment and Evaluation: The Questions Become the Curriculum

Teachers ask a lot of questions. They always have. And it's no different in the writing workshop. What is different, however, are the kinds of questions teachers ask and the ways in which they ask them. Because questioning itself is so much a part of how we assess and evaluate in any situation, it seems wise to start simply by thinking about how we use questions in workshop teaching.

Traditionally, teachers have spent most of their time during the day asking students questions that they (the teachers) already know the answers to: "What is the first stage of mitosis?" or "What's 3 × 7?" or "What do we need to do when we start a new sentence?" These are either drill-and-practice kinds of questions or testing-your-knowledge kinds of questions, and they aren't used much in the real world outside of school—except by adults interacting with young children. Most of us don't waste time asking other people questions that we already know the answers to, just to see if they know, but this has long been the accepted norm of questioning in traditional classrooms.

Most of the questions that teachers ask students in writing workshops, however, are not questions the teachers can answer themselves. Why? Well, it's because we writing teachers like to ask our students very *personal* questions, for lack of a better expression. We like to poke around underneath their "skins as writers" and see what's happening on the inside of their writing lives. And it's not because we're nosy, either. You see, in the workshop, we question students as *writers* because we expect them to be the kinds of people who would have answers to these questions. They are writing every day, after all. And it is this expectation behind our questions that teaches students, over time, one of the most powerful lessons of the workshop. Questioning students as writers teaches *them* to think of *themselves* as people who are supposed to have answers to these questions.

Think about it this way. In the world outside of school, when we have a real question we need answered, we find someone to ask who, we think, is the kind of person who would have an answer to that question. There are certain people we ask about our cars if they are giving us trouble, and other people we would never ask about our cars because we just don't see them as being the kinds of people who know about cars. We know people we will ask about gardening, other people we'll ask about restaurants, and still others we will ask about dating problems. Before we ask an important question, we think to ourselves, "Who should I ask about this?"

Likewise, if someone *asks me* a question, it may be obvious why he or she is asking me this particular question, such as someone asking me about writing or about a good book I've read lately. They see me as the kind of person who would have answers to those kinds of questions. But we may also be asked questions from time to time that make us think (or even respond), "Now why is she asking *me* that question? I don't know one thing about that." Interestingly enough, many students in writing workshops seem to be thinking that too the first time they are approached with questions. Over time, though, if people keep asking me this same kind of question, I start to think, "Maybe I am supposed to have an answer to this." And our students will too.

For example, the first time someone asks a student, "What genre do you think you write best in?" the student sort of mumbles, "I don't know." But if you come back the next day, or maybe the next week, or the week after that and you keep asking, before long he tentatively responds, "I don't know. Maybe fiction? I'm kind of good at stories." You have questioned the student into believing he has an answer to this, and when you get behind this answer, the student is able to build an identity for himself around his answer.

You see, the questions people ask us tell us a lot about what those people think of us, how they see us. Teachers of writing recognize this as a very powerful teaching tool in the writing workshop. They see that the questions they ask students are important to the building of identities, the building of "I am someone who writes." They believe students into being writers by asking the right kinds of questions, over and over. And what an honor for a nine- or ten-year-old student to be asked a question that, really, no one else in the whole world can answer but *her:* "What new things are you trying as a writer?" When her teacher seems genuinely interested in the answer and the student knows she is the only one who can give that answer, it gives that young student a real feeling of control, of ownership, of empowerment—all those big jargon words that basically mean, "I feel *good* about that interaction."

In an important way, then, the questions we ask students in the writing workshop are both assessment and curriculum. They are assessment because they provide us with critical information about how writing is going for our students. But they are also curriculum because the questions themselves teach students important ways to think about their writing and about themselves as writers. Our questions show students very clearly what we value in their work as writers, and they model ways in which we hope students will learn to talk among themselves as writers. We use talk, and particularly questions, in the writing workshop to help students join our literacy clubs, as Frank Smith would say. Once we realize how important teacher questions are both to assessment and to curriculum in the writing workshop, we realize the need to really think about the kinds of things we are asking children about in our teaching. When I think, overall, about the kinds of questions we ask in a writing workshop, I see basically three kinds of questions that get asked: questions of history, questions of action, and questions of process.

QUESTIONS OF HISTORY, ACTION, AND PROCESS

Questions of history are timeline questions. They ask students to think about where they have been as writers, where they are now, and where they are going, often all in relation to each other. "Out of all the writing you've ever done, how is this piece similar? How is it different?" would be questions of history. We ask students questions like these because we want them to think about their own growth as writers on a timeline of growth, to see how some things become easier over time and how others are still hard. Thinking of themselves historically as writers is also important in helping students manage their futures, in knowing what things they need to try and where they need to go next with their writing.

Questions of action simply ask writers about the kinds of things they are doing to support their writing lives, the actions they are taking as writers, such as, "Where have you taken your notebook lately to gather entries?" If we expect them to be active in their writing lives, then we need to ask them again and again about what active things they are doing. Often the phrasing of these questions is very specific. Notice that the question above states a specific action—"Where have you been taking your notebook?"—rather than just "What have you been doing with your notebook?" We can choose to ask about very specific actions when we want to emphasize that we expect students to be doing these things as writers.

Questions of process ask students about the specific processes they use to take ideas through to publication. "What decisions did you make as you were drafting?" is a process question. Like all the others, these questions teach students what we expect from their involvement in the writing process. We expect them to be making decisions along the way, so we ask them about these decisions.

Sometimes a question overlaps these three kinds of thinking. "What format are you planning to use to present this to your audience?" is both a question of process and a question of history because it has that timeline element—asking the student to think about the future by asking him or her to think about planning. Some of the best questions we ask will cause students to reflect on their work in more than one way. What is important as we think about the questions we ask, however, is simply that we are having students think about their work in all of these ways on a regular basis.

If our questions are intended to help lead students' development as writers, then to think about questioning, we need to return once again to the ways in which we hope to see students growing in our workshops. Let's look at some examples of questions that would help students think about themselves as writers in each of the growth areas we hope to see. In each area, we should see questions of history, action, and process, as well as some questions that overlap all three.

Over time in a writing workshop we hope to see writers developing . . .

A sense of self as writers, as well as personal writing processes that work for them

- Out of all the writing you've done, how is this piece similar? How is it different?
- Tell me about yourself as a writer.
- Tell me how you went about writing this piece. What was your process?
- What new things are you trying as a writer?
- What would you say you do best as a writer right now?
- What genre do you feel most comfortable with as a writer?

Ways of reading the world like writers, collecting ideas with variety, volume, and thoughtfulness

- As you look back through your notebook entries, where do you see that it has traveled away from your desk?
- How much are you writing? How often?
- What different kinds of entries are you gathering?
- What kinds of writing exercises are you trying in your writing notebook to push yourself?
- Do you have entries where you started off writing about one thing and ended up somewhere very different?
- What surprises you when you look at your notebook?

A sense of thoughtful, deliberate purpose about their writing, and a willingness to linger with these purposes

- Why are you working on this piece? How did you choose this writing project to pursue?
- What kinds of things have you done inside your notebook and outside it to get ready to write this piece?
- What are your plans for working on this over the next few days (weeks)?
- What plans do you have as a writer for later, after this piece is all finished?

As members of a responsive, literate community

- What kinds of help have you been giving other writers in the room?
- Who are you learning from in the room? What kinds of things?
- Can you think of someone who might be interested in what you're doing as a writer? Would you want to share this with that person?
- Do you have any resources that might help another writer in the room?
- What kinds of help do you need with this piece that you could ask for?

Ways of reading texts like writers, developing a sense of craft, genre, and form in writing

- Where are the places in this piece where you really tried to craft the writing?
- What decisions did you make as you were drafting this?
- Who are the published writers you're learning from? What are you learning from them that you are trying in your own writing?
- How are you going to write this? (a question of form when planning a draft)
- What kinds of things do you know about this genre that you're writing in? What examples of the genre have you studied?

A sense of audience, and an understanding of how to prepare writing to go into the world

- Who is your audience? What kind of stakes are there for this audience?
- What was your process for proofreading this? What things did you check for? What corrections did you make?
- What resources did you use to help you proofread and correct?
- Are there any proofreading things that you know you need help with?
- What format are you planning to present this in for publication (to your audience)?

Notice how, in this sampling of questions, we so clearly communicate what it is we value in the work of the writing workshop. Most all of our expectations for the workshop are represented in some form in one or more of these questions. This is why our questions are so important. They let students know what we expect them to be doing and how we expect them to be carrying on in the writing workshop.

Where Do Questions Fit in the Workshop?

Questions like these can be asked several ways. First of all, it's a good idea to introduce in focus lessons the questions we'll be asking students often; for example, "How did you choose this writing project to pursue?" or "What decisions did you make as you were drafting this?" In these lessons, we explain to students why questions like these are important ones for them to be able to answer, we show them kinds of answers other writers have had to these questions, and we let them know to expect us to be asking them these questions in the future.

Many teachers have students answer some questions like these as part of their portfolios or as some other form of self-assessment. For example, one required section of a portfolio might ask students to show examples and to explain about their work with crafting techniques over time. Another section of a portfolio might require students to show and explain a variety of notebook entries they have gathered outside the workshop. In addition to portfolio-type assessments, students might be asked to answer questions about their plans for writing on planning sheets that are turned in periodically. Many written records in the writing workshop have students answering these types of questions, both for assessment and for managing the work from day to day (see Chapter 18). Teachers use these assessments like they would any others: to plan future teaching by seeing where students need help with their ongoing writing work.

Conferring is probably the main activity in the writing workshop where questions like these are asked. Teachers sit down beside students, look them in the eyes, and ask questions such as, "Would you tell me about how you are drafting this?" Usually when a very specific question like this is asked to *begin* a conference, the teacher has in mind some particular classwide or individual curriculum agenda for that student. Probably more often in our conferences, specific questions like those shown above are used as follow-ups to the request, "Tell me about how your writing is going." We listen to the child to determine what he or she is doing just now as a writer, and then we pursue a line of questioning that makes sense based on that. We should not underestimate the power of really good questions to set the stage for powerful curriculum in our conferences, both in the teaching that comes in response to those questions and in the simple asking of the questions themselves. Remember, our questions teach students to think of themselves as writers.

Share time is the other predictable structure in the writing workshop where questions like these make sense. After a focus lesson where the teacher has offered a question for students to consider applying in their own writing lives and writing work, the share time is often used as a follow-up to that, with students talking in small groups about their answers to the question the teacher has introduced. Over the year, students may be asked to return to certain questions during share time again and again. "What new things are you trying in your writing notebook?" and "What things are you learning from mentor authors?" are two questions I like to come back to over and over as frames for share time. I know that students can learn so much from their different answers to these kinds of questions, making share time a very rich curriculum time.

From Assessment to Evaluation

So far in this chapter, we have been thinking of questions as being essential tools for reflection, assessment, and even curriculum. But what do we do when we also need to *evaluate* student work in the writing workshop? What about when we need to place a *value* on the work for grading purposes or simply in order to get students to think about the quality of the work they are doing as writers? Some of you may be like me and spend lots of your time wishing you didn't have to think about evaluation in terms of grading, but

Writers' Voices on . . .

evaluation

> . . . I believed that the ultimate purpose in writing was to be published. Since then I have become a published writer myself, and I realize how wrong I was. It's what happens beyond publishing that's important. It's the response to my work that matters. (Mem Fox, *Radical Reflections,* 11).

Writers don't get grades from teachers. For writers, the ultimate evaluation comes not from an editor, a publisher, or even a reviewer, but from the reader. Readers decide whether the work of writers is worthy of attention, and it is that evaluation that drives our work. It is that evaluation that must be in our minds even as we begin the work. Writers get "grades" from readers.

Katherine Paterson says,

> The best people to talk about a book, then, are not writers, but readers. . . . My philosophy on publication goes something like this: Once a book is published, it no longer belongs to me. My creative task is done. The work now belongs to the creative minds of my readers. I had my turn to make of it what I would, now it is their turn. I have no more right to tell readers how they should respond to what I have written than they had to tell me how to write it. It's a wonderful feeling when readers hear what I thought I was trying to say, but there is no law that they must. Frankly, it is even more thrilling for a reader to find something in my writing that I hadn't until that moment known was there. But this happens because of who the reader is, not simply because of who I am or what I have done. (*A Sense of Wonder,* 34)

Fox, Mem. 1993. *Radical Reflections: Passionate Opinions on Teaching, Learning, and Living.* San Diego: Harcourt Brace.

Paterson, Katherine. 1995. *A Sense of Wonder: On Reading and Writing Books for Children.* New York: Plume.

for most of us, grading is a reality of our teaching lives that we must think about. And regardless of whether outsiders tell us our students need to be given grades for writing, our students, as *insiders* on their writing lives, need to develop a sense of the quality of their work and of their role in maintaining or improving that quality. This seems to be an important "life skill" that they will use again and again in the other worlds of work they will find for themselves throughout their lives. So we must think about evaluation.

Evaluation requires us to ask questions of value: "How good is this?" "How well did I work at this?" "To what extent did I accomplish this goal?" We don't have to make a huge shift to move from assessment to evaluation, because these kinds of value questions can be attached to any of the assessment questions above. For example, if we take one of the assessment questions we suggested earlier, "Who are the published writers you're learning from?" we can turn this into an evaluation question fairly easily: "How well are you doing in your learning from published writers?" We can ask for a narrative response to this and get a fairly good picture of how well a student is doing. If we ask to see some *evidence* of this kind of learning—maybe specific things the student has tried in drafts, or specific texts he has studied as a writer—we can get an even better picture of how well he's doing at this learning. But if we must push on over into "grade land," the "scale of 1 to 10 land," we are going to have to push this student to place some *value* on how well he feels he is doing at this learning from published writers. To get him to do this, we might show him a scale like the one below and then ask, "On this scale of 1 to 4, where would you place yourself in this area of learning from published writers?"

4 Superior. Lots of studying writers on my own and lots of trying what I'm learning.

3 Good. I've studied some on my own and have tried some things in my writing.

2 Just OK. I've tried what we've done as a whole class with learning from writers, but not much else.

1 Need work here. I haven't really been paying much attention to learning from writers, either with the whole class or on my own.

What we've set up here is a rubric, a scale used for evaluation. If learning to write from writers was something we had been emphasizing in our teaching, we could ask every student in our writing workshop to evaluate him- or herself on this question, "How well are you doing learning from published writers?" Notice that in this rubric, we have been very specific about what each score means in relation to the evaluation question. In other words, "good" is defined specifically in terms of what we are looking for here. The teacher can decide on this definition by himself, or he can collaborate with his students on the definition for each of these.

What is probably more common in the rubrics that I've seen and used for evaluation is a combination of a score and a narrative that explains why the student has evaluated herself in this way in relation to whatever is being evaluated. So the scale above would either say, "Evaluate yourself on a scale from 1 to 4, with 4 being the highest," or it would look like this and have the descriptors but no specifics:

4	3	2	1
superior	good	just OK	need work here

Students would then be asked to write comments that explain why they gave themselves the scores they did. When we use a rubric this way, it does two things. First, it allows students to define these evaluations in individual ways, and second, it allows us to use the same rubric again and again for all kinds of things we might want students to evaluate. What we lose is the specific communication of what's expected in the evaluation, but we can get at this in other ways. For example, look at this evaluation I used at the end of a poetry genre study in my summer writing workshop for third and fourth graders (Figure 17.1). We used a simple 1 to 3 scale, with 3 being the highest.

Notice how I used the evaluation questions to communicate what I expected in student work. For each of the four areas I asked students to evaluate, I asked several layers of questions that helped them know exactly what I wanted them to think about in their work. I had to be careful to make sure these questions matched what I had been focusing on during my instruction in the poetry study. Notice how Bryan explains each of his rankings in the

FIGURE 17.1
Writing Evaluation for Poetry Genre Study

Writing Evaluation
Poetry Genre Study

Name Bryan McManus

Please read the series of questions in each category, and then rate your work on a scale of 1 (lowest) to 3 (highest), with 2 as average. Also, please write comments to explain your rating.

Writers Notebook
How did you do keeping your writers' notebook? Were you careful to write **a lot** of entries in your notebook? Did you push yourself to write **different kinds** of entries? Did you write in your notebook **outside** of our school workshop?

Comments: Rating 2

I usually kept my notebook withme but somethes I forgot it and I dig push my self and I wrote outside of the work shop

Reading Poetry
How did you do reading poetry during our study? Did you read a lot? Did you really try to **study closely** what the poets were doing so you could try it in your own writing?

Comments: Rating 3

I read alot at home and at the workshop... I am still working on using unexpected verbs I learned alot from Dime a dozen

continued on next page

FIGURE 17.1 (continued)

Drafting
How was your process of drafting your poems? Did you use your notebook to try some **draft work**? Did you push yourself to explore **lots of possibilities** with your draft before you decided it was *finished*?

Comments: I tried lots of things to help my draf... thesarus, notebook, other books ect. I explored lots of ideas

Rating 3

Editing and Publishing

How did you do getting your poems ready to publish? Were you very **careful to check** for spelling and punctuation accuracy and find where you needed help? Did you **get help** with things you were unsure about? Were you careful to **publish** the poem in way that was interesting and fitting for the piece?

Comments: In my YAY poem I made the poem into the title and in the room I cut up another poem to make mine.

Rating: 3

context of his own work. It is important that he is able to individualize these, mentioning specifics like his learning from the book *A Dime a Dozen* and his work on using unexpected verbs in his writing (something he got very interested in from his reading of poetry). The narrative comments give students an opportunity to do this.

This student evaluation covered a lot of territory. I designed it to be a comprehensive overview of all the work I had asked students to engage in during the study. Now, I could have designed a much more specific evaluation for any one of the four areas on this comprehensive evaluation. For example, an evaluation of only the writer's notebook might look like the one in Figure 17.2.

Again, I would have to make sure that the criteria I list here match what I am emphasizing in my instruction about writer's notebooks. Students need to be aware of the criteria for evaluation *before* they evaluate themselves. The criteria should be in place early on so that students can match their work to those criteria. Many teachers let students help them decide what the criteria will be for much of the evaluation in the writing workshop by bringing students into the evaluation process right from the start, rather than only at the end.

I tell my teacher education students, "Anything you want your students doing in the writing workshop needs to be a part of your evaluation in some way." "Value" is the root word in "evaluation," and so what we evaluate needs to come from what we value as a writing community. If we think about all the "values" we have talked about in this book so far, we can see that during a school year, we might devise evaluation instruments that let us look at these kinds of things:

- productive use of daily independent writing time;
- attention to using focus lessons to support independent work;
- productive interactions with writing peers;
- Engagement in all facets of the writing process: prewriting (writer's notebooks), drafting, revision, editing, and publishing.

In order to develop evaluation criteria for each of these, we will need to think about the answer to this question: "What does it look like if someone is

FIGURE 17.2 Writer's Notebook Evaluation

Writer's Notebook Evaluation

Name__________________ Date_____________

Please rate your notebook work on a scale of 1 (lowest) to 3 (highest), with 2 being average. Write comments that explain each of your ratings. If you need more room for comments, feel free to use the back.

Notebook Criteria	Rating and Comments
My notebook shows evidence of lots of writing (volume).	_____
I am trying different kinds of entries in my notebook.	_____
I am collecting entries outside of school.	_____
I am writing some entries long enough to deepen the meaning of my ideas.	_____
I reread my entries, think about them, and write more.	_____
I take good care of my notebook (it looks like something I care about).	_____

doing this *well?*" This is where we can break the criteria down into very specific things we'll be looking at. For example, I think one thing someone who is *revising* well is doing is lots of reading and rereading of a draft, so I will find a way to ask about this in any evaluation that looks at student revision.

Now, you may be wondering, "Do we have students evaluate actual pieces of writing?" And the answer is, "Of course." We expect that "engagement in all facets of the writing process" will result in pieces of writing, and so students will need to evaluate these as well. In a genre study of editorials, for example, Amy Arnberg and her fourth-grade students developed the criteria shown in Figure 17.3 to evaluate their finished editorials at the end of the study.

Amy's students evaluated themselves on each of these criteria and then wrote comments to support their evaluations. The criteria clearly reflected the teaching focus during the study—these were the aspects of writing editorials that Amy and her students spent most of their time thinking about and studying, in other words. Again, this is such a critical factor in develop-

FIGURE 17.3 Evaluation Criteria for a Genre Study on Editorials

Editorial Rubric

Elements we are looking for:

Voice:	Is your voice opinionated and strong? Is the *slant* evident?
Beginning:	Does your beginning captivate your audience?
Evidence of Facts:	*Primary sources*—are survey and interview evident? Are *secondary sources* used?
Craft:	Did you pay attention to crafting strategies such as *word choice?*
Ending:	Have you convinced the reader of your opinion? Is your ending powerful?
Structure:	Are the transitions in your article appropriate? Did you stay on topic?
Mechanics:	Is your piece edited for *punctuation*, *spelling*, and *grammar?*

ing evaluations. They must reflect the teaching that has taken place in the workshop.

Now, some questions worth considering: "How honest are students on these evaluations? How reflective of their actual work are their own evaluations of that work?" First of all, let me say that I have found that most children of elementary age are very honest in their evaluations of their work. Sometimes, I have found them even to be too hard on themselves. To ensure that we are getting an honest look at things, these kinds of evaluations need to be accompanied by artifacts that support them whenever they are available. For example, a student who gives himself the highest possible rating on his notebook having lots of writing in it needs to have a notebook with lots of writing in it to go with this evaluation. The student who rates herself highly on having edited her editorial for mechanics needs to have a final draft of an editorial where we can see evidence of that. Students learn pretty quickly that they must be able to back up their evaluations when we ask them, as a matter of course, to show us the evidence that supports these evaluations.

We'll want to think of the kinds of artifacts our students have that can support the various evaluations we'll ask them to do. Here are some of the main kinds of artifacts I have seen used to support student evaluations (often these are collected in portfolios):

- daily logs of what students did during independent writing time;
- writers notebooks, or copies of specific entries that show things we're looking for in the notebooks;
- drafts of writing projects with various things we're looking for labeled in them;
- final writing projects;
- the teacher's conference notes;
- tape recordings of students working together on writing.

So a student evaluation is not something he or she can make up out of the air; there is the expectation in the room that students will have evidence to back them up. Either students need to be able to show something that supports their evaluations, or they need to cite specifics that support them. If they cannot do this, we ask them to rethink their evaluation. For example, in the question we raised above, "How well are you doing learning from published writers?" the student would need to be able, at the very least, to tell us who some of these writers are and what kinds of things he or she is learning from them in order to support a good evaluation on this criterion. Students can either write out these kinds of explanations to go with their evaluations, or they can be asked to explain them in conferences. I have also found that with highlighters, colored pens, and sticky notes in hand, students love to mark up their drafts in ways that point out the decisions that they made as they drafted, another good way for them to show evidence of what they are doing as writers.

Some teachers question whether students should be the sole evaluators of their work; they feel that teachers have a responsibility to evaluate student work as well. There are many different reasons why people feel teachers have this responsibility, and there is not one right answer to the question of whether they should or shouldn't. Every teacher has to make a decision about this. I personally feel that the teacher (and even the student's peers from time to time) should also evaluate the student's work, and not because I think students can't do it on their own. I think, in the end, that students may be the *best* ones to evaluate their work. But I also know that having someone else give us an honest evaluation of our work helps us grow in our own understanding of our work as part of *a larger world of work*. And this is an understanding that I think is important for students to have.

Many teachers complete evaluations like the ones above for each individual student from time to time. I find that most of the time when I do this, the student and I come to the same conclusions in our evaluations. We may have different explanations, but we usually are not that far apart. Sometimes I can see things in a student's work that he or she can't see, and sometimes the other way around. But when we both get a chance to evaluate, we account for both of those ways of seeing.

If grades must be given in writing, then we will need to find some way to translate our evaluations into the grades used by our system. We may simply use these grade markers to begin with as students evaluate themselves, or we may develop some process of translation from rubrics to grades. When both teachers and students are involved in evaluation, then I believe both evaluations should be used in the translation to grades. During any grading period, we want to be sure to have completed a variety of different evaluations (some of them completed more than once over the period) that represent the range of things we want to see students doing in the writing workshop.

Know that assigning student grades in writing will always feel a little awkward. We are trying to measure something that is immeasurable when we do it. There is no purely "objective" way to look at it—a grade in writing will always involve interpretation. It would be much better if we could describe a student's writing work rather than having to put this one incredibly narrow label on it—the *grade*. What we do need to be sure about, however, is that we can describe exactly how a student grade was assigned—where the interpretation came from, in other words.

We'll want to make sure that how students are being evaluated is made clear to all those with a stake in their work, especially parents and next year's teachers. Most writing workshop teachers do lots of evaluation around the process of students' work, in addition to the products of that work. And because we look carefully at students' processes in our evaluations, it becomes quite possible for struggling writers to make good grades in our workshops, and sometimes for very gifted but lazy writers not to make such good grades. How is this possible? You see, we have to believe in the work we are asking students to do in our workshops. We have to believe that this work will help the most struggling writers and the most gifted writers to outgrow themselves, if they invest themselves in it. If we have faith in the work we ask students to do, then I believe we can have confidence in assigning grades based primarily on students' *investment in this work*. After all, what more can we ask of students than that they do their best at what we've asked them to do?

Of course, I posed the question above so it sounded as if no one would argue with me about that. But believe me, there are plenty of people who would argue with me. The world is full of people who want public school classrooms to be very competitive, high-stakes kinds of places. And it is in this world that we have to explain how students are assigned grades in our classrooms. We must be very articulate about this. The explanation, for me, comes down to this. A struggling nine-year-old writer in a third-grade writing workshop didn't ask to be there. We told this student that he or she had to be there. We tell every single child in this country that he or she has to be there. When you think about it in that way, the question, "What more can we ask of students than that they do their best at what we've asked them to do?" seems a bit different. How could children do that, their very best, and still *fail?* It is *the* question that drives all of my thinking about evaluation in public school classrooms.

Assessment, and especially evaluation, will always be a difficult, complex, and even volatile subject of much discussion in schools. But out of this fray of complexity, as teachers of writing we always want to remember that assessment and evaluation are actually forms of *curriculum* in the writing workshop, curriculum that teaches students who they are as writers in so many important ways.

Reference

Grimes, Nikki. 1998. *A Dime a Dozen*. New York: Dial Books for Young Readers.

18

On Loving *Worksheets* in the Writing *Workshop*

"THESE ARE NOT WORKSHEETS!!! HOW MANY TIMES DO I HAVE TO TELL YOU GUYS THAT??" I shouted to anyone who would listen, exasperated as yet another student told me he'd lost the "worksheet" I'd given him last week.

Bravely, a tiny voice from somewhere on the side of the room (at the outskirts of my wrath) spoke up and asked, "Well, what do you want us to call them then?"

She had asked a good question. A really good question, I realized in retrospect. The only better question might have been, "Why *not* call them worksheets?" What the student had lost was one of the dozens of pieces of paper he would get from me over time in the writing workshop, pieces of paper that were meant to help him manage his work as a writer. *Worksheets.* The label was perfect.

Of course, my rejection of that label had come many years earlier when I had done a wholesale rejection of the skill-and-drill world of manufactured worksheets. My friends and I used to joke derisively about our first years of teaching when our biggest planning decision was what time we needed to be in line at the copier. As I thought about it, though, I realized that, in fact, I was still spending a good bit of time at the copy machine. So were most of the teachers I knew who had writing workshops that were humming along during the year. What was it we were all copying?

Worksheets! We were copying worksheets—we *loved* them!

You see, as we've said throughout this book, the writing workshop is a place where a lot of things are happening all at once and in a lot of different ways. There is a lot of *work* going on in a *workshop,* and one of the things that can help to manage that work is *worksheets*—written reminders that help stu-

WRITERS' VOICES ON . . .

moving from instruction to writing

A book about writing isn't enough. Being a writer is a whole way of life, a way of seeing, thinking, being. It's the passing on of a lineage. Writers hand on what they know. . . . Writers are not available for teaching in the way a Zen master is available. We can take a class from a writer but it is not enough. In class, we don't see how a writer organizes her day or dreams up writing ideas. We sit in class and learn what narrative is but we can't figure out how to do it. *A* does not lead to *B.* We can't make that kamikaze leap. So writing is always over there in the novels on the shelves or discussed on class blackboards and we are over here in our seats. I know many people who are aching to be writers and have no idea how to begin. There is a great gap like an open wound. . . . It is my hope that in sharing what I do, I have helped my readers along the writing path. (Natalie Goldberg, *Wild Mind,* xiv–xvi)

The kinds of worksheets Katie is talking about for the writing workshop help writers make that "kamikaze leap" from the teaching about writing to their actual work as writers. The worksheets help to bridge that "great gap" and close that "open wound" by giving students a way to revisit important content when they need it.

Goldberg, Natalie. 1990. *Wild Mind: Living the Writer's Life.* New York: Bantam.

dents manage their ongoing work as writers. Most writing workshop teachers I know design all kinds of worksheets that students paste onto their folders and into their notebooks and onto the walls of their classrooms. Now, these are not "practice-some-isolated-skill" kinds of worksheets. These are worksheets that remind students to think about important aspects of their work as they are writing from day to day, most of them aspects that have been discussed in focus lessons. The written reminders help students revisit these important ideas without having to ask the teacher to go over them again, so in that way the worksheets are another tool to help students be independent as writers during the workshop. They also help students be accountable because they are responsible for whatever information is on the worksheet, whether they have filled it in or whether it is all written reminders from the teacher.

Let's look at some different examples of teacher-designed worksheets for the writing workshop, and as we do, let's think about our different teaching situations and what kinds of worksheets we might develop that would help students manage the work we're asking them to do.

Keeping Track of Independent Work

Many writing workshops have some kind of worksheet in place that simply documents what independent work students engage in each day of writing workshop. This worksheet can be anything from a whole-class chart where students (or the teacher) quickly note their work for the day, to an individual daily log that each student keeps, to a weekly report that includes reflections about what was accomplished that week in the workshop. I have always been partial to "logs" where, at the end of each workshop, students make a quick note of what work they did that day and what work they plan to do tomor row. Having them think about tomorrow helps them be planful about their work. At the end of the week, I like for students to use these logs to reflect on the work they have done over the course of days. These logs become important artifacts when we look at the quality of each child's independent writing work (for evaluation and grading purposes).

Figure 18.1 shows an example of a weekly log from Bryan, a fourth grader in my summer writing workshop.

FIGURE 18.1
Bryan's Daily Log

WRITING WORKSHOP DAILY LOG FOR Bryan

What I did today...	What I think I'll do tomorrow...
Monday	on Tuesday
Tuesday	on Wednesday
Long and fast list made a draft of Yay	finish draft of yay - new words thosarus
Wednesday	on Thursday
finsihed draft of Yay and wrote 3 long and quick enterw	do quick and long drafts and do a first draf of spaceship

continued on next page

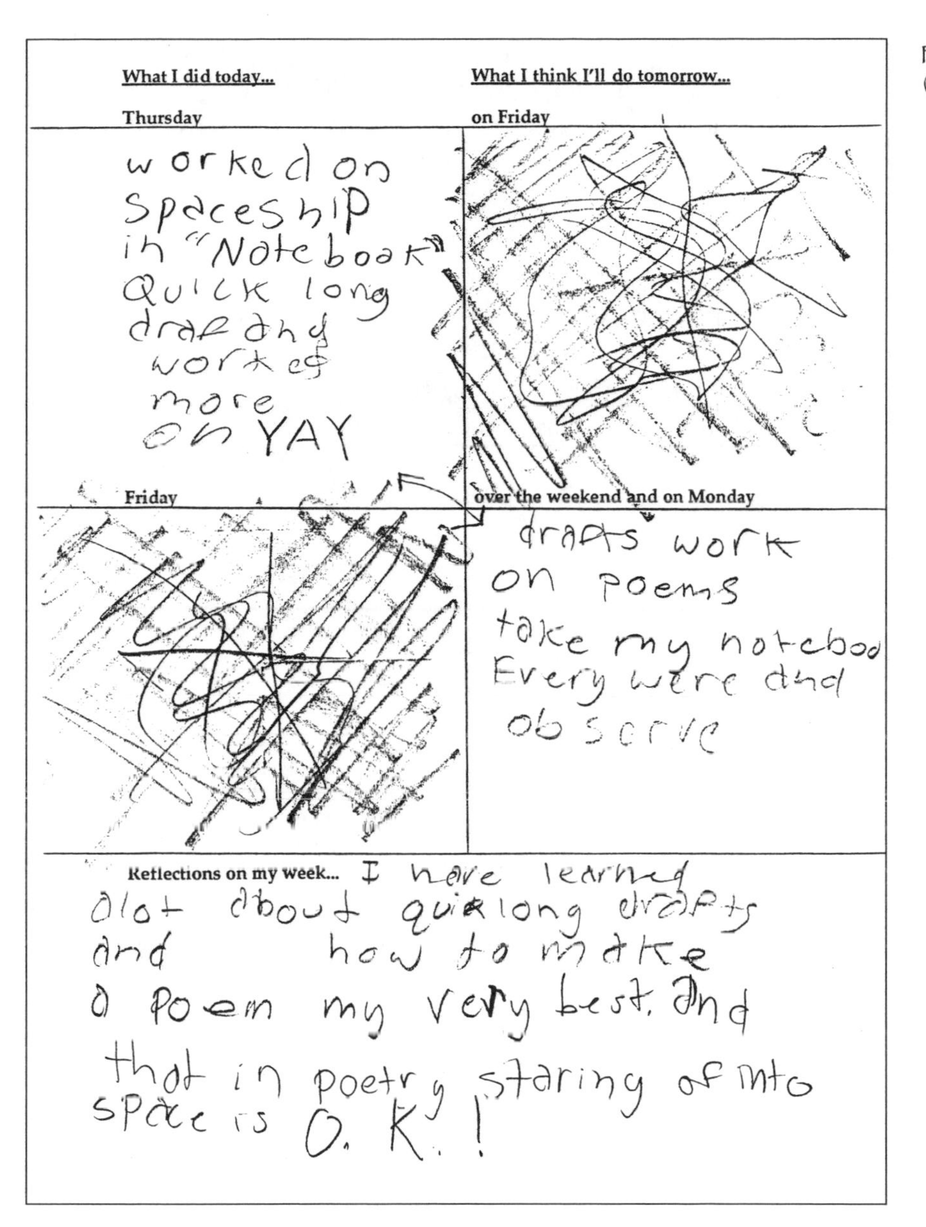

What I did today...

Thursday

worked on spaceship in "Notebook" Quick long draf and worked more on YAY

What I think I'll do tomorrow...

on Friday

Friday

over the weekend and on Monday

drafts work on poems take my notebod Every were and observe

Reflections on my week... I have learned alot about quiklong drafts and how to make a poem my very best. and that in poetry staring of into space is O.K.!

FIGURE 18.1 (continued)

Writing quick self-stick note responses on logs from time to time lets students know that we are closely watching their day-to-day work as writers. On notes like these, we can also make suggestions for things students might try based on the work they have going. In Figure 18.2 you can see how I have written some notes on Brittany's workshop log.

This kind of feedback can, of course, be given during conferencing as well, if the teacher and the child are looking at the log together. I just think that when I write a quick response, it makes a nice trail of "work and response to work" to look back on later when we reflect on our writing over a long period of time. Either way, in written responses or in conferences, I find that when students see that I am paying attention to what they are writ-

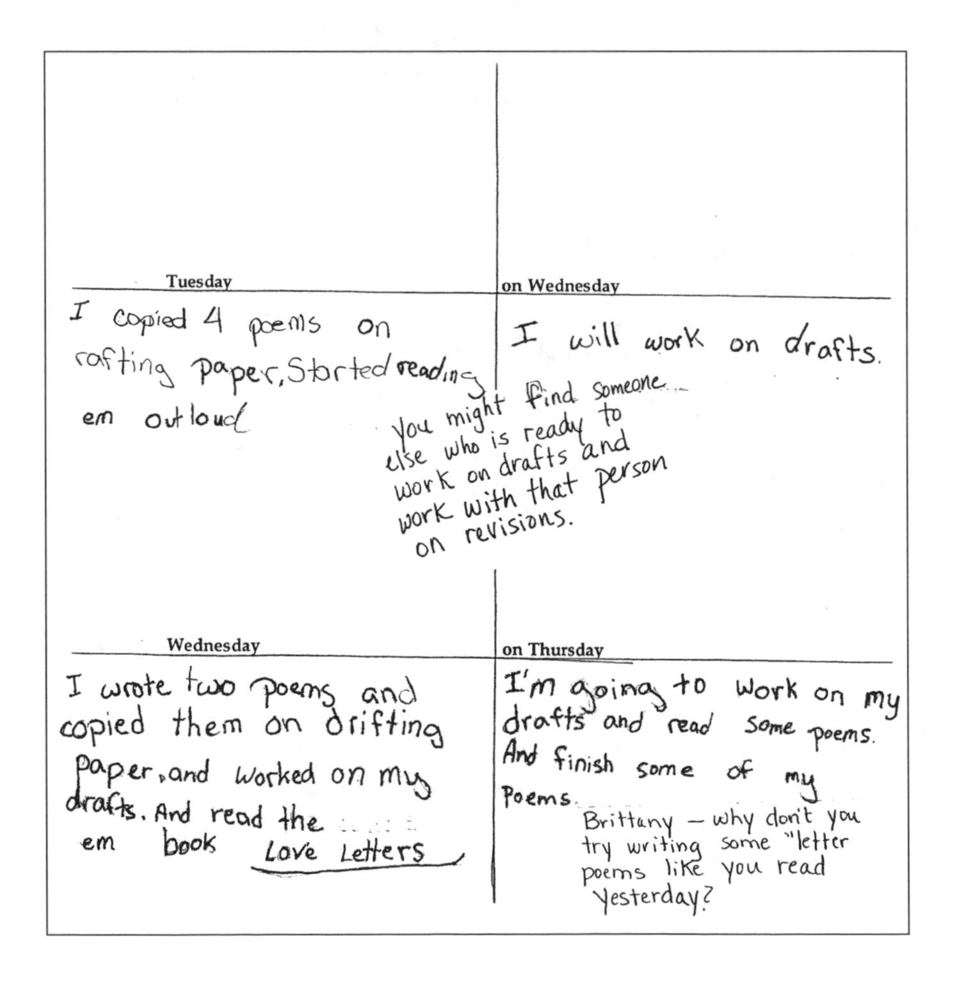

Tuesday	on Wednesday
I copied 4 poems on rafting paper, Storted reading em outloud	I will work on drafts.

you might find someone else who is ready to work on drafts and work with that person on revisions.

Wednesday	on Thursday
I wrote two poems and copied them on drifting paper, and worked on my drafts. And read the em book Love Letters	I'm going to work on my drafts and read some poems. And finish some of my Poems.

Brittany — why don't you try writing some "letter poems like you read yesterday?

FIGURE 18.2
Brittany's Daily Log with Comments

ing and planning in these logs, they take them more seriously. We should expect to see them grow over time in their ability to name the work they are doing and to plan the next steps in that work.

Keeping Track of Individualized and Whole-Class Instruction

While teachers always keep track of individualized instruction in their conference notes, some of them also create worksheets that help students keep track of the important content offered in writing conferences. Often pasted into writer's notebooks or folders, these cumulative worksheets have places for students to make their own records of the content of an individual conference with the teacher. Figure 18.3 shows an example of a worksheet that I like.

My Writing Conference Log

Name:

Date	What to remember from my conference . . .	I'm getting it!

FIGURE 18.3 Worksheet for Recording Conferences

At the end of the conference, the teacher helps the student decide what to jot down that will help him or her remember the essential content of the conference, often including an example if the content is a skill, such as using an apostrophe to make a contraction or knowing a high frequency spelling pattern. The summary of the content should be short, to the point, and serve only as a quick reminder for the student of the teaching that took place. What I especially like on this worksheet is the last column, "I'm getting it!" where students are encouraged to come back and make a note whenever they use or think specifically about the content of the conference in an actual writing situation.

I have seen some teachers keep a single classwide record much like this one where they record the essential content of focus lessons (rather than individual conferences). As these worksheets fill up with the content of focus lessons over time, they are kept in a notebook binder, usually divided into units of study, that students may use as a reference tool during independent writing time. Making several copies of these worksheets and putting them in different binders allows the teacher to have more than one copy of this valuable reference tool floating around the room. In a way, by collecting the content of the focus lessons, the class creates its own "writing textbook" for the year.

Supporting Independent and Collaborative Work

Most of the worksheets designed by writing workshop teachers are meant to support students' independent and collaborative work. You may remember from Chapter 6, in which we discussed getting started with independent writing time, that we suggested some kinds of reminders we might give students to paste into their notebooks. You may want to take a quick look back at these. One of them outlines the range of activities students can engage in during the workshop, and the other offers notebook strategies students can try when they feel "stuck" in their writing. I consider both of these to be worksheets, and I make all kinds of them to support my teaching of writing in different situations. Basically, anything we put in writing that can be used independently by students as a resource or as a reference for their writing I call a worksheet—something that helps them do their writing work. We can design worksheets that summarize or outline big ideas about work that students will be engaged in again and again during the workshop.

Two of the smartest writing workshop teachers I know are colleagues at the same grade level in the same school (lucky school, huh?). These two teachers, Kathleen Burda and Kirsten Morgan, seem to be constantly thinking of ways they can support their students to do engaging, independent work in their writing workshops. The result of this thinking is a fairly large "paper trail" of all kinds of neat worksheets, designed specifically with their classrooms in mind, that students use day in and day out to support their writing. So, although we could sample from the large collection of teacher-made writing worksheets I have collected through the years, I think it is more powerful to see a range of teacher-developed worksheets that are being used in a single writing workshop—or in this case, two workshops working side by side. Kirsten and Kathleen have been kind enough to let us take a peek at some worksheets that are representative of the ones they developed for their workshops in the fall of 1999.

One type of worksheet both Kathleen and Kirsten have used in their rooms is actually a basket of tiny worksheets on laminated pieces of paper. These are worksheets that students go and get during independent writing time if they want to "work out" as writers, need new ideas for what to try as writers, or if they just find themselves at an in-between place in their writing and need something to do during independent writing time. After using them, students return the worksheets to the basket for other students to use later. These worksheets are called "Try its," and they are suggestions Kathleen and Kirsten have found in books by professional writers. They are careful to include the writer's name and the name of the professional book where they found the suggestion so that students know this isn't just some made-up teacher assignment: It's advice from a writer in the world outside school. Figures 18.4 and 18.5 show two samples of "Try it" worksheets.

FIGURE 18.4
Sample "Try It" Worksheet

Try it!

Georgia Heard in *Writing toward Home* (78–79) suggests this:

- Find a photograph of yourself as a child—it can be of you alone or it can include other people. Run your eyes over it. Write down quickly everything you think and feel. Sometimes description only lets you wander around outside looking in. One way to become part of the photograph's world, to go more deeply into it, is to imagine yourself speaking as the child you were. What would you say? What would you hear or smell?
- You can also find a photograph of something in the world—from the newspaper, old magazines, photographs you've seen repeatedly that have become symbols of a certain time or situation. Find a photograph that sparks emotion in you when you look at it. Remember, the point is not just to write a description but to drift, dream, let poetry happen, let images connect you deeply to what you see.

So the "Try its" are there for students to use when they want or need to use them during the independent part of the workshop. Some of them will likely be offered as focus lesson possibilities (as opposed to writing assignments) in a unit of study on living a writing life, but many of them will simply wait there for students to discover the writing possibilities they contain. These are worksheets that clearly help students manage their independent writing in the workshop.

The worksheet shown in Figure 18.6 is one Kirsten gave all of her students to paste in their notebooks. On it she has outlined the "writing project stages" for them. The sheet summarizes a process that Kirsten had been teaching her students for several weeks. She wanted them to have it as a reminder of what they had learned about doing writing projects, as they would be continuing to plan and carry out writing projects on their own during the year.

FIGURE 18.5
Sample "Try It" Worksheet

Try it!

Ralph Fletcher in *A Writer's Notebook* (26–27) suggests this:

I often find myself using too many general words in my writer's notebook: *good, nice.* These words don't give much of a picture as to exactly what was going on. When this happens, I stop and try to "crack open" these words by using specific examples.

- Not "My Grandpa is really nice," but "My Grandpa pulled out his chest of war stuff and let me try on his old uniform."
- Not "His mother is super neat," but "She irons everything, even her ten- and twenty-dollar bills."
- Not "My Uncle Paul does lots of silly stuff," but "My Uncle Paul drinks his coffee out of a glass measuring cup."

You can do this yourself. Reread your writer's notebook and look for places where you are using vague, general words: *fun, cool.* Circle those words. Ask yourself: What are the details underneath these words? What little things will bring to life what I'm writing about? Write these details in your notebook. You don't even have to use complete sentences; a list will do.

The "tracks of Kirsten's teaching" are evident throughout this worksheet; there is insiders' language ("mentor books") and even a quote from Betsy Byars that was significant in getting the class thinking about writing in notebooks. It is so important that we, as workshop teachers, design our own worksheets for our own classrooms. The sheets should feel like records of the work *we* do in *our* rooms; they should not have a "fill-in-any-classroom-here" quality to them. And their development is a very evolutionary process. Over time, teachers like Kirsten will redesign the same worksheets many times, making them match new insights and understandings that necessarily shift the explanations used in the teaching of writing.

FIGURE 18.6 Writing Project Stages

Writing Project Stages

Writing in writer's notebook

- gathering "scraps" ("Plenty of good scraps are as important in writing a book as in the making of a quilt"—Betsy Byars.)
- writing, writing, writing; VARIETY

Project planning (gathering around seed)

- choosing a seed idea
- choosing a purpose and an audience
- choosing "mentor" books
- writing anything related to seed (in notebook)
- planning a format (interview, poetry, letter, picture book . . .)

Drafting

- using a structure that fits the idea
- writing a rough draft on looseleaf paper (skip lines, one side of the page only)

Revising

- reading aloud and listening for things that need changing
- asking for feedback from a small group
- developing a powerful beginning and ending
- using author's craft

Typing (first round)

- typing and saving a revised draft
- printing one copy

continued on next page

FIGURE 18.6 (continued)

Editing

- proofreading and correcting alone (by hand, not on the computer until the final copy)
- proofreading and correcting with friend(s)
- proofreading and correcting with the teacher

Final copy (second round of typing and saving)

- making final corrections
- changing font, size, spacing when appropriate (e.g., adding page breaks)
- printing one copy

Publishing

- binding the book (when appropriate)
- cutting and pasting (when appropriate)
- illustrating (when appropriate)

Celebration!

- sharing the project with the class
- presenting the gift to a recipient

Kirsten and Kathleen developed the worksheet shown in Figure 18.7 together to help students manage the choosing of seed ideas for writing projects. Again, the sheet summarizes the teaching that has gone on in the two classrooms, but it also has room for students to do some actual written planning on the worksheet itself.

Notice that this worksheet is meant to capture a line of thinking that Kirsten and Kathleen want their students to engage in as they make this important decision about which seed ideas for writing projects to pursue first. It's a line of thinking they've been teaching their students about in

FIGURE 18.7
Choosing Seed Ideas

Moving into Writing Projects

You are looking for something in your notebook that you want to pursue—an idea that you want to develop. THIS IS JUST A BEGINNING, a seed idea for a writing project.

1. Read through your notebook, looking and listening for writing that catches your attention.
   - Katherine Paterson says that "writing comes from ideas that make a sound in my heart."
   - Choose a few entries (or parts of entries) that seem special to you (maybe an idea that comes up repeatedly, maybe something that is important or interesting to you).
2. Start an idea page in your notebook.
   - List possibilities you found during step 1.
   - For whom would this make a good gift? Or could it serve another purpose?

Possible Idea	*Possibility for a Gift or Other Purpose*

3. Narrow your choice to one idea you'll work on first. (Decide which one stands out from the crowd or seems to have the most potential right now.)

focus lessons and conferences. But as individuals begin to use it to make actual decisions about what they will pursue as writers, the worksheet brings them back to that teaching, putting its essential content right at their writing fingertips.

Like most writing workshop teachers, Kirsten and Kathleen depend on their students to help themselves and to help each other do the very best writing they can—at all stages of the process, but especially during drafting and revision when writers need lots of feedback and support. The two worksheets shown in Figures 18.8 and 18.9 were designed to help students during the drafting and revision of writing projects. The first one was created for individual writers. Both Kirsten and Kathleen were having a predictable problem with students assuring them that yes, they had used the entire line of thinking for revision of their drafts. But then in conferences, when it became clear that they had not really used all the tools for revision they had been asked to use, they quickly responded with, "Oh, I forgot to do that." This worksheet was to help them remember (Figure 18.8).

Now, neither Kirsten nor Kathleen envisions her students ten years from now, and maybe not even ten weeks from now, needing this ten-step plan for revision, checking to make sure they've done number eight before they move on to number nine. But a lot of their students, being new to writing workshops and new to the process of deeply engaged revision, need it *now*, to help them remember what writers think about and do as they revise. So in addition to helping them use a process for revision that would improve their writing, this worksheet also helped them be accountable to their teachers who wanted to know that they were at least trying all the revision tools they had been taught to use so far in the year.

Both these smart teachers had worked with their students on how to help each other with writing in ways that were productive. They designed the worksheet shown in Figure 18.9 early in the year to help students remember the suggestions they had given them for giving good feedback to a fellow writer.

As they helped each other with drafts of writing projects, Kathleen's and Kirsten's students used the "Rough Draft Reader Tips" worksheet to help them remember the kinds of thoughtful feedback they could give a writing partner. Each one of the questions offered as a "tip" had been discussed and demonstrated as a feedback technique during a previous focus lesson. Worksheets like these are meant to follow good teaching, not take its place.

FIGURE 18.8
Project Progress Worksheet

Project Progress

Planning

1. What is my seed idea?

2. What mentor book(s) am I using?

3. What will my writing project have in common with my mentor book(s)?

Drafting

4. Have I finished my rough draft? (When the answer is yes, go on to step 5.)

Revising

5. Have I read my draft out loud to myself and corrected the problems I hear? (When the answer is yes, go on to step 6.)
6. Have I used author's craft to improve my writing? (When the answer is yes, go on to step 7.)
7. Have I read my draft to my group? (When the answer is yes, go on to step 8.)
8. Did I revise the areas that did not make sense to my group? (When the answer is yes, go on to step 9.)
9. Does my beginning grab the reader's attention and set the right mood? (When the answer is yes, go on to step 10.)
10. Does my ending leave the reader thinking about the ideas I have shared?

FIGURE 18.9
Rough Draft Reader Tips

Rough Draft Reader Tips

Try these ways of giving response to the writer . . .

- In your own words, explain what you think the writer is talking about in the piece.
- Does the piece make sense to you?
- Do you think there are any places in this piece that need more details or more explanation?
- Do you think there are any parts of this piece that are not necessary or helpful to the meaning?
- What parts of this writing seem especially strong?
- Look for places where the writer can use author's craft to improve this writing. Explain what type of craft would help in these places.
- Can you suggest any mentor books or other types of writing that could help this writer?
- What other comments or advice can you think of that might be helpful to this writer?

Now, one of the keys to understanding the power of worksheets like the ones you've seen above is to know that students must learn to use these resources when it makes sense for them to use them. In other words, they must use them when they are engaged in the kinds of work the worksheets support, and when they feel like they need some extra support for that work. These are not worksheets that Kirsten and Kathleen hand out to all their students and, holding their hands, have them all complete together. Likewise, these are not worksheets that students even "complete" so that they can say, "I'm finished." How do you finish something that is designed to be used over and over again? You see, the worksheets themselves are not THE work of the writing workshop. They are tools students use when they need them and as long as they need them that support THE work: getting important writing done.

Creating Our Own Worksheets

I remember when I first told some of my colleagues that I was going to have a chapter on worksheets in this book. I got kind of a startled reaction. Certainly, the way I've been using that label throughout this chapter is in direct contrast to the more traditional way of using it, but I hope my definition for "worksheet" (a piece of paper that is used to help manage or support a writer's work in the writing workshop) has made sense. Worksheets designed for our writing workshops make good management sense, because they give us and our students the confidence that comes from simply having some things in writing. But worksheets like these are also important curriculum tools, giving students quick and easy access to some of the most important content they need to help them do their writing. As we design worksheets and begin to watch them being used in the writing workshop, we need to keep several things in mind. We need to . . .

- Make sure that any worksheet we create comes straight from the teaching we are doing. We shouldn't be afraid to incorporate our own and our students' own particular ways of saying things into the language of the worksheet.
- Watch very carefully to make sure that our worksheets are helping manage or support good writing work, but are not taking over that work. We don't want worksheets to overpower and become more important than the work they are supposed to support.
- Related to this, we don't want too many worksheets in use at any given time. We need to decide which curriculum issues are most important to support at any given time, and make worksheets for these only.
- Worksheets that help manage and support talk in the workshop might sound like they are being used as *scripts* for talk, and this is to be expected at first. We'll need to watch this over time, however. Students should move farther and farther away from scripted talk once they have become comfortable with the kinds of talk we're asking them to try on the worksheet.

- With any of the worksheets that support independent and collaborative work, our long-range goal is for students to grow out of needing their support. We need to watch and to celebrate (in public ways) when we see that students have internalized the "work" of a worksheet or are inventing new ways of their own to get that work done.
- The worksheets we use can help parents and other outsiders (administrators) understand the work of the workshop in important ways. We must find ways to share them (as information) with these groups.

References

Fletcher, Ralph. 1996. *A Writer's Notebook: Unlocking the Writer within You.* New York: Avon Books.

Heard, Georgia. 1995. *Writing toward Home: Tales and Lessons to Find Your Way.* Portsmouth, N.H.: Heinemann.

19

Publish or Perish, and Predictable Problems along the Way

The writing workshop is full of all kinds of options, but the one thing, the main thing, that is not optional is publishing. The only way students can get enough experience with the whole process of writing is to take pieces all the way through that process—often. I tell students in my writing classes that they must publish or perish! That is the driving requirement of a professional writer's life (it puts food on the table), but it is also the driving requirement of a student's life in a writing workshop (evaluation is tied to publication). We begin the year with that expectation in place. We say to our students, "This year, you will publish." But probably before we even tell them what "publish" means exactly, before we even help them understand why it is so important, we should go ahead and tell them when at least some of their publications will be expected. We might even give them some deadlines on the first day of school. Writers thrive on deadlines.

I remember when I was in elementary school—it must have been about fourth grade—and my teacher announced at the very beginning of the school year that the science fair would take place on a certain day in April. *April.* When she first told us, that date sounded like it was in another lifetime, far away from the one in which we lived. But this teacher *loved* the science fair, and she wanted us to love it too. Every time she talked about it, she would mention that date in April. Before long, that date took on almost mythical proportions in our classroom. We were *living* for that day, and we planned for it with an ardent fervor most of us had never experienced in our young lives. I don't remember a lot about my project for the fair, but I do remember so well living in anticipation of that day and getting everything ready. I remember the energy of having a real deadline that was marked on a calendar and waiting for me in the future of my work.

As we have gained experience over the years, we writing workshop teachers have come to see the need to harness some of that same energy I felt so long ago as a fourth grader waiting on the science fair. It is the energy of a deadline, a moment in time that a writer can work toward with anticipation. You see, the one thing that can get a writer going and move her forward like nothing else is a deadline looming in front of her—especially if she has to publish to eat (publish or perish, remember?). So in reality, we probably need to say to our students, "This year, you will publish, and your first publication is due September 15th. Your next, October 7th. Your next, October 23rd. Your next, an informational article, November 28th. . . .

Perhaps the first worksheet we give our students should be a school-year calendar with publication dates marked on it. Some of these dates will be open publications, completely up to the student's choice, and some of them will coincide with genre studies and will have the kind of writing that is required to be published noted as well. But a calendar with publication deadlines can really set our workshops in motion. Deadlines send the message to students that writing to publish is serious, that it's expected, and look, here's when it's due. It also sends this wonderful message of possibility, of a whole year stretching out in front of you: "What are all the cool things you'd like to

Writers' Voices on . . .

deadlines

First day of classes yesterday and my Advanced Narrative Writing group looks lively. They're to return on the 16th with a maximum of 500 words of narrative on the theme "A Bad Half Hour." I told them that I intended to begin, and work beside them, on a new novel; so I should set a date now for giving them my first installment. If I allow the 16th and the 18th for the discussion of their own first pieces, then I could offer them mine on Tuesday, 23 January. (Reynolds Price, *Learning a Trade*, 585)

Katie speaks of the need for writers to have deadlines, to know what is expected and when. Notice here how Reynolds Price not only sets such expectations for his students, but also for himself. Indeed, whether imposed by a contract, suggested by an editor, or merely set as a target by the writer, a deadline can provide the needed target toward which we aim.

Price, Reynolds. 1998. *Learning a Trade: A Craftsman's Notebooks, 1955–1997.* Durham, N.C.: Duke University Press.

do with writing over the year to get ready for publication at these different times?" Students can use a calendar full of deadlines to envision the writing lives they want to lead that year, and start making plans for their work.

Now the question, of course, is how many publications and how often? There's not a single answer to that; there are just things to think about that will help us answer that from year to year. But before we think about those things, we need to define what we mean by "publishing." The questions of "how many" and "how often" have a lot to do with how we define publishing.

What Is Publishing Anyway?

In the world outside of school, when you see a piece of published writing, it really means three things. One, it means that the writing you see was accepted for publication by the publisher. Two, it means that the writing is finished. And three, it means that the writing is now available to the public. It has an audience waiting for it. These are the three concepts we need to help us define publishing in the writing workshop as well.

Having Work Accepted for Publication

First, our students are lucky because most all of the ideas they have for writing will be "accepted by the publisher." They don't have to enter the competitive world of publishing where they must shop their ideas around by sending out manuscripts and hoping someone will want them. Certainly, I think we should encourage students to enter that competitive world of publishing if they'd like. There are all kinds of magazines, journals, and newspapers that accept manuscripts from children, and there are also a lucky few children who've had book manuscripts taken on by major publishers. But in our writing workshops, students work more like very famous writers: Their manuscripts are *solicited*. If they have some good reason to want to work on a piece of writing, then we say to them, "Go for it. We'll *publish* it." So the idea of being "accepted for publication" is very much in place in the workshop as students are working on various writing projects.

Being Finished

The next concept, then, is the idea that a piece of writing that is published is *finished*. In the world of publishing outside school, the author and the publisher (usually represented by an editor) must come to an agreement that the piece is finished. Now, sometimes one of them will believe this to be true before the other, and in that case they have to talk and negotiate until they can come to some agreement about how to get it finished so that both are satisfied. This author-publisher relationship is very similar to the student-teacher relationship around publishing in the writing workshop. Both the student and the teacher need to come to an agreement that a piece is finished. Being able to reach this agreement begins with the teacher making it clear what the definition of "finished" is for publishing in the workshop.

Being finished with a piece of writing is the final destination of a journey a writer takes, and, as anyone who writes will tell you, no two journeys for any two pieces of writing are exactly alike. For one thing, some take a lot longer than others, and this isn't necessarily tied to the length of the piece of writing. Some may require more research, others more drafting and revision, and still others just seem to keep demanding that you "write more, write more." But regardless of the kind of trip you take, coming to the place of being finished is a journey.

Now, there are some fairly predictable ways of traveling we do on most of our writing journeys, and these need to be communicated clearly to students in writing workshops. What do we expect? What does it mean for the journey to *be finished*? From writing ourselves, and from studying what professional writers say about their writing processes, we've learned that the journey often looks a lot like this:

- It begins with a good reason to write. An idea that won't leave us alone. A specific audience or cause we need to address with writing. A desire to write in a certain genre. A passion for a topic. Having a good reason to write gives us what lots of writing teachers call a *seed idea* for writing.
- We develop the seed idea. We think about it a lot. We collect entries on it in our writer's notebooks. We live in the world with the seed idea very present in our thinking, collecting related ideas from our living. We may research or do some intentional gathering of information or ideas related to the seed idea.
- We begin a draft. At some point, we have to start. We have to say, "Now I am making this piece of writing." We may do some planning about how we will write it before we start, or we may just start drafting and see what happens.
- We continue drafting, weaving revision and editing (proofreading) into the process. Some will just get the draft down and then work back through it to revise. Others will draft very slowly, revising a lot as they go. Most will do some combination of the two. Most writers go ahead and fix proofreading errors if they see them while drafting. They're not concerned with them at that point; they just fix them if they see them.
- We get some feedback. Some writers will do this all along the way. But certainly as the drafting begins to take shape, most writers have a "test audience" of readers they trust to give them good feedback. They use this feedback to support their drafting and revision. Professional writers not only use their friends, but also their editors for this.
- We "fine-tooth comb" the writing once we feel the meaning and the wording are what we want it to be, making sure, one more time, we haven't overlooked anything that needs to be edited.
- If the publisher agrees that the piece is ready, then the writing is published—put into a suitable format to go out into the world of readers.

So there it is, in a big, general way—the writing process, the journey we take to being finished with a piece of writing. Now, it seems important to mention here again that while most journeys have all these steps embedded in them in one way or another, the steps aren't all carried out in the exact same ways from one piece of writing to the next. Writers go about them in different ways, for one thing. But also, different kinds of writing and different reasons to write require different ways of going at this process.

Let me explain it this way. This book you are reading now was a very long, slow journey through this process that took over a year to complete. But I actually use this same process, all of it in a single morning sometimes, to write something like a letter of recommendation for a student. I have my reason to write: I've been asked to write by the student. I develop my "seed idea" by thinking about what I know about this student. I usually do some research by going to look through the student's folder at the transcript and teaching evaluations, and at the work he or she did in my class. I find out about the audience for the letter: who will be reading it. Then, I begin writing the letter. I am a slow drafter (I revise a lot as I go), so it might take me forty minutes or so to get two or three short paragraphs. I usually call Rick, my officemate, over and ask him to read it. I revise based on what he says. I "fine-tooth comb" it one last time, load some letterhead paper in the printer, and print it out. And voilá! I've used the same year-long process I used to write this book—in a single morning—to write a letter.

When we communicate to our students what we mean by "being finished" with writing, we tell them it means being at the end of the journey outlined above. But we must know, and they will have to learn, that there is not *one way* to go on this journey. Each writer finds his own way with each different piece of writing that he sets out to publish. Later, we'll think more about how a student will account for this journey in his or her writing. For now, let's move on to the last concept we need to understand about publishing.

Making Work Available to the Public

The word "publish" comes from the same root as the word "public," and being finished with a piece of writing means that it is ready for the public. There is an audience waiting for it. There *needs* to be an audience waiting for it, or else none of the steps on that journey was worth taking. Like a welcoming party who greets you at the airport, readers need to be waiting there for us when our writing journey is finished. We didn't need to publish if we weren't going to go public; we could have kept the writing in our notebook or journal for our eyes only.

For publishing to make any sense at all in our writing workshops, students need to feel the pull of readers waiting for them. From the first steps writers take on the journey toward being finished, they need to have a sense of who the audience is that's waiting for them at the end. This question, "Who is your audience?" needs to be a driving force behind publication in our workshops, just as it is a driving force in any writer's work. Actually, it's the response of that audience to our writing that is the driving force, but you can't have the response without the audiences who read your writing. Now, in each other, students have a built-in audience waiting for them in the workshop. But we are guilty, I think, of relying too much on this one audience over and over again and not doing enough to help our students find audiences outside the classroom—audiences who matter to them and who will wait anxiously for them to finish pieces of writing.

Our students need to be publishing things for audiences outside the writing workshop as well as for the other students who are writing alongside them. They need to publish things for family (aunts, uncles, cousins, little sisters, grandfathers), friends, pen pals, younger students, older students, community members, teammates, classmates, soulmates. They need to publish things for readers of newspapers, magazines, stories, letters, poetry, cookbooks, comic books, how-to books, joke books. They need to use writing in public ways to advertise, complain, request, acknowledge, announce, solicit, plead their cases. Mem Fox says that students need to spend more time writing letters than writing stories in our writing workshops because the audiences are more specific and the chances for response more promising and immediate. That may be true, but it is also true that we can invest lots more teaching energy into helping students find real readers (who will respond) to all kinds of the writing that they will do in our workshops. As a matter of fact, there may not be a more important use of our teaching energy than this. Writers need readers, and we need to help them find those readers.

So to answer the question we started this section with, a publication in the writing workshop is any piece of writing that goes on a journey ending

WRITERS' VOICES ON . . .

writing for an audience

> I love imagining the reader reading what I've written because, I suppose, I've had such terrific responses in the past. I just can't resist messing around with writing.
>
> I can't not try because my sense of audience is so strong. . . . I can see and hear my imagined readers very clearly. I can't even sign a birthday greeting without going into battle with the blank side of the card . . . .
>
> But I'm a teacher, too. As a teacher, I believe that the most important relationship is the one between the child and the book. I try, as a teacher-writer, to write energetically to capture attention. I try to write rhythmically and repetitively to ensure that my words dance inside the child's head long after the story is finished. I try to use touching, crazy, scary, rowdy themes that will deliver an appropriate meaning to my young reader without my preaching or talking down. I try to use the best words I can find, the most exciting words . . . in case my book is the only one my young reader will ever own. I try to write so the gorgeous little kid in my head will experience, as she reads, a range of emotions from heartbreak to elation, because she must *feel* something in order to want to return to the book. (Mem Fox, *Radical Reflections,* 138)

Karen Hesse has a different view:

> When I begin a new work I truly don't know what audience will most appreciate the finished book. In nearly every project I've published to date, the main character draws me into the story. The cadence of voice, the insistence, the inflection, the rhythm, suggests what will happen to the character, what the character most wants, and what is keeping the character from satisfying that want. By the end of the first draft I usually know who my audience will be for the completed project, and when I begin the revision process I keep age range and interest level somewhat in mind. But above all I try to be true, first and foremost, to the protagonist. No matter how complex the situation, if it is interpreted authentically through the sense of the narrator, the story will be told as it should, without my needing to censor or interpret for the reader. (in Judy O'Malley, *BookLinks,* 54–57)

Writers hold the audience in mind as they craft their work. They must consider who will receive their words in the process of choosing and placing those words with care. Some begin writing with no specific audience in mind, whereas others think of a specific individual. In the end, however, we must consider for whom we write. No one of us writes in a vacuum. Even if we are alone on a desert island with nothing but paper and pencil, we have an imagined audience for the work we do. Why else would we do it?

Fox, Mem. 1993. *Radical Reflections: Passionate Opinions on Teaching, Learning, and Living.* San Diego: Harcourt Brace.

O'Malley, Judy. 1999. "Talking with . . . Karen Hesse." *BookLinks* 9, no. 1 (September): 54–57.

with an audience of readers. The published piece might be a letter, a song, a short story, an article, an editorial, a collection of poems, a play, a book review, a memoir, an information book. . . . Anything that can be written specifically for an audience. That's the key. The journey to being finished begins by knowing that there is an audience of readers waiting for us at the end. Having got to this definition for publishing, I believe we can go back now and think about the questions of "how many" and "how often" students should publish in the writing workshop.

Thinking about How Many and How Often

Publishing a Lot

The first thing to think about in response to both these questions is that students need to publish a lot. The only way they get experience with all parts of the writing journey we described above (the writing process, if you will) is to use that process over and over to do important work for them. I see that, in many classrooms, students are not publishing nearly enough during the year to gain the valuable experience they need to learn to control all aspects of the writing process; they don't get around to editing enough to learn what they need to know to be good editors, in other words.

I think one reason students don't publish more is that, in too many writing workshops, publishing has come to mean this huge fanfare we put on where students make these elaborate books with elaborate pictures, and then we invite everyone we know to come in and hear the students read them, and we have some elaborate refreshments afterwards. And when we think of doing more of this, it is overwhelming. No way can we do more of all that. But we don't need to. That's not publishing! That's a *celebration of things students have published,* and we can do that once or twice a year if we want, but our students need to be publishing way more than that.

Making deadlines for student publishing doesn't mean we have to also make plans for big writing celebrations. It simply means that students agree to be finished with a piece of writing at that time, having gotten the writing ready for its intended audience. We may very well spend some time on that deadline day having students share their publications with each other, but it doesn't have to be this big (or)deal. If the students have written with a specific audience in mind, and have done a good job getting the writing ready for that audience, then the real celebration will be when that audience reads the writing and responds to the writer.

So with the idea in mind that publishing can happen more as a matter of course in the writing workshop, we know that we want for students to publish a lot during the year. Our whole approach to setting deadlines for writing, then, begins with this assumption: We'll need a lot of them. We'll spread that school calendar out in front of us and we'll think, "Where can I set some deadlines for my writers?"

A Calendar of Deadlines for Writers

As we're looking at the school calendar, we need to think about the teaching we are planning for the year. We know we want a lot of publishing, but how will students manage it around the teaching we have going on in the room? Genre studies almost always end with students publishing pieces written in the genre under study, so these will be a given. While students will choose the topics and audiences for these pieces of writing, we will require that the publications be written in the genre under study. We'll need to look at our unit of study planning for the year to help us make deadline decisions for genre studies. We can write these in first. If we're not sure about what genre we want to study in, say, April but know we want a genre study to happen in that month, then we can schedule a deadline with a note, "genre TBA."

Other units of study don't necessarily have to end with a publication, though for some of them, it often makes sense to end this way. For example, a study of how writers co-author might end with a publication that is co-authored, or a study of how writers use punctuation marks in different ways to make meaning might end with a publication where students have paid special attention to crafting in this way. We might look at the different units of study we're planning for the year, then make some deadline decisions based on these and fill these in next. What we don't want is a calendar filled up almost entirely with publications tied to *our* plans as the teacher. There must be plenty of room for *their* plans as writers too. So with the total number of publications that will be required over the course of the year, we aim for a balance of ones that meet specific teaching objectives we have, and ones that totally come from student purposes for the writing.

Now, one problem we run into when we think about a calendar full of publishing deadlines is that different pieces of writing take different amounts of time to finish. A short piece of memoir may take just over a week from start to finish, while an editorial requiring extensive research and lots of drafting to get the tone right could take a month. And though we do want students publishing a lot, we also want to see them developing the ability to work on something for a long time. Big publishing projects take a long time. So how do we account for this in our planning? We have a couple of options. One good option is to have longer spaces of time between some publication deadlines; we let students know this ahead of time, and they know that we expect them to work on "bigger" writing projects during that time.

You see, part of students' learning to manage their writing has to do with learning to manage their time. If they see that they are expected to publish at least four pieces in September and October, but that only one will be required for the whole month of January, they will need to plan to work on shorter things early on and work on more involved publishing projects in January. Think of a deadline as a time when a writer needs to have something she has committed to finishing, finished. If a student has a very big project she wants to work on, even more than a month-long project—say a play with several acts and scenes to it—then she commits to being finished with that play on a publication date in late April, knowing she will work on this project off and on all year long. Writers could have several publishing projects going on at once (just as most professional writers do), but to help them manage these projects, they need to be able to set different deadlines for each of them across the year—which leads us to another option to consider.

We can spread out that calendar, write in all the publishing deadlines for the year (or the semester, or the grading period, depending on how long-range we want to be), hand this to students, and let them begin to make some writing plans around the dates we've set down for them to be finished. We need to know that these plans will evolve and sometimes even change, and we probably don't need students to make plans for all the deadlines across the year right from the start. The calendar is something that we work with as we go along; we pencil things in, committing ourselves most ardently to the deadlines that loom closest.

We might do what some teachers have done and set a required number of publications for the year (or a semester, or a grading period), set the dates for only those tied to classwide genre studies, and then let students set their own deadlines for other required publications in a given period of time. This way, if students wanted to spend a long time on projects that are very involved, they will know that they have to balance that time with projects they can finish in shorter spans of time, and they will make working schedules on their calendars that account for that.

Whether we are comfortable letting students set their own writing deadlines probably will have to do with the experience of our students as writers and with our own comfort with writing workshop teaching. You may be thinking, "But if they set their own deadlines, then they will all be finishing things at different times." True, but that's true even if we set the deadlines. Some students will have a required piece finished for publication days before the deadline and even days before other students have finished theirs. These students either have to work on other publications for a later date, have to work on things they want to publish that are beyond what is required, or simply have to work as writers in notebooks, gathering material they will use in the future.

Think of it this way. The deadline is the day students are responsible for letting us see a finished piece of writing. It's not the day all of them will finish. Neither is the day before. Some of them will have been finished a week earlier with the piece of writing we will see on that day, and some of them won't be finished on that day at all. That's right. Some won't be finished. It happens to all writers. It happened to me while writing this book. A week before my finishing deadline with NCTE, I had to write a letter and ask for an extension. I explained why I was not finished, and I outlined my plans for finishing by a new deadline.

Students who cannot finish their published pieces on time probably need to write letters requesting extensions, as professional writers must do. We may decide to require some part of evaluation to be tied to meeting deadline expectations. There are sometimes consequences in a writer's life when he or she doesn't meet a deadline. But I would recognize that there are sometimes legitimate reasons why a writer cannot be finished with a piece of writing by the time he set out to be finished with it. I think the key is to look at the work of the student who is asking for an extension. Does the work this student has been doing each day (or not doing, as the case may be) explain why he is not ready? We might also look at a student's history of meeting deadlines in the workshop, and if it is an ongoing problem, we would make it a specific goal for that writer to work harder on meeting them.

In the end, however we decide to go about setting them, I believe we need to get students working toward publishing deadlines right from the start. And we need lots of them during the year. We need to think ambitiously. If our students have individual writing portfolios at the end of the school year with fifteen to twenty pieces of published writing in them, imagine how much experience they will have gained in all aspects of the writing process. Now, again, that doesn't mean fifteen to twenty *elaborate* publications. It simply means pieces of writing that have been on a journey ending with an audience of readers.

I know that the idea of managing writing deadlines and managing calendars for publishing across a year seems like a very challenging one. And it is challenging—no question about it. But we know from experience that without at least trying to commit to some deadlines in our teaching of writing, then the publishing won't happen as often, and students won't get this valuable experience of moving toward that in their writing. We'll need a spirit of adventure about experimenting with publishing deadlines in our teaching of writing, making ourselves ready for the bumps and setbacks we'll experience as we move our students into more ambitious publishing. But I believe the challenge is one worth taking because, after all, being able to take that writing into the world is what gives our students the power they need for all their writing tomorrows.

Show and Tell: The Finished Piece

The only way for us to have ambitious goals for student publishing is to let go of our need to have our hands in the process the whole time, every time. If we slow students down enough to keep up with them all, they will not be publishing enough. It's that simple. We have to trust the process of writing itself to do the teaching when we're not there, and let students press on as writers. If we establish a process for finishing writing that will be published, and if we hold students accountable for it, then they can go through this

WRITERS' VOICES ON . . .

publishing

Many nonwriters assume that publication is a thunderously joyous event in the writer's life, and it is certainly the biggest and brightest carrot dangling before the eyes of my students. They believe that if they themselves were to get something published, their lives would change instantly, dramatically, and for the better. Their self-esteem would flourish; all self-doubt would be erased like a typo. Entire paragraphs and manuscripts of disappointment and rejection and lack of faith would be wiped out by one push of a psychic delete button and replaced by a quiet, tender sense of worth and belonging. Then they could wrap the world in flame. . . .

But the fact of publication is the acknowledgement from the community that you did your writing right. You acquire a rank that you never lose. Now you're a published writer . . . .

But eventually you have to sit down like every other writer and face the blank page.

The beginnings of a second or third book are full of spirit and confidence because you have been published, and false starts and terror because now you have to prove yourself again. . . . What I know now is that you have to wear out all that dread by writing long and hard and not stopping too often to admire yourself and your publishedness in the mirror. Sometime later you'll find yourself at work on, maybe really into, another book, and once again you figure out that the real payoff is the writing itself, that a day when you have gotten your work done is a good day, that total dedication is the point. (Anne Lamott, *Bird by Bird,* 210–211, 215)

Whoa, what can I say to add to this? Publication is a BIG event for any writer, and it does bring a rush of emotions. On the plus side, there is satisfaction, accomplishment, pride, joy. It feels wonderful. Then there's the dread. My work is out of my hands and in the hands of readers—will they love it as I have? Did I leave out something important? Could I have made it better if I had just spent one more week with it? If people love it, will I ever be able to do anything to equal it? If people hate it, will anyone ever want to read my work again? Yikes! This publishing stuff is dicey. Once again, it's the writing that matters; it's the work itself that we thrive on. Let publication be what it is—just one more part of the work of writers.

Lamott, Anne. 1995. *Bird by Bird: Some Instructions on Writing and Life.* New York: Anchor Books.

process on their own. If we are conferring on a daily basis, we will likely catch them at some point in most steps of the process; but even if we don't, they can still carry on. We can look at the completed process with them when they're finished. Remember that our goal during independent writing is for us to match our teaching (conferring) to students' writing, not for them to match their writing to our teaching. We don't want them to feel like we have to hold their hands through the process.

The key, then, is for students to know what it means to move a piece of writing from "start to finish." Many teachers use their focus lessons and conferences at the beginning of the year to take the whole class through this process together, their goal being for students to know how to publish independently afterward. Later in the year, they will slow down different parts of the process for deeper study, but at first, the objective of the instruction is just to show students what they need to do. After that, they can get pieces ready for publication on their own, but they'll need to know exactly what they will be accountable for in doing this.

In many writing workshops, students know that declaring a piece of writing as "finished" means that they are ready not only to show the nice, neat final draft of the piece, but it also means that they are ready to tell the whole story of the journey of that piece of writing, as well as show the artifacts that accompany that journey. We ask students to do this because it makes them accountable for doing what a writer must do to finish a piece. We also do it because we know that as students think about the writing processes they use to publish, their thinking becomes curriculum for them. They learn about the process by stepping away from it and thinking about how it went for them.

Some teachers find it helpful to have students use a standard reporting procedure for showing and telling the story of the published piece of writing. They ask students to write narrative reflections to questions about the processes behind their published pieces, and then to attach all artifacts that support these reflections. Figure 19.1 shows an example of a set of questions that helps students tell the stories of how their published pieces came to be finished. If we wanted students to answer these questions on an actual form like this, we would need to leave spaces for their reflections. Students might also be asked to evaluate both this process and the piece of writing itself, rating themselves on how well they did on things. In that case, we would add a place for them to use a scoring rubric alongside their reflections.

Notice that the questions in Figure 19.1 follow very closely the "journey to being finished" we described earlier as we defined what it means to publish something.

To these reflections, students will attach copies of drafts, perhaps copies of related notebook entries or notes from conferences with peers—anything that shows some of the work they are describing having done. What students tell us about their writing process should be supported by what they *show* us

FIGURE 19.1
A Reflection Sheet for Published Writing

Name ______________________
Title of published piece ______________________
Genre ______________________

1. How did the idea for this piece start? Who is the audience for this piece?
2. What kinds of things did you do to develop this idea before you began drafting it? What notebook entries did you do around this idea before you began drafting it?
3. Describe your process for drafting and revision. Explain some actual decisions you made while drafting and revising this piece. Include details about what kinds of help you got from other writers.
4. What was your process for editing (proofreading) this piece? What were some specific things you changed while editing?
5. How did you decide on the format for publishing the finished piece?
6. If your intended audience has read this already, what was the response? If not, what are your plans for getting this to your audience?

of their writing. I need to *see* lots of notebook entries if a student says he developed this idea extensively in his notebook before drafting it. I need to *see* a final draft that looks as if it has been "fine-tooth combed" if the student said she was very careful in her editing. And based on what I know about the student as a writer, what he shows me needs to look like his best work. We must leave some room for "best work" to be defined in different ways for different writers. I want to see a struggling writer work just as hard at drafting as a gifted writer, but I know that the results of her efforts may have a different look to them.

The other key for us to remember as teachers is that we should expect that the way students engage in this process should shift and change with different publications. It needs to be OK if some pieces just kind of "came out that way" and required very little revision. It needs to be OK if sometimes a student went very quickly from an idea to a draft, with little development in between. These are all things that happen to real writers from time to time. The thing to watch for are patterns over time. If a student hardly ever tries much revision, or rarely develops an idea in his or her notebook before starting to draft it, then this issue needs to be addressed in our response to this student. This needs to become a goal for the student to work on in future writing projects.

Curriculum to Support the Process

Throughout the year, our students will need curriculum support for all these processes we are asking them to use in order to finish writing for publication. Starting with where writers get their ideas, to how they develop them, to how they draft and revise them for important audiences, all the way to possibilities for publishing, we will need to develop curriculum that supports students as they publish. There will be many challenges along the way. There always are. From my own experience working with young writers and from talking to many teachers who work with young writers, some of the hardest parts of all are these:

- **The difference between notebook writing and drafting.** Students struggle with this difference, and so they struggle with moving from one to the other. I try to help students understand that once the draft starts, the writer has begun *making something*. The notebook writing is sort of like collecting what you need in order to make something. The draft is when you actually begin making it.
- **Revision.** Students tend to think of revision almost exclusively as "fixing what's wrong." I struggle to help them understand that revision is more about seeing what else is possible in a draft: seeing what could be left out, what could be added, what could be cleverly worded, what other endings there might be. Revision is "playing around with the possible" in a lot of ways. Curriculum that helps students learn specific things to try while revising can really help match this struggle. Also, helping students get some distance from drafts—by putting them away

for awhile and working on something else—can help. The possibilities are easier to see on a piece of writing when you haven't looked at it for awhile.

• **Knowing when enough is enough.** Perhaps the most elusive aspect of the writing process for even the most experienced writer is knowing when to stop working at drafting and revision. I have seen more students who stop too soon than those who go on and on, but "how much is enough" is an elusive question. Sometimes we stop because our deadline is looming, but we want students to know more about how to make this decision than just that. We want curriculum that helps them think about how writers know they have gone as far as they need to go with a piece of writing.

• **Giving and receiving responses to writing.** Many students who haven't had much experience in writing workshops will struggle with how to respond to one another in ways that support the writing. The best curriculum that we will offer across the year for this part of the process will come through our conferring. Every time we confer with a student, we are demonstrating how to respond to a writer.

• **Editing.** The struggle here is not in getting students to edit. It's that many students don't know enough yet to do a very good job of it when they do it. They miss a lot of things because they just don't know them yet. They need outside editors to help them when the stakes for their writing are very high, just like professional writers have. But they also need explanations that will help them understand the editing things they are missing so that they can get better at it. We need to look for patterns of things that they are missing, and in a follow-up conference after a project, we can work on one or two of these. Then we expect to see them finding and fixing those things on the next go-round. If we happen to catch them in the act of editing in a conference before the piece is finished, we can offer needed explanations then. But we don't have to catch them all then. Remember, being finished means the writer has done the best editing he or she can do; it doesn't mean the writing is perfect.

So these are some of the hardest parts of the writing process for many young students, and any given group of writers—as well as any individual writer—is likely to have their own particular struggles with the process. But this is why having them publish a lot is so critical to the success of the workshop. The more experience students have in managing this process with different kinds of writing for different audiences, the more control they will have over it. Remember that it is better for them to publish a lot, knowing that not every piece will be brilliant or that every journey to being finished with a piece will be the best one the student ever makes. Just keep them traveling. . . .

Suggested Readings

Books on Teaching and Related Issues

Atwell, Nancie. 1998. *In the Middle: New Understandings about Reading, Writing, and Learning*. Portsmouth, N.H.: Boynton/Cook.

Avery, Carol. 1993. *. . . And with a Light Touch: Learning about Reading, Writing, and Teaching with First Graders*. Portsmouth, N.H.: Heinemann.

Bomer, Randy. 1995. *Time for Meaning: Crafting Literate Lives in Middle and High School*. Portsmouth, N.H.: Heinemann.

Calkins, Lucy McCormick. 1994. *The Art of Teaching Writing*. 2nd ed. Portsmouth, N.H.: Heinemann.

Calkins, Lucy McCormick, with Shelley Harwayne. 1990. *Living between the Lines*. Portsmouth, N.H.: Heinemann.

Cambourne, Brian, and Jan Turnbill, eds. 1994. *Responsive Evaluation: Making Valid Judgments about Student Literacy*. Portsmouth, N.H.: Heinemann.

Fisher, Bobbi. 1998. *Joyful Learning in Kindergarten*. Portsmouth, N.H.: Heinemann.

Fraser, Jane, and Donna Skolnick. 1994. *On Their Way: Celebrating Second Graders as They Read and Write*. Portsmouth, N.H.: Heinemann.

Glover, Mary Kenner. 1999. *A Garden of Poets: Poetry Writing in the Elementary Classroom.* Urbana, Ill.: NCTE.

Graves, Donald H. 1994. *A Fresh Look at Writing.* Portsmouth, N.H.: Heinemann.

Graves, Donald H., and Bonnie S. Sunstein, eds. 1992. *Portfolio Portraits.* Portsmouth, N.H.: Heinemann.

Hansen, Jane. 1998. *When Learners Evaluate.* Portsmouth, N.H.: Heinemann.

Harvey, Stephanie. 1998. *Nonfiction Matters: Reading, Writing, and Research in Grades 3–8.* York, Maine: Stenhouse Publishers.

Harwayne, Shelley. 1992. *Lasting Impressions: Weaving Literature into the Writing Workshop.* Portsmouth, N.H.: Heinemann.

Heard, Georgia. 1989. *For the Good of the Earth and Sun: Teaching Poetry.* Portsmouth, N.H.: Heinemann.

———. 1998. *Awakening the Heart: Exploring Poetry in Elementary and Middle School.* Portsmouth, N.H.: Heinemann.

Hindley, Joanne. 1996. *In the Company of Children.* York, Maine: Stenhouse.

Peterson, Ralph. 1992. *Life in a Crowded Place: Making a Learning Community.* Portsmouth, N.H.: Heinemann.

Ray, Katie Wood. 1999. *Wondrous Words: Writers and Writing in the Elementary Classroom.* Urbana, Ill.: NCTE.

Romano, Tom. 1995. *Writing with Passion: Life Stories, Multiple Genres.* Portsmouth, N.H.: Boynton/Cook.

Short, Kathy G., and Jerome Harste, with Carolyn Burke. 1996. *Creating Classrooms for Authors and Inquirers.* Portsmouth, N.H.: Heinemann.

Tierney, Robert J., Mark A. Carter, and Laura E. Desai. 1991. *Portfolio Assessment in the Reading-Writing Classroom.* Norwood, MA: Christopher-Gordon Publishers.

Books about Writing and the Writing Life

Addonizio, Kim, and Dorianne Laux. 1997. *The Poet's Companion: A Guide to the Pleasures of Writing Poetry.* New York: Norton.

Asher, Sandy. 1996. *But That's Another Story: Famous Authors Introduce Popular Genres.* New York: Walker.

Barrington, Judith. 1997. *Writing the Memoir: From Truth to Art.* Portland, Ore.: Eighth Mountain Press.

Burroway, Janet. 2000. *Writing Fiction: A Guide to Narrative Craft.* 5th ed. New York: HarperCollins.

Dillard, Annie. 1990. *The Writing Life.* New York: HarperPerennial.

Fletcher, Ralph. 1993. *What a Writer Needs.* Portsmouth, N.H.: Heinemann.

———. 1996. *Breathing In, Breathing Out: Keeping a Writer's Notebook.* Portsmouth, N.H.: Heinemann.

———. 1996. *A Writer's Notebook: Unlocking the Writer within You.* New York: Avon Books.

———. 1999. *Live Writing: Breathing Life into Your Words.* New York: Avon Books.

Fox, Mem. 1993. *Radical Reflections: Passionate Opinions on Teaching, Learning, and Living.* San Diego: Harcourt Brace.

Gardner, John. 1983. *The Art of Fiction: Notes on Craft for Young Writers.* New York: Vintage Books.

Gerard, Philip. 1996. *Creative Nonfiction: Researching and Crafting Stories in Real Life.* Cincinnati: Story Press.

Goldberg, Natalie. 1986. *Writing Down the Bones: Freeing the Writer Within.* Boston: Shambhala.

———. 1990. *Wild Mind: Living the Writer's Life.* New York: Bantam.

Gutkind, Lee. 1997. *The Art of Creative Nonfiction: Writing and Selling the Literature of Reality.* New York: John Wiley.

Heard, Georgia. 1995. *Writing toward Home: Tales and Lessons to Find Your Way.* Portsmouth, N.H.: Heinemann.

Hemley, Robin. 1994. *Turning Your Life into Fiction.* Cincinnati: Story Press.

Kaplan, David Michael. 1997. *Revision: A Creative Approach to Writing and Rewriting Fiction.* Cincinnati: Story Press.

Kovacs, Deborah, and James Preller. 1993. *Meet the Authors and Illustrators: 60 Creators of Favorite Children's Books Talk about Their Work.* Vol. 2. New York: Scholastic Professional.

Kowit, Steve. 1995. *In the Palm of Your Hand: A Poet's Portable Workshop: A Lively and Illuminative Guide for the Practicing Poet.* Gardiner, Maine: Tilbury House.

Kuusisto, Stephen, Deborah Tall, and David Weiss, eds. 1995. *The Poet's Notebook: Excerpts from the Notebooks of Contemporary American Poets.* New York: Norton.

Lamott, Anne. 1995. *Bird by Bird: Some Instructions on Writing and Life*. New York: Anchor Books.

LeGuin, Ursula K. 1998. *Steering the Craft: Exercises and Discussions on Story Writing for the Lone Navigator or the Mutinous Crew.* Portland, Ore.: Eighth Mountain Press.

Lyon, George Ella. 1999. *Where I'm From, Where Poems Come From*. Spring, Texas: Absey & Company.

Macauley, Robie, and George Lanning. 1987. *Technique in Fiction*. 2nd ed. New York: St. Martin's.

Magee, Rosemary M., ed. 1987. *Conversations with Flannery O'Connor.* Jackson: University Press of Mississippi.

McDonnell, Jane Taylor. 1998. *Living to Tell the Tale: A Guide to Writing Memoir.* New York: Penguin.

Murray, Donald M. 1990. *Shoptalk: Learning to Write with Writers*. Portsmouth, N.H.: Heinemann.

———. 1996. *Crafting a Life in Essay, Story, Poem*. Portsmouth, N.H.: Boynton/Cook.

Oliver, Mary. 1994. *A Poetry Handbook*. San Diego: Harcourt Brace.

Olmstead, Robert. 1997. *Elements of the Writing Craft*. Cincinnati: Story Press.

Paterson, Katherine. 1995. *A Sense of Wonder: On Reading and Writing Books for Children*. New York: Plume.

Powell, Dannye Romine. 1995. *Parting the Curtains: Voices of the Great Southern Writers.* New York: Anchor Books.

Price, Reynolds. 1998. *Learning a Trade: A Craftsman's Notebooks, 1955–1997.* Durham, N.C.: Duke University Press.

Roorbach, Bill. 1998. *Writing Life Stories*. Cincinnati: Story Press.

Stern, Jerome. 1991. *Making Shapely Fiction*. New York: Dell Publishing.

Stilman, Anne. 1997. *Grammatically Correct: The Writer's Essential Guide to Punctuation, Spelling, Style, Usage and Grammar.* Cincinnati: Writer's Digest Books.

Strunk, William, and E. B. White. 1999. *The Elements of Style*. 4th ed. Boston: Allyn and Bacon.

Swallow, Pamela Curtis. 1999. *A Writer's Notebook: The Ultimate Guide to Creative Writing*. New York: Scholastic.

Welty, Eudora. 1990. *The Eye of the Story: Selected Essays and Reviews*. New York: Vintage Books.

Wooldridge, Susan G. 1997. *Poemcrazy: Freeing Your Life with Words.* New York: Three Rivers Press.

Zinsser, William, ed. 1987. *Inventing the Truth: The Art and Craft of Memoir.* Rev. ed. Boston: Houghton Mifflin.

———. 1988. *On Writing Well: An Informal Guide to Writing Nonfiction.* New York: Harper & Row.

Authors

Photo by Mark Haskett

Katie Wood Ray teaches courses in language arts education at Western Carolina University in Cullowhee, North Carolina. She is the author of *Wondrous Words: Writers and Writing in the Elementary Classroom* and the co-author (with Lester L. Laminack) of *Spelling in Use: Looking Closely at Spelling in Whole Language Classrooms*, both NCTE publications. She has taught by herself and alongside other teachers, and her experiences in writing workshops have taken her from middle school classrooms in South Carolina, to K–5 classrooms in the New York City Public Schools, to K–8 classrooms in the rural mountains of western North Carolina. In every teaching setting, she has encountered the "hard parts" in many forms, but she has also found the joy that comes from working through them and helping students find the power of writing in their lives.

Photo by Mark Haskett

Lester L. Laminack is professor and chair, Elementary and Middle Grades Education, at Western Carolina University in Cullowhee, North Carolina, where he teaches graduate and undergraduate courses in literacy education. He is an active member of the National Council of Teachers of English and currently serves (with Katie Wood Ray) as co-editor of the NCTE journal *Primary Voices K–6*. He is a former member of the Whole Language Umbrella Governing Board, a former member of the Governing Board and Secretary of the North Carolina Association for the Education of Young Children, and a current member of the Board of Directors for the Center for the Expansion of Language and Thinking. He has served as the Basic Reading Consultant to Literacy Volunteers of America since 1987.

His academic publications encompass five books (including *Learning with Zachary*, *Spelling in Use*, and *Volunteers Working with Young Readers*) and several articles published in journals such as *The Reading Teacher*, *Science and Children*, *Language Arts*, *Primary Voices*, and *Young Children*. In addition, he is the author of two children's books, *The Sunsets of Miss Olivia Wiggins* and *Trevor's Wiggly-Wobbly Tooth*.

The Writing Workshop

Composed by Precision Graphics in Galliard and Papyrus.
Typefaces used on the cover were Adobe Garamond,
Adobe Berkeley, Emigre Triplex Condensed,
and ITC Zapf Dingbats.
Printed by IPC Communication Services
on 60-lb. Lynx Opaque.